CORPOREAL AESTH/ETHICS

BEFORE YOU START TO READ THIS BOOK, take this moment to think about making a donation to punctum books, an independent non-profit press,

@ https://punctumbooks.com/support/

If you're reading the e-book, you can click on the image below to go directly to our donations site. Any amount, no matter the size, is appreciated and will help us to keep our ship of fools afloat. Contributions from dedicated readers will also help us to keep our commons open and to cultivate new work that can't find a welcoming port elsewhere. Our adventure is not possible without your support.

Vive la Open Access.

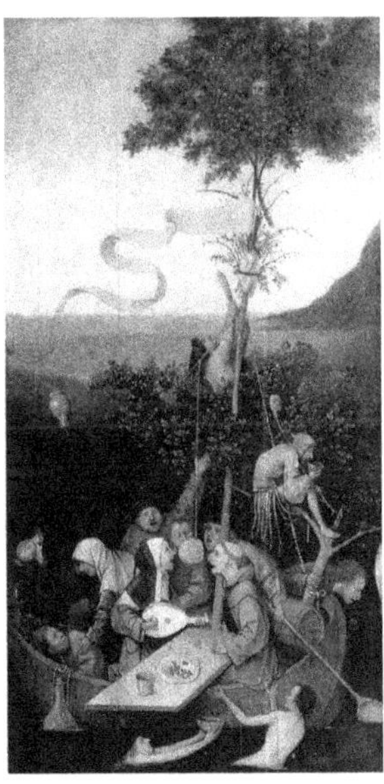

Fig. 1. Detail from Hieronymus Bosch, *Ship of Fools* (1490–1500)

CORPOREAL AESTH/ETHICS: THE BODY IN BRACHA L. ETTINGER'S THEORY AND ART. Copyright © 2026 by Anna Kisiel. This work carries a Creative Commons BY-NC-SA 4.0 International license, which means that you are free to copy and redistribute the material in any medium or format, and you may also remix, transform, and build upon the material, as long as you clearly attribute the work to the author (but not in a way that suggests the author or punctum books endorses you and your work), you do not use this work for commercial gain in any form whatsoever, and that for any remixing and transformation, you distribute your rebuild under the same license. http://creativecommons.org/licenses/by-nc-sa/4.0/

Published in 2026 by MAI: Feminism and Culture
an imprint of punctum books, Earth, Milky Way.
https://punctumbooks.com

ISBN-13: 978-1-68571-214-3 (paperbound)
ISBN-13: 978-1-68571-215-0 (PDF)
ISBN-13: 978-1-68571-299-0 (EPUB)

DOI: 10.53288/0499.1.00

LCCN: 2026932367
Library of Congress Cataloging Data is available from the Library of Congress

Editing: SAJ and Vincent W.J. van Gerven Oei
Book design: Hatim Eujayl
Cover image: Bracha L. Ettinger, *Eurydice, The Graces, Demeter,* 2006–2012, oil on canvas, 50 × 41 cm. Collection: Fiorucci, Monaco, featured at the exhibition Bracha Lichtenberg Ettinger: Eurydice — Pieta in Muzeum Śląskie (Silesian Museum), Katowice, July 7–September 2, 2017. © Courtesy of the artist.
Cover design: Vincent W.J. van Gerven Oei

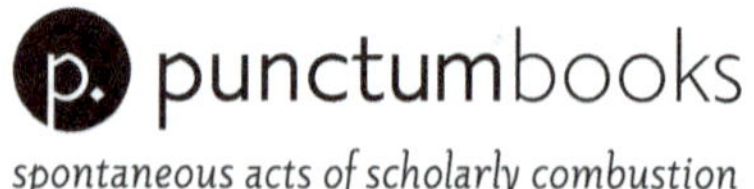

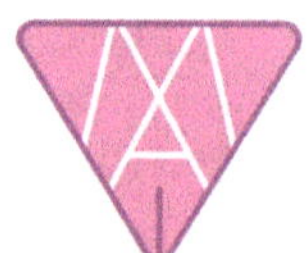

spontaneous acts of scholarly combustion

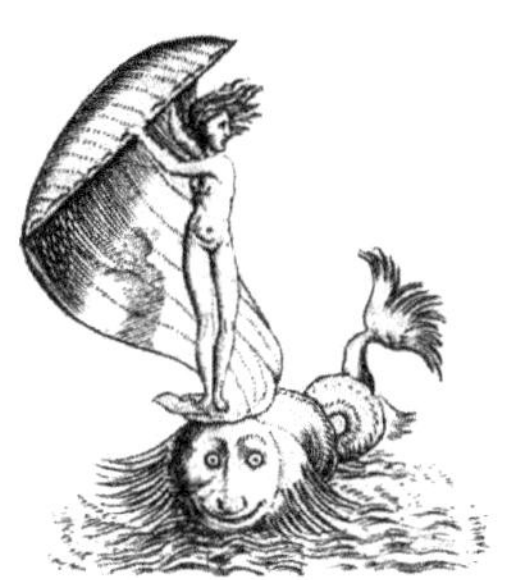

HIC SVNT MONSTRA

Corporeal Aesth/ethics

The Body in Bracha L. Ettinger's Theory and Art

Anna Kisiel

Contents

Acknowledgments

Any book is a collective endeavor. *Corporeal Aesth/ethics* — being essentially a book on togetherness — is no exception in this respect. I am happy to use this space to thank those without whose commitment and understanding I would not have written it.

Thank you to the magnificent team of punctum books — especially Vincent and SAJ — for the opportunity to publish my book with you, in open access, no less! I owe a debt of gratitude to Anna Backman Rogers and Erika Kvistad, whose insightful comments helped me develop as a writer. Thank you, Anna, for believing in this project; it is a privilege to be part of MAI community and have a chance to contribute to this cutting-edge imprint. My thanks also go to Roma Sendyka and Katarzyna Więckowska, the reviewers of my PhD thesis, which laid the foundation for this book.

I am deeply grateful to Wojciech Kalaga for ceaseless support and guidance; I would like to thank you for encouraging me to follow my ideas, offering wise words of advice, and having faith in my abilities.

A warm thank you to Bracha L. Ettinger for your kindness and generosity, towards me and towards the world; Bracha, it is a great honor for me to use your artworks in this book. And thank you to Anna Chromik, who introduced me to matrixial theory in 2012 and has inspired me ever since.

I am lucky to have met dozens of wonderful people in my professional life. Thank you to my colleagues: at the University of Silesia in Katowice, wsb University, and the University of the National Education Commission in Kraków; at the University of Silesia Press; in editorial teams of journals that I am or was a member of; and that I have met at academic conferences or collaborated with in any other way.

Finally, a loving thank you to my family and friends for your warmth and patience; I am truly fortunate to be surrounded by so many kind-hearted people. Most importantly, there are no words to convey the depth of my gratitude for the love and commitment of my husband Michał; your endless rereads and remarks, and your unwavering belief in me have given me strength to carry on with this book — and so many other projects! Last but not least, there has been one recent addition in my life that cannot be omitted here, especially since motherhood is one of the key themes of this book. Lilia, my inherently kind and generous baby girl, has allowed me to complete the final stages of the publishing process without much protest. Lilia, being your mother is a wondrous adventure.

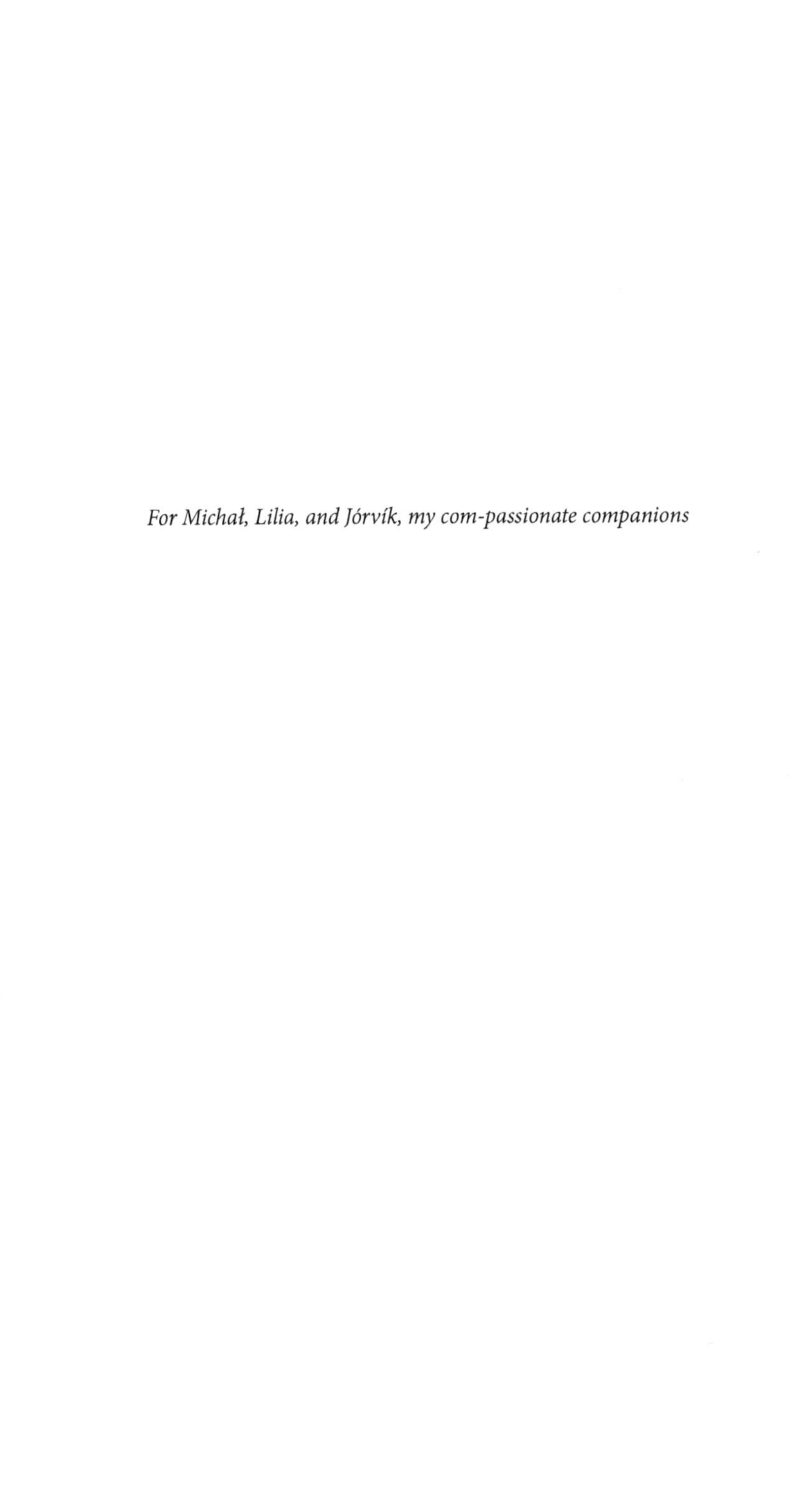

For Michał, Lilia, and Jórvík, my com-passionate companions

Introduction

Corporeal Aesth/ethics endeavors to trace the body in Bracha L. Ettinger's oeuvre and investigate the humanizing potential of this rich category. Born in 1948 in Tel Aviv to the Holocaust survivors Bluma and Uziel Lichtenberg, Ettinger is a clinical psychologist, Lacanian psychoanalyst, visual artist, and theoretician of the matrix. In my book, I focus on her matrixial psychoanalysis and artistic practice in an attempt to take a closer look at corporeality — the notion which resurfaces in these two areas, but has never occupied a central position in Ettingerian criticism; as I believe, the status of the matrixial body needs to be studied, clarified, and foregrounded as it may be read as a primary ethical site in a psychoanalytical sense.

The primary concern of my project is the work of Ettinger as a matrixial theorist. The founding concept of Ettinger's psychoanalysis is the *matrix,* which ought not to be mistaken for a womb although it carries such a connotation. Similarly to the phallus, as defined by Jacques Lacan, the matrix in Ettinger's theory gains a status of a signifier of difference. This type of difference is non-phallic and non-gendered. Instead of being grounded upon separation or male–female dichotomy, it embraces connectedness, shareability, fragility, openness, and hospitality — the qualities inspired by the intrauterine period, pregnancy, maternity, and, in general, potentialities of the female body. Thus, the matrix stands for an intimate encounter between several becoming-subjects modeled after the prenatal period; this does not, however, mean that it forms an opposition to phallic paradigms. Rather, the matrixial borderspace theorized by Ettinger functions as a supplement to the psychoanalytic concepts of Lacan and Sigmund Freud. While the matrix as a concept questions the phallus and castration as the only means of forming subjectivity, it does not challenge their significance in the postnatal period. In her proposition of a supplementary subjectivizing realm, Ettinger scrutinizes the postulates of Lacan with regard to their possibly phallocentric structure, and she re-reads Freud (for instance, she returns to *Muttersleibphantasien,* or phantasies of the mother's body, a term partly abandoned by Lacan); such analyses allow her to rethink a space for femininity at the threshold of phallus-oriented psychoanalysis. Calling for the co-existence instead of the rejection of paradigms, Ettinger expands the Symbolic order onto the logics of "between/and" and "both/and" alongside that of "either/or." As a result, Ettinger questions the primacy of the binary stratification and integrity of the subject, and stresses the value of matrixial severality (which should not be mistaken with subjectless or meaning-less symbiosis or fusion) as an equally universal experience. While Freudian–Lacanian psychoanalysis provides a major point of reference in the discussion of the matrixial theory, Ettinger is also indebted to other thinkers and areas. Her next crucial inspiration is derived from Gilles Deleuze and Félix Guattari's schizo-analysis. Although Ettinger's approach is not anti-Oedipal, it is focused on such notions as becoming, affect, and connectedness, which instantly redirect us towards Deleuze and Guattari's propositions. Ettinger also turns to Emmanuel Levinas's ethics of the Other and Julia Kristeva's conceptualization of the Platonic *chora.* Importantly, even though Ettinger's focal point is the prenatal/pregnancy phase and, thus, the female body, Ettinger dissociates herself from any form of essentialism. Finally, Ettinger is indebted to French cultural feminism. It is especially visible in her theoretical writings as she uses *écriture féminine,* a literary strategy devised by Hélène Cixous.[1] In the course of this project I refer to these contexts as they make it possible to provide a more complete picture of Ettinger's multi-layered — yet evanescent — notion of corporeality.

In her reading of Ettinger's theory, Griselda Pollock provocatively argues that it commits "blasphemy"[2]; what I would like to propose is a notion that supplements such a view of this system. When considering blasphemy, Pollock refers to two basic assumptions of the matrix: one of the prenatal period as a formative time-space for the becoming-subject, and the other of severality as a subjectivizing quality that precedes separation. In psychoanalysis, as Pollock notes, both thinking of the subject-before-birth and thinking of the subject indispensably linked with its intimate Others are impossible, or even "psychotic and perverse."[3] Feminism, on the other hand, is claimed to fear falling into essentialism or biological determinism whenever the

---

1   Ettinger's *écriture féminine* will be discussed in Chapter 4. However, at this point let me briefly comment upon the satisfaction and challenge embedded in analyzing Ettinger's theoretical works. Many of neologisms and terms coined by Ettinger seem to be employed to add some nuance to the original terms they expand ("wit(h)ness with-out an event," for instance, is a direct reference to Dori Laub's description of the Holocaust as an "event without a witness"). Some function like puns (for example, "with-in" suggests the combination of "with," "in," and "within" in a case when neither of these prepositions alone gives justice to the complex phenomenon it describes). They seem to be intended to inspire the reader and open them to new layers of connotations and denotations, but, aside from that, they cannot be reduced to a single element in a system. That is why, as a literary scholar, I study the layers of meaning of Ettinger's neologisms and wordplays, but I find it rather difficult — unbeneficial even — to provide the reader with simple definitions of these terms.

2   Griselda Pollock, "Introduction. Femininity: Aporia or Sexual Difference?," in Bracha L. Ettinger, *The Matrixial Borderspace*, ed. Brian Massumi (University of Minnesota Press, 2006), 13. Pollock uses the notion of blasphemy after Donna Haraway's "A Cyborg Manifesto." There, blasphemy is a creative act that has to be differentiated from apostasy. See Donna Haraway, "A Cyborg Manifesto: Science, Technology, and Socialist-Feminism in the Late 20th Century," in *International Handbook of Virtual Learning Environments*, ed. Joel Weiss et al. (Springer, 2006), 117.

3   Pollock, "Introduction. Femininity," 14.

issue of the female body is raised. Nevertheless, Ettinger's intention is not to antagonize or disregard these two fields, but to contribute to and thus expand them. Different difference is an Ettingerian notion that in my view seems to embrace the essence of the relation of the matrixial theory to both areas delineated above. Different difference cannot be conceived of in terms of exclusion or opposition; rather, it constitutes a border-Other to the classical psychoanalytic theorization of binary +/– difference. Similarly, Ettinger introduces a system that neither has to be rejected nor expects its predecessors to withdraw since it works within the borders of psychoanalytic paradigms. Moreover, even though the matrixial theory does not refrain from using the female-maternal flesh as a departure point for further investigations, it does not question feminism or women's rights, again placing itself as *different* rather than *definitive* difference to them. The matrixial realm, therefore, builds the relation with psychoanalysis and feminism upon mutuality, proximity, and correspondence, but also upon a "blasphemous" challenge.

Not only a matrixial theorist and psychoanalyst, Ettinger is also a visual artist. Ettinger's artistic activity, which is another key concern of my book, constantly intermingles with her theoretical considerations. Ettinger states, "While painting produces theory, theory casts light on painting in a backward projection. [...] For me, painting and theory are not different aspects that attest to the same thing, but are rather differentiated levels of working-through."[4] The experience of creating and witnessing art thus becomes one of the grounds for the emergence of the matrixial theory and its inseparable companion; these two aspects of Ettinger's oeuvre constantly inspire and unfold one another, which is why in this project I read them together. Emphatically, Ettinger's aesthetic practice cannot be reduced to one genre or medium. This project focuses mainly on her paintings, but it also refers to several works on paper, drawings,

---

4   Bracha L. Ettinger, "The With-In-Visible Screen," in Ettinger, *The Matrixial Borderspace*, 94. Emphasis in original.

sketches, and notebooks; apart from these, Ettinger's artistic output includes video works, installations, and photography.

While the techniques of the particular artworks analyzed are explored in detail in the course of the book, I find it essential to outline the underpinnings of Ettinger's most famous series, *Eurydice,* as these paintings recur in all five chapters. The majority of *Eurydices* are based on a historical black and white photograph from 1942 which depicts women and children from the Mizocz ghetto waiting to be executed.[5] Naked, the victims stand in a row; among them, we can see women of different ages, one of them visibly pregnant, some holding babies, and a little girl. We can also spot male soldiers behind them.[6] In the series, the Mizocz picture functions as a background which Ettinger re-works. She begins by using a photocopy machine, suspending its work before the full copy is produced; the final effect is never predictable whereas the copy remains unfinished, which testifies to the aforementioned between/and logic. Next, Ettinger engages in further manipulations, for instance covering the image with layers of paint or adding other pictures to the canvas. This procedure, the use of the photograph, and other themes present in these pieces provide us with numerous implications which require a further analysis and — as I am convinced — contribute to the proposed reflections on the proto-ethics of the matrix.

The primary point of interest in *Corporeal Aesth/ethics* — the body — occupies a paradoxical position in Ettinger's oeuvre. To start with the theory, the notion of the matrix is based on the womb, but it serves as a psychoanalytic model; consequently,

---

5   Throughout the book, by *Eurydices* in italics I mean the series whereas by Eurydices in roman typeface I refer to the women from the Mizocz ghetto.

6   As my project is devoted to ethics, I decided not to include this image — I feel neither ethically secure nor entitled to do so. The photograph is, however, available online. It can be accessed in the online archives of the United States Holocaust Memorial Museum; the Museum website also provides more information about the photograph. Reference number of the photograph: #17877, https://collections.ushmm.org/search/catalog/pa1065461.

the body in this system ought not to be understood via essentialism or biological determinism as it is argued to be used in a non-ideological manner. Omnipresent in the matrixial domain, (female) corporeality becomes a metaphorical rather than actual site. Namely, it may be read as a space of relations between subject and Other(s), or between becoming-subjects; it may also be theorized as an origin of ethics. Simultaneously, in critical examinations of Ettinger's theory, the significance of the body appears to be treated either as unquestionable and obvious, or as an element that ought not to be spoken of: that is, as a dangerous territory. As a result, it is not analyzed sufficiently, which leaves numerous blank spaces and inadequacies. In art, the presence of the female body appears to be more straightforward. Ettinger's artworks frequently feature feminine tropes and associations, and women often become points of reference in the titles themselves (among others, Eurydice, Saint Anne, Medusa, and Ophelia). Moreover, the pieces host actual women, for instance, those from Mizocz, Ettinger herself, and Bluma Lichtenberg. Finally, it is the combination of theory and art in the context of corporeality that makes my project important — so far no one has devoted full attention to the body in these two dimensions of Ettinger's activity. There are numerous articles and books on Ettinger's art that tackle the question of corporeality, in which theory is more of an addition or context,[7] but when it comes to theoretical discussions on this subject, or discussions on how theory and art are inseparable when it comes to Ettinger, there is a gap here that I wish to fill. In my view, the body — and especially the female body — constantly resurfaces in Ettinger's

---

7   See, for instance, Catherine de Zegher and Griselda Pollock, eds., *Art as Compassion: Bracha L. Ettinger* (ASA Publishers, 2012); Bracha L. Ettinger, *Bracha Lichtenberg Ettinger: Artworking 1985–1999* (Ludion, 2000); Bracha L. Ettinger, *And My Heart Wound-Space* (Wild Pansy Press, 2015); and Anna Chromik, "Eurydice and Pieta, Fire and Water, Rescue and Evacuation: Traces of Trauma in Bracha Lichtenberg Ettinger's Art," in *Bracha L. Ettinger: Eurydyka — Pieta / Eurydice — Pieta,* ed. Anna Chromik (Muzeum Śląskie, 2018), 33–37.

thought and art, and yet is virtually absent, never reaching the status of the main subject, in Ettingerian critique.

My intention is to prove that the body can be identified as both the origin and the potential of matrixial ethics, or proto-ethics, grounded upon the correspondence of theory and art. As such, I have a number of objectives here. In general terms, I aim to investigate the ethics of the body in Ettinger's psycho-analysis, and to explore the trans-connectedness of theory and aesthetics with reference to corporeality and its ethical dimensions. More specifically, I examine the relationships of bodies (especially I/non-I, and mother/child) and differences arising between them; also, I exercise the potentialities of the body in the system that is claimed to be neither essentialist nor biologically determined. The related goal is an analysis of the Ettingerian corporeality with regard to the gender distinctions it is said to evade, and, in the process, an assessment of the validity of this critical claim. Finally, I turn to the chosen thinkers engaged in Holocaust studies and Judeo-Christian theology as these two fields provide an indispensable context for both the theory of the matrix and Ettinger's artistic activity. When combined, the outlined aims work in favor of emphasizing the inherent significance of the body in Ettinger's oeuvre and opening up its scope and implications.

As I am trained in literary studies, the approach I adopt is predominantly a hermeneutic reading of Ettinger's thought and art, which embraces juxtapositions of systems and analyses of corporeal tropes. What is at stake here is not only to highlight the undermined — yet foundational — notion of the body but also to discover its implications in the contexts and spaces in which it has been merely noted (if so) yet not studied in detail. Simultaneously, in my encounters with Ettinger's art, I frequently allow myself to go further — towards a more affective interpretation. Ettinger's artworks often strive to challenge the borders of representation; as Brian Massumi notes, "The parts and paintings couple not because they look alike, but because they feel alike. If there is resemblance, it is in the feeling: it is of relived feeling to itself."[8] My slightly affective readings, as proposed in the following chapters, by no means renounce representation, but endeavor to move towards its limits; I wish to show how the selected artworks interweave with and contribute to the matrixial theory. One of the inspirations for such an approach is a notebook entry, the scan of which was available at the exhibition *Bracha Lichtenberg Ettinger: Eurydice — Pieta* in Silesian Museum in Katowice (July 7–September 2, 2017, curated by Anna Chromik). It was dated May 2013, and one of the inscriptions read, "My thinking results from this feel-know-seeing. [… I]t is paradoxical and looks sounds illogical — but it has another kind of logic." The triad of feel-know-seeing can be acknowledged as a set of principles that guide my interpretative practice, in which the theory (know) and observation (see) are accompanied by affect and sensation (feel). Focusing only on formal elements would be reductive because of both the character of Ettinger's artworks and her theoretical reflections, which put an emphasis on non-normative transfer of knowledge. I suggest such an approach provides deeper insights into Ettinger's thought and art.

This project of matrixial humanism of or from the body might turn out to be promising for various fields of study. To begin with, the system I develop here may be considered beneficial for the theoretical approaches the matrixial domain is grounded upon, especially psychoanalysis; since the matrixial theory itself offers a supplement to Freudian–Lacanian psychoanalysis, my attempt at foregrounding the body might offer some fresh insights into the area as well. Similarly, rethinking ethics through corporeality may be considered a chance for feminism to regain the female body, exercise its potentialities, and affirm the maternal-female corporeality outside the essentialist or biologically determined frames. For literary studies, the proto-ethical matrixial space may prove useful as a methodology or an interpretative strategy that helps unmask and explore

---

8   Brian Massumi, "Afterword. Painting: The Voice of the Grain," in Ettinger, *The Matrixial Borderspace*, 207.

trans-subjective relations within the practices of writing and reading.[9] Also, the delineated system appears to be especially significant in the context of the need to preserve the memory of the Shoah — the memory that is inevitably fading over time. With no alive eye-witnesses to possess the knowledge and experience of the Holocaust, these seem doomed to be lost soon; yet, if we apply the matrixial paradigm concerning the shareability of traces of trauma and other information originating in the non-I, this situation may not be hopeless. To use Paul Celan's words often referred to by Ettinger herself, "The world is gone, I have to carry you"[10] — now, in the dusk of the era of direct witnesses, we need to accept the responsibility to take over the burden and, consequently, work through the trauma of the Holocaust for and instead of those who cannot do it anymore. The proposed project tries to theorize a space for such a possibility.

* * *

I coined the phrase "corporeal aesth/ethics" and decided to use it for the title of the book as I believe it grasps the essence of my endeavors to foreground the body as the source and site of humanism. As we encounter Ettinger's art, we instantly find it to be inseparable from its ethical aspect. Also, Ettinger's art-working goes hand in hand with her theoretical propositions to the point that it becomes impossible — and unnecessary — to judge what is more important in this dyad. Thus, "aesth/ethics" is aimed to suggest that, in Ettinger's case, art and ethical reflection are intertwined to the extent that we can conceive of an aes-

---

9   Of course, the matrixial theory is used to read literature and poetry even by Ettinger herself. See, for instance, Bracha L. Ettinger, "*Fascinance* and the Girl-to-m/Other Matrixial Feminine Difference," in *Psychoanalysis and the Image: Transdisciplinary Perspectives,* ed. Griselda Pollock (Blackwell Publishing, 2006), 60–93, and Bracha L. Ettinger, "Demeter–Persephone Complex, Entangled Aerials of the Psyche, and Sylvia Plath," *ESC: English Studies in Canada* 40, no. 1 (2014): 123–54. Still, I believe that the matrixial aesth/ethical dimension as a tool for literary studies is yet to be discovered.

10 Paul Celan, "Great, Glowing Vault," in *Breathturn,* trans. Pierre Joris (Sun & Moon Press, 1995), 233.

thetic type of ethics, an ethical type of aesthetics, and anything in-between such categorizations as the clear-cut boundaries of these fields are no longer tenable. Art, theory, and ethics — these three aspects, as I intend to show, are deeply embedded in the capacities of corporeality.

The book is divided into two parts. In Part One, comprised of three chapters, Ettinger's works hold a central position; they are contextualized, introduced, and explored in terms of relationships between corporeality and ethics. Part Two, which embraces two chapters, is devoted to two encounters with the matrixial realm — Ettinger's partners in these encounters are theology and Holocaust studies, respectively. Together, both parts testify to the body as a humanizing space.

Chapter 1, "The Matrix: Contexts, Tropes, Implications" foregrounds the elementary category of Ettinger's thought. Since some of Ettinger's theoretical postulates are still relatively unknown and are prone to being misunderstood, in this chapter I develop a theoretical and contextual cartography of the matrixial realm. The matrix and the notions directly linked to it — co-naissance, severality, communicaring, subjectivity-as-encounter, and hospitality — are scrutinized and juxtaposed with the notions of Freud, Lacan, and Kristeva. Such analyses help me reveal the corporeal roots and humanizing implications of Ettinger's concepts. The chapter also takes a closer look at Ettinger's paintings from the *Eurydice* series and the *No Title Yet (Saint Anne)* series that are united by their womb-connotations; I try to identify their entanglement in aesth/ethics and to understand their peculiar hospitality.

While the first chapter thrives on a conviction that the matrix and its related notions both are grounded upon corporeality and allow for an ethical interpretation, Chapter 2 expands this idea, inquiring whether the Ettingerian notion of the body can be established as the root of matrixial ethics and reflecting on the potential of such a statement. "Human(e) Origins: The Female Body as an Ethical Site" begins with the recognition of female corporeality as a primary space where the becoming-subjects meet; this reading is supported by Levinasian ethics and schizoanalysis. Thereafter, this chapter covers the possibility of knowledge and meaning of and in the body, and the humanizing implications of this Ettingerian postulate; what is tackled are the questions of tracing sense beyond language and of experiencing the trauma (instead) of the Other. Finally, bodily encounters and trans-historical human(e) linkages are observed in the chosen "Eurydicial" artworks.

The closing chapter of the first part, "Femininity and Universality: Gender(lessness) of the Matrixial Body," faces questions concerning the universal character of the theory of the matrix and the arguably privileged status of women in Ettinger's oeuvre. It not only examines to what extent the matrix and the matrixial feminine difference are universal, neutral, or gendered, but also asks about men's access to the matrix. In the chapter, I touch upon such issues as essentialist and biologically determined interpretations of the system, women's rights, and different treatment of males and females in matrixial theory and Ettinger's art. Furthermore, I propose the notion of the "Ettingerian mythos" and look into its two variants — the theoretical mythos, including biblical and mythological figures, and the private one of Ettinger's family members in her art — in order to seek potential gender patterns.

Chapter 4, entitled "Through/With/In the Body: Theological Resonances of the Matrixial Specificity," is devoted to Ettinger's dialogue with Judeo-Christian theology, mediated by such philosophers as Jean-Luc Nancy, Giorgio Agamben, and Jacques Derrida. To be more precise, the chapter studies the resonances between incarnation and the logic of the matrix, and scrutinizes the matrixial notions (com-passion, covenant, and the Ettingerian interpretation of sacrifice) with regard to their religious connotations. In my search of biblical traces and openings in the matrixial corporeal aesth/ethics, I also look at an encounter with Ettinger's *Eurydices* through the prisms of revelation and messianic time.

The final chapter encompasses the issue that is inherent in the discussed oeuvre, Ettinger being a member of the second generation after the Holocaust. "In-Appropriate(d): Art, Humanism, and the Body after Auschwitz" is the only chapter in which art prevails over the matrixial theory. Hosting the Mizocz women and thus being embodiments of the feminine experience of the Shoah, Ettinger's paintings are collated with such issues as appropriation/appropriateness, Marianne Hirsch's Nazi gaze, Agamben's *homo sacer,* the Levinasian face of the Other, Derridean hauntology, and the psychoanalytic gaze along with its matrixial revision. In the chapter, I recognize the dangers of Ettinger's art in the context of the Holocaust, and simultaneously probe its ethical potential in the face of this unthinkably tragic event. My objective is to prove that, despite certain ethical risks this kind of art inevitably carries, Ettinger's marriage of theory and aesthetics makes a promise of re-conceptualizing humanism by means of corporeality and embodied encounters.

PART I

WITH-IN THE MATRIXIAL REALM

1

The Matrix

Contexts, Tropes, Implications

> [I]t is the Several, the more-than-one or less-than-one, the
> *"Un-en-moins"* (One-less), and the not-all that become a
> transgressive borderline, never all-encompassing, never
> limitless.
>
> — Bracha L. Ettinger, "The Matrixial Gaze"[1]

What is left of Eurydice after Orpheus's deadly gaze? When looking at Ettinger's *Eurydice* paintings created between 2000 and 2010, the viewer does not find the photograph serving as a background for the whole series — the picture of naked women and children from the Mizocz ghetto taken in 1942 just before their execution. Instead, one is left with the smears of paint that make any points of reference indiscernible. In *Eurydice*, No. 47 (2001–2006), one may — or may not — see the female figures standing as if in a row; one might recognize shades of faces, hair, and bodies (fig. 1). If not, one can at least observe and experience the color, rhythm, and pulse of the image. Indeed, pulsating reds and purples pierce the viewer with their intensity. The red color connotes passion and love, but also blood and dan-

---

1   Bracha L. Ettinger, "The Matrixial Gaze," in Bracha L. Ettinger, *The Matrixial Borderspace*, ed. Brian Massumi (University of Minnesota Press, 2006), 69. Emphasis in original.

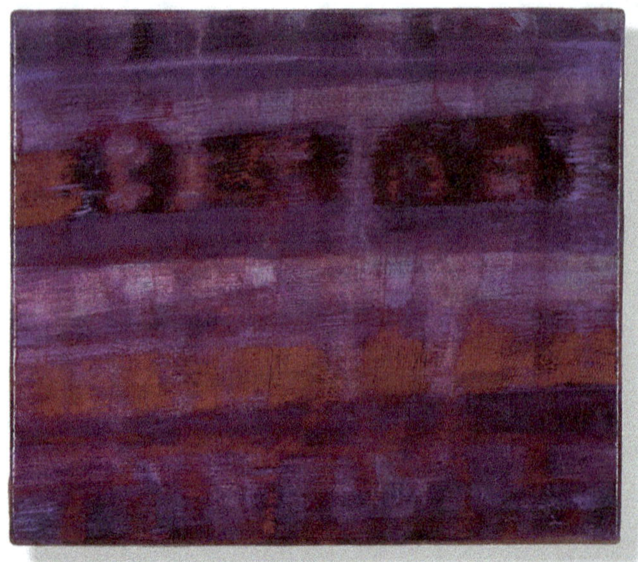

Fig. 1. Bracha L. Ettinger, *Eurydice,* No. 47, 2001–2006, oil on paper mounted on canvas, 23.3 × 27.7 cm. Collection: Ben Naftaly, Tel Aviv. © Courtesy of the artist.

ger, while both purple and red — as the colors of bruises — are related to the wound. If we choose to follow this trope, red and purple can serve to remind us of the past trauma or of its traces carried in the body. Moreover, as Brian Massumi notes, in the *Eurydice* series there is "less the image than the sensation of its remaining in its fading, re-arising: rhythm,"[2] which within psychoanalytical and feminist readings indicates Julia Kristeva's notion of the *chora.*[3] Therefore, perhaps there is nothing left to see when it comes to the women from the original photographs;

---

2   Brian Massumi, "Afterword. Painting: The Voice of the Grain," in Ettinger, *The Matrixial Borderspace,* 203.

3   Julia Kristeva, *Revolution in Poetic Language,* trans. Margaret Waller (Columbia University Press, 1984), 26.

still, *Eurydice,* No. 47 seems to expose us to bodily and maternal reminiscence of their presence.

This chapter will explore the model of relations in the triad of the matrix, body, and ethics found in Ettinger's theory and art. As I will show, the matrix — the basic unit in the Ettingerian system — and its related notions (severality, communicaring, co-naissance, subjectivity-as-encounter, and metramorphosis) originate in the materiality of the body and are open to ethical reading. This contention serves the purpose of preparing the ground for examining ethical implications of the Ettingerian notion of corporeality. The scrutiny of the first level of Ettinger's thought allows me to map the complexity of this territory and to provide the reader with the necessary terminology. While exploring the notion of the matrix, I will need to revisit its key psychoanalytic contexts; however, my aim is by no means to rehash concepts taken from Sigmund Freud, Jacques Lacan, or Kristeva that have been extensively explored elsewhere,[4] but rather to highlight their assumptions that Ettinger corresponds with, is inspired by, or questions in her research on sexual difference. Finally, I will focus on Ettinger's womb-like paintings, their traumatizing hospitality, and ethical potential.

The Matrix and the Phallus

The fundamental element of Ettingerian psychoanalysis, the matrix is defined as a supplementary sphere of subjectivity formation and a signifier of difference, subsequently named as feminine, but which is in fact non-gendered, non-Oedipal,

---

4   For the feminist rereadings of these notions, see, for instance, Luce Irigaray, *This Sex Which Is Not One,* trans. Catherine Porter and Carolyn Burke (Cornell University Press, 1985); Elizabeth Grosz, *Volatile Bodies: Toward a Corporeal Feminism* (Indiana University Press, 1994); Elizabeth Grosz, *Sexual Subversions: Three French Feminists* (Allen & Unwin, 1989); and Judith Butler, *Gender Trouble: Feminism and the Subversion of Identity* (Routledge, 2007).

and non-phallic.[5] This difference is not based on opposition, but rather it comprises the potential to meet and share, inspired by the prenatal encounter.[6] The womb, referred to by the Latin roots of the word *matrix*,[7] is perceived here as a space of difference that emerges in togetherness — the archaic space of an originary meeting, whose participants have an impact on each other. The extreme closeness they experience is connected with the notion of boundaries, which are either challenged or not yet defined fully. Ettinger's proposition responds to a pronounced hiatus in Freudian–Lacanian understanding of sexual difference, but it does not aim at expunging the phallic stratum.

In Freud's and Lacan's accounts of psychosexual development, the penis is a biological organ that provides a basis for reconsidering subjectivity while the phallus gains the status of a primary signifier of difference. In Freudian thought, the penis has a significant cognitive impact and establishes a major point of reference because of its apparent visibility during psychological development, which is starkly offset by the female sexual organ which is read or culturally understood to be non-existent especially for the male subject up to the age of puberty.[8] The phallus, in Lacan's proposition, is not an "organ," a "fantasy," or

---

5 For the matrix as a signifier, see, for instance, Griselda Pollock, "Introduction. Femininity: Aporia or Sexual Difference?," in Ettinger, *The Matrixial Borderspace*, 6–7 and 21, and Bracha L. Ettinger, "Weaving a Woman Artist with-in the Matrixial Encounter-Event," in Ettinger, *The Matrixial Borderspace*, 184.

6 For a comprehensive study of the matrixial feminine difference, see Griselda Pollock, "Mother Trouble: The Maternal-Feminine in Phallic and Feminist Theory in Relation to Bracha Ettinger's Elaboration of Matrixial Ethics/Aesthetics," *Studies in the Maternal* 1, no. 1 (2009): 9–10.

7 See Ettinger, "The Matrixial Gaze," 64.

8 Sigmund Freud, "The Infantile Genital Organization (An Interpolation into the Theory of Sexuality)," in *The Standard Edition of the Complete Psychological Works of Sigmund Freud*, vol. 19: *The Ego and the Id and Other Works (1923–1925)*, ed. and trans. James Strachey with Anna Freud (Hogarth Press, 2001), 145. In Freudian psychoanalysis, it is the castration complex — the discovery that not everyone possesses a penis resulting in the fear of losing it — that is significant in one's development.

an "object"[9]; here, male genitals provide nothing more than a conceptual space. Deprived of corporeality, the phallus becomes the category reigning over the Symbolic and Imaginary orders. More specifically, the phallus is pronounced "the signifier of the Other's desire."[10] The subject cannot know what the desire of the Other — including the mother — is, which is why the phallus is doomed always to fail. In his "Encore" seminar, Lacan goes as far as to claim that the phallus is "the signifier that has no signified."[11] The phallus is thus inextricably linked to lack, failure, impossible desire, and inadequacy. In the Freudian–Lacanian system, it nevertheless remains the main formative aspect of sexual difference: "the signifier of signification itself,"[12] as Bruce Fink has it. It is marked as a universal point of reference for both sexes. There is no other sexual organ than the male one during the phallic phase of an infant's psychosexual development described by Freud[13]; likewise, there is no female signifier analogous to the phallus in Lacanian psychoanalysis.[14] When turn-

9 Jacques Lacan, "The Signification of the Phallus," in Jacques Lacan, *Écrits: The First Complete Edition in English*, trans. Bruce Fink, Héloïse Fink, and Russel Grigg (W.W. Norton & Company, 2006), 579. It ought to be kept in mind that in Freud the distinction between the phallus and the penis is implied rather than clearly stated.

10 Ibid., 583.

11 Jacques Lacan, *The Seminar of Jacques Lacan, Book XX: On Feminine Sexuality, the Limits of Love and Knowledge, Encore 1972–1973*, ed. Jacques-Alain Miller, trans. Bruce Fink (W.W. Norton & Company, 1999), 81. Bruce Fink explicates it as follows: "[W]e might say that the phallus is the signifier of the barred relationship (or missing relationship) between the signifier and the signified (hence, the missing sexual relationship)." Bruce Fink, *Lacan to the Letter: Reading* Écrits *Closely* (University of Minnesota Press, 2004), 85.

12 Fink, *Lacan to the Letter*, 139.

13 Freud goes as far as to claim that in this phase of development there is "not a primacy of the genitals, but a primacy of the *phallus*." Freud, "The Infantile Genital Organization," 142. Emphasis in original.

14 Lacan claims that the phallus is the only formative element when it comes to sexual difference as it "is a symbol to which there is no correspondent, no equivalent." Jacques Lacan, *The Seminar of Jacques Lacan, Book III: The Psychoses 1955–1956*, ed. Jacques-Alain Miller, trans. Russell Grigg (Routledge, 1993), 176.

ing directly to the possibility of femininity in the phallic phase, Freud speaks frankly that there is none since "[t]he antithesis here is between having a *male genital* and being *castrated*."[15] Here, femininity appears only at the stage of puberty, when the vagina gains the function of a "shelter," or an envelope for the male sexual organ.[16] Lacan takes these statements further, maintaining infamously not only that "*woman* does not exist," but also that she "is *not whole (pas toute)*"[17]; he also sees maternity as the only functional position for a woman to occupy in a sexual relationship.[18] Simultaneously, aware that they take into consideration the male perspective only, both theorists suggest that they may miss the feminine side; womanhood and female sexuality thus remain unsolved mysteries of the "dark continent."[19]

The related issue is that of envy, which in Freudian–Lacanian psychoanalysis is read through the prism of a girl's supposed lack. Freud claims that in case of a girl, the initiation of the phallic phase is linked to the observation that a male child possesses something she does not — a penis. She is said to identify herself as missing the male organ. By extension, and as a result of this "wound to her narcissism," a woman "develops, like a scar, a sense of inferiority,"[20] not only of herself, but also of the

---

15 Freud, "The Infantile Genital Organization," 145. Emphasis in original.

16 Ibid.

17 Lacan, *On Feminine Sexuality*, 7. Emphasis in original. For an eye-opening reading of Lacan's views on sexual difference and anatomical difference, lack, and femininity that differs from that proposed by Ettinger, see Jacqueline Rose, "Feminine Sexuality: Jacques Lacan and the *école freudienne*," in *Sexuality in the Field of Vision* (Verso, 2020), 49–81.

18 Lacan, *On Feminine Sexuality*, 35.

19 Sigmund Freud, "The Question of Lay Analysis: Conversations with an Impartial Person," in *The Standard Edition of the Complete Psychological Works of Sigmund Freud*, vol. 20: *An Autobiographical Study, Inhibitions, Symptoms and Anxiety, Lay Analysis and Other Works (1925–1926)*, trans. James Strachey with Anna Freud (Hogarth Press, 2001), 212. For Freud referring to the phallic phase of development, see Freud, "The Infantile Genital Organization," 143, and Lacan, *On Feminine Sexuality*, 63 and 72.

20 Sigmund Freud, "Some Psychical Consequences of the Anatomical Distinction between the Sexes," in *The Standard Edition of the Complete Psychological Works of Sigmund Freud*, vol. 19: *The Ego and the Id and*

female sex in general. Freud associates penis envy with jealousy, deterioration of the daughter–mother relation,[21] and humiliation, which — in his view — is indispensable to a girl's movement towards femininity.[22] Penis envy thus becomes one of the formative aspects of feminine sexuality. Interestingly enough, in Freud's writings there is no mention of any possibility of womb envy.[23] This is criticized by, among others, Karen Horney, Melanie Klein, and Joan Riviere.[24] Riviere reflects on the notion of womb envy as follows:

Other Works (1923–1925), ed. and trans. James Strachey with Anna Freud (Hogarth Press, 2001), 253. See also Sigmund Freud, "On the Sexual Theories of Children," in *The Standard Edition of the Complete Psychological Works of Sigmund Freud*, vol. 9: *Jensen's "Gradiva" and Other Works (1906–1908)*, ed. and trans. James Strachey with Anna Freud (Hogarth Press, 2001), 217–18.

21 Freud, "Some Psychical Consequences," 254.

22 Ibid., 255–56. A comprehensive study of the concept — including the writings of Sigmund Freud, Karen Horney, Melanie Klein, Luce Irigaray, John A. Friedman, and Maria Torok, to name a few — is presented in Nancy Burke, ed., *Gender & Envy* (Routledge, 1998). The notion of penis envy is also employed by Jacques Lacan.

23 In Freudian psychoanalysis, the very existence of the womb is supposed to be denied by children. Freud writes that when questioning the origin of babies, a child jumps to the conclusion that they have to be born through the anal aperture, which is based on the belief that women (including the mother) possess a penis, the male sexual organ being a universal human trait. As Freud argues, "it was only logical that the child should refuse to grant women the painful prerogative of giving birth to the children. If babies are born through the anus, then a man can give birth just as well as a woman" (Freud, "On the Sexual Theories of Children," 219–20). This claim is interpreted by Ettinger as an act of defending male narcissism under the cover of a universal one, arguably applicable to both men and women (Ettinger, "The Matrixial Gaze," 54). Melanie Klein also observes the insufficiency of Freud's take on narcissism; on the key importance of the mother's body in children's development, see Melanie Klein, *The Psychoanalysis of Children,* trans. Alix Strachey (Grove Press, 1960).

24 See Karen Horney, "The Dread of Woman: Observations on a Specific Difference in the Dread Felt by Men and by Women Respectively for the Opposite Sex," in *Feminine Psychology* (W.W. Norton & Company, 1973), 133–46; Melanie Klein, "Love, Guilt and Reparation," in *The Writings of Melanie Klein*, vol. 1: *Love, Guilt and Reparation and Other Works, 1921–1945* (The Free Press, 1975), 306–43; Melanie Klein, "Envy and Gratitude,"

> [I]t is often not realized how much boys envy girls, and espe-
> cially envy women (their mothers) for their breasts and milk,
> and above all for the mysterious capacity women's bodies
> have of forming and creating babies out of food and what
> men give them.[25]

She also notes that even though the male envy is as frequent as its female counterpart, it is more concealed. As Riviere argues, firstly, boys possess the penis from the beginning, while girls have to wait until their breasts develop, thus being deprived of the weapon against jealousy; secondly, the womb remains inside as a secret female quality unavailable for possession and comprehension.[26] Yet, the debate about penis and womb envy does not lead to developing a more affirmative, non-dichotomous frame.

Ettinger's matrixial project shifts the emphasis from lack, castration, and jealousy to proximity, interconnectivity, and exchange. What we witness here is the pronouncement of another dimension that supplements the phallic one. Ettinger puts forward a hypothesis that while in the prenatal phase the matrixial subjectivity formation is more significant, after birth it gives way to the reign of the phallus. Yet, it does not mean that the matrixial sphere dissipates — it can resurface in the postnatal phase.[27] How is, then, the matrix/womb relation posited with reference to the phallus/penis dichotomy? Similarly to the womb, the penis as an organ forms the ground for the reconsideration of subjectivity in psychoanalysis. The phallus is

---

in *The Writings of Melanie Klein*, vol. 3: *Envy and Gratitude and Other Works 1946–1963* (The Free Press, 1975), 176–235; and Joan Riviere, "Public Lectures: Hate, Greed and Aggression," in *The Inner World and Joan Riviere: Collected Papers, 1920–1958*, ed. Athol Hughes (Karnac Books, 1991), 168–205. D.W. Winnicott also explores the relationship between envy and motherhood; among other examples, he observes in a patient "a very obvious envy of the mother's productive capacity." D.W. Winnicott, *Therapeutic Consultations in Child Psychiatry* (Routledge, 2018), 91.

25 Riviere, "Hate, Greed and Aggression," 189.

26 Ibid., 191–92.

27 See Ettinger, "The Matrixial Gaze," 84–85.

by no means an actual male organ; instead, as Ellie Ragland-Sullivan emphasizes, it ought to be understood as one of "structuring principles of human identity"[28] and as "the symbolic or representational agent of separation"[29]; the phallus is a signifier of difference that arises as a result of a series of splits in child development. The matrix is based on a similar mechanism since anatomy is by no means essentialized here: It only serves as a model; echoing the womb's attributes, the matrix simultaneously transfers it "from nature to culture."[30] We read:

> The womb and the prenatal phase are the referents to the Real to which the imaginary Matrix corresponds. But as a concept, the Matrix is no more — but no less — related to the womb than the Phallus is related to the penis. That is, Matrix is a symbolic concept.[31]

The womb — just as the penis — is treated as an opening to the reconsideration of difference. Identifying as a Lacanian psychoanalyst, Ettinger does not aim at formulating a counter-proposal to the underpinnings of Freudian–Lacanian system; instead of trying to reverse the hierarchy, she conceptualizes the coexistence of these two modes instead.

Ettinger's notion of the matrix resonates with Kristeva's theorization of the semiotic *chora*; the key difference between the two proposals lies in different positioning of the feminine element in the model of the psychosexual development. Kristeva's contribution to Lacan's phases of development, the *chora* is a postnatal yet pre-Imaginary "rhythmic space," which "precedes evidence, verisimilitude, spatiality, and temporality."[32] It is a paradoxical

---

28 Ellie Ragland-Sullivan, *Jacques Lacan and the Philosophy of Psychoanalysis* (University of Illinois Press, 1987), 80.

29 Ibid., 55.

30 Ettinger, "Weaving a Woman Artist," 181.

31 Bracha L. Ettinger, "Woman-Other-Thing: A Matrixial Touch," in *Matrix – Borderlines* (Museum of Modern Art, 1993), quoted in Pollock, "Introduction. Femininity," 17.

32 Kristeva, *Revolution in Poetic Language*, 26.

source of signification that eludes "all discourse."[33] Grosz delineates the infant–mother relationship in the space of the *chora* as follows: "The *chora* is a function of the child's unmediated (imaginary) relation to the mother's body, even though the child does not, at this point, recognise itself as separate or distinct."[34] In this maternal-corporeal receptacle, the boundaries of the self are not yet cognized by the infant. Still, when the becoming subject is supposed to enter the Symbolic, signification and difference need to come to dominate, hence ending the aforementioned borderless existence determined by drives. In the thetic phase, understood as "the threshold of language,"[35] the maternal connection is put to an end, and one of the processes responsible for it — along with the mirror stage and the identification of castration — is abjection. Belonging neither to the realm of a subject nor to that of an object, an abject is claimed to finalize the detachment from the mother, but it is also precarious for the infant due to the constant danger of being thrown back into the *chora*.[36] To experience abjection is to face the return of the repressed — bodily fluids, corpses, excrement, filth, or even certain foods — which results in a bodily, involuntary reaction. Yet, despite the hazard of dismantling the subject's (seemingly) established boundaries, abjection is identified as requisite for primary narcissism and, accordingly, for the entrance to the Symbolic.[37] It is so because, as Grosz puts it, "'proper' subjectivity and sociality require the expulsion of the improper, the unclean and the disorderly."[38] Ultimately, what is also expelled is boundless intimacy and communicability between the mother and the infant, the latter starting to abide to the law of the father.

What is, then, the position of the feminine/maternal in Kristeva's contribution? Starting with pregnancy, for Kristeva it is

---

33 Ibid.

34 Grosz, *Sexual Subversions,* 44. Emphasis in original.

35 Kristeva, *Revolution in Poetic Language,* 45.

36 Julia Kristeva, *Powers of Horror: An Essay on Abjection,* trans. Léon S. Roudiez (Columbia University Press, 1984), 13.

37 See ibid., 2, 12–13.

38 Grosz, *Sexual Subversions,* 71.

subjectless — it is the phase in which identity is inexistent.[39] In "Women's Time," she argues:

> Pregnancy seems to be experienced as the radical ordeal of the splitting of the subject: redoubling up of the body, separation and coexistence of the self and of an other, of nature and consciousness, of physiology and speech. This fundamental challenge to identity is then accompanied by a fantasy of totality — narcissistic completeness — a sort of instituted, socialized, natural psychosis.[40]

Inextricably linked to series of separations and scissions, the maternal body becomes the mediator between the natural and the cultural.[41] Finally, under a Kristevan reading, the woman who has become a mother begins to perform a phallic role for an infant.[42] Importantly, although the woman/mother and her body play significant roles in the infant's development, this schema is still rooted in incompleteness and split. Maternal corporeal space quickly becomes threatening, so it needs to be rejected in order for the infant to enter the paternal realm, that is, the realm of law and stability.

Both Ettinger and Kristeva endeavor to theorize the formation of feminine subjectivity based on female corporeality instead of the negative difference of "man *versus* woman" and "penis *versus* womb." However, while in Kristeva's thought the feminine flesh remains dangerous, Ettinger's matrixial theory attempts to go beyond this impasse. The following excerpt outlines the basis of the relationship between the body and the matrixial theory:

---

39 See Julia Kristeva, "Motherhood According to Giovanni Bellini," in *Desire in Language. A Semiotic Approach to Literature and Art,* ed. Léon S. Roudiez, trans. Thomas Gora, Alice A. Jardine, and Léon S. Roudiez (Columbia University Press, 1980), 237–43.

40 Julia Kristeva, "Women's Time," trans. Alice Jardine and Harry Blake, *Signs: Journal of Women in Culture and Society* 7, no. 1 (1981): 31.

41 See Kristeva, "Motherhood According to Giovanni Bellini," 238.

42 See Kristeva, *Revolution in Poetic Language,* 47.

> In building subjectivity-as-encounter upon the borderlink-ing between the subject-to-be and the becoming-mother, between the fetus and the female body-and-psyche, we should avoid the mistake of looking for the sense of the matrixial encounter in nature [...]. Yet anatomy makes a dif-ference that we should open to conceptualization.[43]

Ettinger distances herself from any form of essentialism or bio-logical determinism, but she simultaneously does not overlook the potential that feminine corporeality can provide. Such an approach enables her to read female bodily specificity as an inspiration, model, and vehicle for a new sense of subjectivity: the subjectivity before and beyond the split into entirely sepa-rate entities. Pregnancy becomes an opportunity to reconsider the relationship between the *I* and the *non-I:* to de-radicalize the Other, here understood as the co-participant in sharing and mutual change. Such an encounter is thus a *humanizing* event in a twofold sense of the word — it makes the becoming-subject both human and humane.

Introducing the concept of the matrix, Ettinger proposes an alternative take on pregnancy. The aforementioned claim on the challenged frontiers between the I and the non-I can by no means be perceived as a "fusion with the mother,"[44] as Kristeva has it. In the matrixial, the boundaries are fragile, fluid, and possible to be surpassed — or even suspended — but they are not absent as their lack would eliminate the possibility of sub-jectivity. Griselda Pollock clarifies that the matrixial domain is grounded upon two (or more) subjects "sharing space but never fusing, encountering but never dissolving their boundaries, jointly eventing without ever knowing fully the other's event."[45] Hence, there is no question of them merging into one as their relation would then turn into symbiosis, a state in which sub-jectivity is impossible. Instead, we ought to focus on the issue

---

43 Ettinger, "Weaving a Woman Artist," 181.
44 Kristeva, *Revolution in Poetic Language,* 47.
45 Pollock, "Mother Trouble," 14.

of linkages between the mother and the becoming-infant, who — despite not knowing each other — are precariously connected. Moreover, in contrast to Kristeva, in Ettinger's proposition, pregnancy and the prenatal phase are the inspirations for the inclusive and subjectivizing sphere of the matrix instead of being associated with separation and splitting, and thus psychosis and non-subjectivity. In short, Ettinger's aim is to expand the scope of psychoanalysis by including the subjectivizing potentiality provided by female corporeality.

As I have argued, Ettinger proposes a new understanding of difference. In this proposal, difference is always minimal — it prescribes closeness yet does not vanish or lead to non-subjective symbiosis or fusion. Moreover, it reaches beyond the phallus along with its binary paradigms, but this does not mean that it is connected with psychosis or mysticism.[46] This is why this type of difference is claimed to be "primary and originary"[47] — it comes before the phallic subjectivizing domain, thus not succumbing to its rules. Pollock delineates the matrixial difference as follows:

> [A] sexual difference originally "in the feminine," in an encounter of several subjective/subjectivising elements in the corpo-Real of becoming-life occurring in the shared borderspace of several becoming subjectivities, unknown and unknowable to the other, whose becoming the non-I other mutually co-affects in unpredictable and yet *subjectivising* ways.[48]

As we learn, the matrixial difference is feminine, but it is not posed as an opposition to the masculine difference; instead, it is grounded upon shareability and encounter between subjects-to-become, who — despite being anonymous — transform each other in the sphere of the matrix. The matrixial feminine differ-

---

46 See Ettinger, "Weaving a Woman Artist," 178.
47 Ibid., 184.
48 Pollock, "Introduction. Femininity," 3. Emphasis in original.

ence serves as a supplementary one, being not anti-phallic, but non-phallic or beyond-phallic. For this reason, it is also called *an-Other* difference — it is not supposed to function as the absolute Otherness to the phallic stratification.

It is also crucial to keep in mind that in Ettinger's thought, the "feminine" difference is not exclusive to women. In her writings, Ettinger makes it clear that while it is female corporeality which constitutes a point of reference for the notion of the matrix, the matrixial borderspace is not limited to women only; namely, human beings can experience the matrixial domain since their origins lie in the same space — the space of the feminine/motherly body.[49] Simultaneously, Ettinger does not claim that masculine and feminine potentialities of (re-)connecting with the matrixial are exactly the same; on the contrary, while both females and males "experience the womb as an archaic *out-site* and *past-side*," only females are exposed to it as an "*in-site/future-side*."[50] Agreeing that females are privileged due to this differentiation as they have more possibilities to enter this sphere, Ettinger emphasizes that males are by no means excluded from the access to the matrix.[51] Finally, in the matrixial understanding of the term, one's gender is the result of a subjectivizing cut and thus a product of phallic stratification, which is claimed to come when the matrixial sphere withdraws. Therefore, naming this difference "feminine" indicates its originary space instead of being an essentializing act that rejects the phallus-grounded paradigms and male subjectivity as formed in the postnatal phase.

The matrixial theory, in fact, endeavors to fill the blank spots of classical psychoanalysis acknowledged by Freud himself. One of the most significant hints Freud provides us with in this context can be found in "The 'Uncanny,'" in which *Muttersleib-phantasien* are identified among the sources of the feeling of

---

49　Bracha L. Ettinger, "Wit(h)nessing Trauma and the Matrixial Gaze," in Ettinger, *The Matrixial Borderspace*, 143.
50　Ibid., 143. Emphasis mine.
51　See ibid., and Ettinger, "Weaving a Woman Artist," 179.

uncanniness. As Freud notes, referring to the etymology of the uncanny, "*Unheimlich* is in some way or other a sub-species of *heimlich*."[52] When scrutinizing the ambiguity of the term in both language and psychoanalysis, Freud claims that uncanniness is not about fear in itself; it concerns the return of something that should have been left hidden, a repressed experience that used to be familiar. He clarifies it on the example of some people's fear of waking up in a coffin, realizing they have been buried alive:

> And yet psycho-analysis has taught us that this terrifying phantasy is only a transformation of another phantasy which had originally nothing terrifying about it at all, but was qualified by a certain lasciviousness — the phantasy, I mean, of intra-uterine existence.[53]

Freud, therefore, distinguishes between experiences that cause anxiety twice — before repression and as a result of it — and those that provoke anxiety only when repressed. The latter type is linked with the female body, identified as homely, originary, and universal (as it is the site where all human beings emerge), and at the same time uncanny.[54] Regarding this passage, Ettinger puts forward the thesis that we can trace the matrixial — or maternal womb/intrauterine — complex here.[55] Nevertheless, as the theorist stresses, the moment the matrixial withdraws in

---

52 Sigmund Freud, "The 'Uncanny,'" in *The Standard Edition of the Complete Psychological Works of Sigmund Freud*, vol. 17: *An Infantile Neurosis and Other Works (1917–1919)*, ed. and trans. James Strachey with Anna Freud (Hogarth Press, 2001), 226. Emphasis in original.

53 Ibid., 244.

54 Ibid., 245.

55 Ettinger links this concept to the matrixial phantasy. She writes, "While *castration phantasy* is *frightening at the point of the emergence of the original experience before* its repression, the *matrixial phantasy* (from *matrice,* for womb) is not frightening at the point of its original emergence, but becomes frightening when the experience is repressed. [...] Thus for both complexes the same affect, that of anxiety, accompanies the return of the repressed." Ettinger, "The Matrixial Gaze," 47. Emphasis in original.

the postnatal phase marks the beginning of the domination of the castration and Oedipus complexes. All in all, the return of the maternal repressed, as conceptualized by Ettinger, portrays the fundamental status of the corporeal connection between the mother and the infant.

The womb-inspired structure of relationships shatters the dominant dichotomies, such as active/passive, inside/outside, and I/non-I. First, in classical psychoanalysis, the womb tends to be seen on the one hand as a passive envelope — which Freud makes explicitly clear, for instance when discussing the puberty phase[56] — and on the other hand as a symbiotic, non-subjective space. In the matrixial model, the womb is shown as an archaic site of sharing with one's non-I's and, as Ettinger calls it, of "active/passive co-emergence."[57] Due to this change, the active/passive dualism ceases to apply. There is no possibility to divide the two instances as they constantly intertwine in the matrixial encounter. Next, the inside/outside binary is also disturbed when it comes to the womb. As Ettinger emphasizes, in the matrixial realm becoming-subjects "share and are shared by the same vibrating and resonating environment, where the inside is outside and the outside inside," and, as we read further on, "inside and outside vibrate together."[58] The boundaries between the seemingly clear distinctions become uncertain and fluid as they perpetually cooperate, producing a space that above all welcomes and privileges meeting and the experience of being together. Finally, as to the I/non-I differentiation, it does not cease, but it becomes more prone to alterations; the boundaries between the subjects may be stretched, suspended, or moved in the intimate matrixial meeting, but this happens

---

56 In "The Infantile Genital Organization" we read, "Maleness combines [the factors of] subject, activity and possession of the penis; femaleness takes over [those of] object and passivity. The vagina is now valued as a place of shelter for the penis; it enters into the heritage of the womb." Freud, "The Infantile Genital Organization," 145. Additions in square brackets in the original.

57 Ettinger, "The Matrixial Gaze," 64.

58 Ettinger, "Weaving a Woman Artist," 186.

without the abandonment of the self. In this mode, the focus is on exchange and transformation, both of which influence its participants substantially, and the boundaries are indeed unstable, yet not irrelevant.

The matrixial borderspace may seem paradoxical, or even controversial. Its underpinnings appear to be in ongoing dissonance with the phallic logic. Yet simultaneously we may note that such a deconstruction of dichotomies is first and foremost an attempt to reach their margins in order to define difference anew. Herein, femininity is freed from the burden of passivity, but also from its other burdens — it is no longer a negative term to masculinity, a minus, a container, or a potentially psychotic entity.

Trans-Subjective Matrixial Ethics

One of the basic attributes of such a recuperation of femininity is severality, seen as the originary instance of co-existence and relation between oneself and the Other. Pollock maintains that "in this model, there never was a celibate, singular subject becoming all on its own."[59] There is always more than one subject in the process of becoming. Severality is seen as the first experience of being with and embracing the Other, staged before the Other's rejection resulting in the entrance into binarized language.[60] Based on the female bodily specificity and the late prenatal encounter, it becomes the originary condition of the ethical relation between subjects. Ettinger describes the ambiguous structure of the term as follows:

> [I]t is the Several, the more-than-one or less-than-one, the *"Un-en-moins"* (One-less), and the not-all that become a transgressive borderline, never all-encompassing, never lim-

---

59 Pollock, "Introduction. Femininity," 4.
60 See Ettinger, "The Matrixial Gaze," 72.

itless. Multiple and plural matrixial subjectivity is therefore also singular and partial.[61]

Severality always includes at least one partner-in-difference, but it does not equal multitude. Moreover, the subject is never complete during an encounter with the non-I — neither of them is a fixed or stable entity; hence, apparent "fullness" is not the aim of the matrixial. Yet, even though it implies partiality as a principle, the notion of severality puts an emphasis on intimate shareability that occurs between two (or more) subjects before and beyond the act of rejection.

A number of properties of the concept can be found in the etymology of the word "several." In Anglo-French, Middle French, and Latin, it stands for "existing apart," "separate," and "different," whereas since the 1530s "several" has meant "more than one."[62] These meanings comprise the lack of fusion or symbiosis — what we are dealing with in the matrixial is a certain division into separate entities that are nevertheless strongly connected with each other; the limits of the self, though challenged, are not abandoned here.[63] Ettinger emphasizes the minimal difference that needs to exist for subjectivity to emerge. At the same time, the subjects are partial per se since they are still in the process of becoming, that is, in a state of openness to change. Such incompleteness is by no means comfortable: It seems that it is not accidental that there is some degree of "severity" in the word "severality." Pollock summarizes it as follows:

This is not about cosy mothers and babies, symbiosis and fusion, nor fantasies of return to oceanic self-loss which are so common in phallic invocations of the maternal body as

---

61 Ibid., 69. Emphasis in original.

62 *Online Etymology Dictionary*, s.v. "several," https://www.etymonline.com/word/several.

63 This is why this structure of relations is not symbiotic, but reciprocal and asymmetrical. The boundary between two subjects participating in a covenant is maintained, but there is a possibility of changing, moving, or transcending it.

subjectless otherness and origin from which the subject must be separated to be a subject at all. It invokes a dimension of subjectivity, co-existing with, but shifting the phallic, in which the subject is fragile, susceptible, and compassionate to the unknown other who is, nonetheless, a *partner* in the situation, but a partner-in-*difference*.[64]

The matrixial experience is not "cosy," safe, and easy since it requires vulnerability and an ability to share and be shared, to transform and be transformed; it is based on proximity that challenges the notions of selfhood and individuality, but without confusing the I with the non-I.

Severality is modeled on the physical proximity of two or more becoming subjects, witnessed in the late prenatal/pregnancy phase, in which there is no privileged subject position. The mother and the child are equally important in this covenant: There is no question of superiority of one over another, for they base their relation on reciprocity. Nevertheless, they are recognized as different, and their dissimilar experiences do not merge while being shared. Hence, just as the mother–child relationship is asymmetrical, so is the matrixial meeting. The subjects connecting in severality continuously transform each other while transforming themselves, engaging in humanizing intimacy, but without making a pretense that their change can in any way be predicted, channeled, or equally distributed. There is no symmetry concerning the flow of information between the subjects, in a sense that what one gives is not what the other receives — what can be communicated is an affective partial trace coming from the non-I by no means mastered by them. All in all, the relationship between the mother and the child in the severality of the prenatal phase, if transferred to the field of psychoanalysis, provides it with such features as reciprocity and togetherness in not-yet-binarized difference.

The notion of severality contributes to the paradigm shift in psychoanalysis. The phallic logic is the logic of cut, in which the

---

64 Pollock, "Mother Trouble," 5–6. Emphasis in original.

paradigm is based on exclusion — on the principle of either/or. In this system, the woman is always posed as negative, or the radical Other for the man. As a result, the emergence of subjectivity is conditioned by split, rejection, or castration — one needs to separate oneself from the Other in order to become a subject. Matrixial psychoanalysis gives us another possibility: Before and beside this set of cuts indispensable in the phallic stratification, the logic of inclusion is at work. This is exactly where the matrixial meets Gilles Deleuze and Félix Guattari's notion of becoming. To summarize, in schizoanalysis, becoming always aims at a certain "goal" — becoming-woman, becoming-animal, or finally becoming-imperceptible, where becoming-woman is only one of many stages. Becoming extracts "particles between which one establishes the relations of movement and rest, speed and slowness that are *closest* to what one is becoming, and through which one becomes."[65] Therefore, becoming is an active, continuous, and rhizomatic struggle to become-somebody/something. For Ettinger, this process is potentially humanizing since it is always performed in severality and leads to a mutual transformation of co-participants. Becoming is hence always becoming-*with*-somebody/something, or becoming-*together*.[66] From the matrixial perspective, one is becoming precisely because one is engaged in the act of connecting oneself with the anonymous yet intimate Other. Due to such a re-consideration, the woman — as well as the mother — ceases to be merely the first stage leading towards a greater aim, and instead she is seen as a meaningful and active partner-in-becoming.

The underlying feature the partners in the matrixial domain ought to possess is *hospitality*. This ambiguous term, inspired by the womb and including both being a host and being a guest, is essential in the ethical reading of the matrix.[67] Without hos-

---

65 Gilles Deleuze and Félix Guattari, *A Thousand Plateaus: Capitalism and Schizophrenia,* trans. Brian Massumi (University of Minnesota Press, 1987), 318. Emphasis in original.

66 See Pollock, "Introduction. Femininity," 15.

67 The meaning structure of the word embraces "from Old French *ospitalité* 'hospitality; hospital,' from Latin *hospitalitem* (nominative *hospitalitas*)

pitality — along with fragility, openness, response-ability, and matrixial desire to link with the Other — the very entrance to this sphere is impossible as one needs to go beyond the phallic structure of relations and relinquish one's narcissistic tendencies in order to participate in the humanizing encounter with the Other fully. Pollock writes that hospitality "is a matrixial transformational potentiality for the human subject."[68] In this sense, it facilitates the further flow of knowledge, affects, traumas, and desires between the becoming subjects, which has ethical implications, such as the ongoing humanizing change. Hospitality can be linked to *communicaring* — an Ettingerian neologism described by Catherine de Zegher simply as "caring within sharing,"[69] which, however, has a more convoluted range of meanings. Communicaring embraces transferring and sharing knowledge; being protective, empathetic, and responsible; and involving community or commonness. Its Latin counterpart, *communicare,* adds to the Ettingerian notion such actions as imparting, uniting, and participating.[70] Both hospitality and communicaring invoke proximity between and with-in subjects; precisely, it is severality of the feminine corporeal specificity that becomes the borderspace of the humanizing resonances of workings incited by these two notions.

What seems to embrace the core of the Ettingerian approach to relations between subjects and their bodily underpinnings is co-naissance. A multileveled structure of the notion provides us with numerous hints concerning its meaning and significance. *Conaissance* in French means "knowledge," while *naissance* means "birth." The prefix *co-* gives us a sense of sharing. Moreover,

---

'friendliness to guests,' from *hospes* (genitive *hospitis*) 'guest; host.'" *Online Etymology Dictionary,* s.v. "hospitality," https://www.etymonline.com/word/hospitality.

68 Pollock, "Introduction. Femininity," 28.

69 Catherine de Zegher, "Drawing Out Voice and Webwork," in *Art as Compassion: Bracha L. Ettinger,* ed. Catherine de Zegher and Griselda Pollock (ASA Publishers, 2012), 135.

70 *Online Etymology Dictionary,* s.v. "communication," https://www.etymonline.com/word/communication.

the word *co-naissance* is connected with *reconnaissance,* which, as Pollock notes, means both "acknowledging an other" and "cognitive understanding at a second take."[71] This subtle wordplay immerses us in the broad scope of the notion. Co-naissance is therefore a non-cognitive and non-linguistic comprehension of togetherness and shareability, which reveals a quality of belatedness. The shared birth of several subjects implies that the feminine body is something more than a mere container, since it is a space of emerging relations that are mutually affective and performed in closeness, but also a sphere facilitating the transmission of non-linguistic knowledge.

The logical outcome and the underlying feature of all of Ettinger's concepts discussed so far is a new dimension of subjectivity: subjectivity-as-encounter. Inspired by the originary encounter in the womb, responsible for the creation and maintenance of life, it becomes the first instance of subjectivity, subverting the primary position of separation. As severality is a prerequisite for this form of subjectivity to occur, unity, autonomy, and self-sufficiency are put into question. Yet this state of ambivalence and vulnerability is the condition without which it is impossible to partake in new connections, as Deleuze would put it. Ettinger delineates this paradoxical subjectivizing mode as follows:

> In subjectivity-as-encounter — where an-other is not an absolute separate Other — [relations-without-relating] turn both of us into partial-subjects, still uncognized, thoughtlessly known to each other, matrixially knowing each other, in painful fragility.[72]

This excerpt, connoting the prenatal state, not only sheds light on what kind of knowledge is being transferred, but also depicts the relationship between partners in the covenant. In the matrixial sphere, any Other turns into a co-existing border-Other, which makes the encounter profoundly ethical. In such a space, there

---

71 Pollock, "Mother Trouble," 7.
72 Ettinger, "Wit(h)nessing Trauma," 144.

is no place for rejection, aggression, or total Otherness that has to be either incorporated as the same or made an enemy. Moreover, the information that is being passed on in the encounter is non-cognitive and seemingly empty from the phallic viewpoint; it originates in the non-I and can be processed only affectively, fueling transformations to come.

The encounter with the experiences of the Other, often traumatic and threatening to one's sense of integrity, is the greatest prospect of the matrixial model. Occurring before split, subjectivity-as-encounter is based on extreme proximity between subjects that do not necessarily know each other; still, there is a certain intimate element that circulates between them, be it knowledge, memory, or pain. The relationship between them is unnameable in terms of binarized language: It happens on the affective, rather than language-based level. Yet if we are able to abandon comfort and security, this transfer becomes profoundly humane instead of being unconceivable and devastating; this intimate sharing can be described as "hurting while healing"[73] — it is distressing, but it provokes almost boundless closeness with the Other. This, in turn, leads to new distribution of the processed affective information, which may often be traumatic and impossible to be handled by a singular subject.

It is the very act of shattering the boundaries between the I and the non-I that is responsible for the chance for subjectivity-as-encounter. A shift from "borderlines" into "thresholds"[74] postulated by Ettinger makes the non-phallic encounter before and beyond rejection possible since subjects with unalterable frontiers not only are unwilling to sacrifice their stability (thus depriving themselves of the possibility of engaging in the matrixial encounter), but also preserve the status quo of the radical Otherness, which is impossible to be changed within

---

73 Bracha L. Ettinger, "Trans-Subjective Transferential Borderspace," in *A Shock to Thought: Expression after Deleuze and Guattari,* ed. Brian Massumi (Routledge, 2002), 236.

74 Ettinger, "Wit(h)nessing Trauma," 144.

the phallic frame. The fluidity of borders is the attribute of subjectivity-as-encounter that carries an ethical promise of such a connection in which the division into what is mine and what belongs to not-me — or where I end and where the Other begins — is less significant than the very act of becoming-together.

The question of frontiers clarifies the new subjectivizing dimension Ettinger proposes, which has to be carefully distinguished from pre-subjectivity. Even though subjectivity-as-encounter is inspired by the intrauterine period, identifying it as a form of pre-subjectivity undeservedly locks it in this phase, prohibiting its return in the later stages of development. A more proper name for it seems to be *inter*subjectivity — the prefix *inter-* conjures up togetherness, reciprocity, and mutuality, emphasizing that subjectivization happens between two or more subjects. However, the most adequate means to describe this notion is provided by yet another prefix: *trans-*. Always partial and never complete, matrixial subjectivity not only is formed together with the anonymous yet intimate non-I, but also transcends such a relation. *Trans*-subjectivity is inextricably linked to a change of its participants and to a transfer of knowledge beyond comprehension, but not beyond sense; this type of subjectivity crosses the boundaries of subjects, inducing their fragile transformation. Ettinger notes that subjectivity in such an understanding "accompanies the phallic subjectivity all along its voyage in time and place, even if its sources are in the 'pre-.'"[75] Matrixial subjectivity continues to resurface occasionally in the moments of extreme openness to the Other, breaching the order of the phallus.

Trans-subjectivity also stems from a change in the understanding of the relation between the orders of the Real, the Imaginary, and the Symbolic. As Ettinger notes, the "late" Lacan describes these registers as interconnected, as if in an inextricable braid; in this braid-like structure, "the knowledge of the Real marks the Symbolic with its sense and its thinking no less

---

75 Ettinger, "Weaving a Woman Artist," 183.

than the Symbolic gives meaning to the Real via signification and concepts."[76] In the matrixial mode of connectedness, a braid crosses the boundaries of singular subjects, interweaving the fragments of knowledge originating in non-I's.[77] Traces of traumas, phantasies, or affects gain the possibility of going beyond one's psyche and of reaching the Other in an always already-mediated form. To be precise, in trans-subjectivity we can find "a *signifiance* between no-meaning and sign,"[78] unthinkable from the phallic point of view, and *almost*-impossible from the matrixial one. The trans-subjective sphere, therefore, not only links the three registers more closely together, but also reveals fields of knowledge that Oedipus and the castration paradigm cannot conceive of.

The matrixial encounter is not an experience that is closed in the Real, which would render it unintelligible and psychotic. The Real — described by Sean Homer as an "indivisible brute materiality that exists prior to symbolization" and that eludes the two other orders[79] — is strongly linked to the female bodily specificity. Yet, while referring to the feminine corpo-Reality, the matrix transcends the pre-subjective frame. Moreover, it changes the perspective on the relation between the three registers as it occurs in all of them. We read:

Matrixial events *do not remain* on the level of the corpo-Real in relation to affective space-time-body instants or in relation to interconnectivity. Retunings of distance-in-proximity are beyond-the-phallus psychic events that testify to the matrix in the fields of the Real, the Imaginary, and the Symbolic — the three distinct-yet-linked interfaces of each event. With the matrix of the Imaginary and the Symbolic, we identify and locate inscriptions of traumas and phantasies veiling transformed traces of archaic relations-without-relating

---

76 Ibid., 189.
77 Ibid.
78 Ibid. Emphasis mine.
79 Sean Homer, *Jacques Lacan* (Routledge, 2005), 82.

between *I* and unknown *non-I* [...], and shared matrixial *objets a.*[80]

The fact that matrixial events are not reigned by phallic paradigms does not sentence them to materiality and incomprehensibility of the Real. On the contrary, the matrix resurfaces in all the orders, participating in the transfer of disruptive information of the anonymous Other(s). Moreover, shared knowledge is never complete or unaltered—it is in the process of constant change, thus disturbing the question of origin; in other words, the trauma of the non-I also partially touches the I in the matrixial encounter. Importantly, in the Ettingerian system, castration is recognized as not the only path towards the Symbolic order. Ettinger identifies yet another way—a process she calls metramorphosis, which is claimed to take place before and beyond such phallic paradigms as gender distinction, castration, and separation.[81] Metramorphosis is a process of transmission occurring among partial-subjects, whose results are change and "affective 'communication.'"[82] Fragments and traces of events, traumas, phantasies, encounters, and other phenomena are transferred through this change-inducing process which always happens in severality[83] and asymmetry, but not supremacy.[84] The entrance to the metramorphic route is grounded upon involvement and closeness up to the point of partial relinquishing of one's borders. All these qualities contribute to the power of metramorphosis to lead the becoming-subject from the Real towards the Symbolic.

---

80 Ettinger, "The Matrixial Gaze," 69. Emphasis in original.

81 See ibid., 69–70.

82 Ettinger, "Wit(h)nessing Trauma," 143.

83 As Ettinger claims, metramorphosis occurs "between subject and object, among subjects and partial-subjects, between me and the stranger, and between some partial-subjects and partial-objects." Ettinger, "Weaving a Woman Artist," 181.

84 Bracha L. Ettinger, "Matrix and Metramorphosis," *differences* 4, no. 3 (1992): 201.

Multileveled matrixial trans-connectedness described in this section constantly reveals its ethical potential. Due to such terms as severality, becoming-together, communicaring, co-naissance, or subjectivity-as-encounter, the position of the Other changes significantly. The Other ceases to be in radical dissonance with the I, turning into the border-Other instead. The implications of such a change are profoundly humanizing since the border-Other is the Other in proximity, but also full of empathy, open, and shareable, while the I — in this relationship — does not have the necessity or need to reject them. Furthermore, in the matrixial realm, each borderline may become a threshold for transfer and trans-formation — processes which carry knowledge otherwise inaccessible; it is, for example, this knowledge of the non-I shared in the encounter that is potentially ethical. Partial subjectivity that emerges out of such a transmission of intimate information between the participants is also based on matrixial closeness, paradoxical in its structure. Proximity experienced in the matrix is almost boundless, yet not symbiotic; still, it links seemingly contradictory time-spaces of several subjects provided that they are fragile and open to an encounter. Matrixial closeness ought not to be comprehended in phallic terms as it escapes their classification, resembling symbiosis, fusion, or psychosis but being none of them. The ethics of the domain theorized in Ettinger's writings corresponds to its aesthetic realization, where we — as viewers — may witness traces of corporeality, motherhood, and humanizing covenant.

Almost-Boundless Canvas Space

Massumi writes that in Ettinger's case "painting is a crowd dynamic."[85] Indeed, she creates "crowds" of paintings that constitute different series, out of which the *Eurydice* series is most famous. In fact, there are not only crowds of paintings in it, but also these are the paintings of crowds as the *Eurydices* are grounded upon the already mentioned photograph from the

---

85 Massumi, "Afterword. Painting," 206.

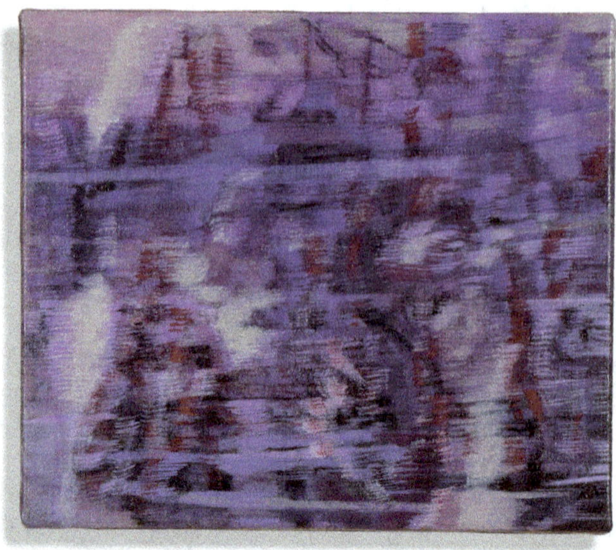

Fig. 2. Bracha L. Ettinger, *Eurydice,* No. 44, 2002–2006, oil on paper mounted on canvas, 23.1 × 27.8 cm. © Courtesy of the artist.

Mizocz ghetto depicting the moment just before the execution of a group of naked women with children. The series undergoes evolutionary changes; one of them is the gradual disappearance of the source picture. It seems that its final moment — or its stage of becoming-imperceptible — comes after 2000; while in the paintings produced before this year the women can still be found to a greater or lesser degree, since 2000s we, as viewers, have been left with nothing but trust. It is the paintings from this period — *Eurydice,* No. 44, No. 45, No. 47, and No. 50, and *No Title Yet,* No. 2 and No. 3 (both subtitled *Saint Anne*) — that are of interest here.

All the mentioned paintings from the *Eurydice* series share technique and color scheme. Mechanical lines that appear on the canvas due to the movement of the paint brush resemble the effect the photocopy machine produces. As to the colors, in *Eurydice,* No. 44 (2002–2006), purples dominate, with the

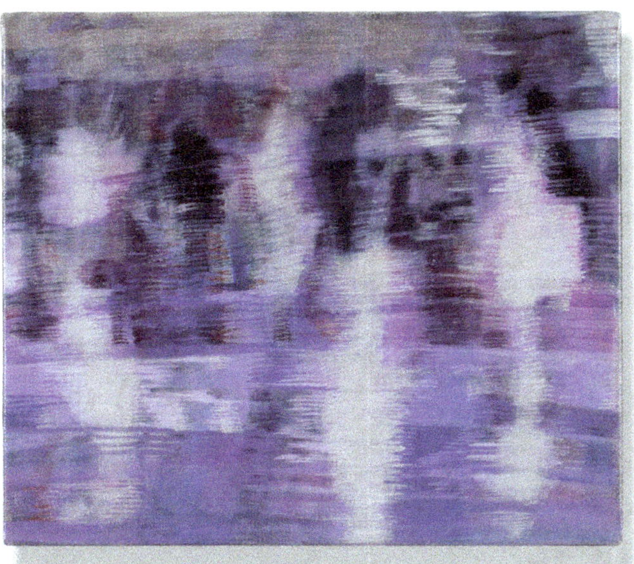

Fig. 3. Bracha L. Ettinger, *Eurydice,* No. 45, 2002–2006, oil on paper mounted on canvas, 24.2 × 29.7 cm. Collection: Menning and Massumi, Toronto. © Courtesy of the artist.

occasional touch of red and pale, fading hues (fig. 2). The light elements gain in strength in *Eurydice,* No. 45 (2002–2006), similar in terms of purples, but visibly brighter, with more pale spots; when the red color is concerned, it is almost inexistent in this piece (fig. 3). *Eurydice,* No. 47, already mentioned in the first part of this chapter, lacks the light described in the previous works (fig. 1). Herein, it is the red color that begins to struggle for supremacy, making the artwork look as if more covered with paint; yet, the red still does not overpower the purples. Such a tendency is continued in *Eurydice,* No. 50 (2006–2007) (fig. 4). Intense and overbearing, the red color pulsates out of the picture boundaries while purple withdraws. Simultaneously, in contrast to the previous works, the horizontal lines are bright here, connoting the photocopier with greater strength. The color scheme, although evolving through these works of art, is unceasingly intense, be it purple, red, or the mixture of both. Despite their

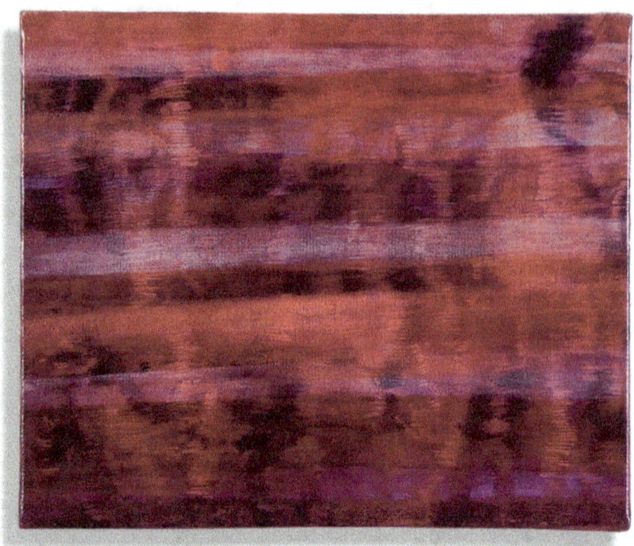

Fig. 4. Bracha L. Ettinger, *Eurydice,* No. 50, 2006–2007, oil on paper mounted on canvas, 25.3 × 31.1 cm. Collection: Museum of Angers. © Courtesy of the artist.

differences, these paintings seem to flow together, sharing certain vigor and agitation,[86] to be grasped in their color and the artistic method respectively.

The features mentioned above contribute to the "feminine" character of the paintings in the matrixial sense of the term. If we take *Eurydices,* No. 47 and No. 50 into consideration, their blood-colored, rhythmical, and pulsating fluidity can be argued to reach the viewer with utmost power because of its connota-

---

86 In an article concerning Ettinger's recent painting (including *Eurydice,* No. 50 and the *No Title Yet* series to be commented upon later in this section), Erin Manning notes the artist's movement "from suspension to agitation." While the question of suspension remains relevant in the context of these artworks, the noun "agitation" perfectly describes Ettinger's technique to be witnessed in them. Erin Manning, "Vertiginous Before the Light: The Form of Force," in *Art as Compassion,* ed. Zegher and Pollock, 174.

tions with the womb environment, connoting the *chora*. Yet, as we will see further on, the femininity explored here goes beyond the *chora*. Still, these attributes are strictly linked to the female corpo-Real, as Ettinger often names it, because they are the origins of such theoretical propositions as severality, blurred borders, togetherness, and exchange. As can be seen, the images are womb-like in both their resemblance to the feminine bodily specificity in its physiological sense and their symbolic layer. The latter element is considered to be the more relevant one since — as Pollock argues — it is not as much "content" as "*gesture*"[87] that matters in Ettinger's artistic activity. This emphasis on gesture is related to its affective potentiality. Once again, *Eurydice, No. 50* can exemplify it well. Namely, the image relies above all on our senses, sensibility, and sensations as there is nothing else left to follow but color, occupying a central position here. Therefore, when it comes to the workings of the aforementioned features, it is the affect that Ettinger's womb-like paintings are supposed to provide us with, sending us back to the matrixial borderspace.

The layers of paint in these *Eurydice* paintings cover the source photograph with more precision than the previous artworks from the series. However, is the very existence of this image — or its visibility — relevant at all? In No. 44, the women from Mizocz are imperceptible. Simultaneously, in the light, central-left part of the painting, a half-profile face resurfaces. The pale paint brushes resemble the skin on the face, probably of a woman, as suggested by the shape of cheeks. The darker stains are like a mouth — open as if in awe — and an eye, looking away. Yet, this impression is a subjective one: Each spectator may see a face somewhere else in the image, which makes an encounter with it both volatile and uncertain. *Eurydice, No. 45* appears to give us more in terms of the women's bodies; the light smears of paint connote female shapes whilst faces can be seen

---

87 Griselda Pollock, *After-Affects / After-Images: Trauma and Aesthetic Transformation in the Virtual Feminist Museum* (Manchester University Press, 2013), 3. Emphasis in original.

in the upper part of the artwork. It may be, however, the case that such an association is possible only when we are familiar with the historical document hidden underneath the layers. In No. 47, the situation is similar: There is a "crowd" of faces possible to be grasped. *Eurydice,* No. 50, however, does not give us this opportunity, relying on the mentioned bodily tropes instead of the actual distinguishable body-like shapes. What we witness in these paintings is a movement from a purely aesthetical encounter to an ethical one, occurring on two levels. One of them may be perceived as historical; it is connected with the knowledge of the background of Ettinger's artworks from this series — the traumatic and tragic history behind them. However, there is also an-Other level — ahistorical, or maybe timeless — grounded upon openness to an unknown Other. One of the underlying theses of the matrixial theory is that one does not need to know one's non-I's to affectively experience the fragments of their events, pain, or traumas. Indeed, due to Ettinger's gesture, the *Eurydice* figures are in a sense made accessible — ready for an encounter. Yet, what they require is receptivity — one has to be able to receive affective information and share it, already transformed.

We may identify the mentioned artistic strategies as hospitable invitations to the matrixial sphere of reciprocity. The reason for such a claim is related to the complex notion of boundaries in these artworks, which gradually lose their stability. In other words, internal borders become increasingly dispersed and elusive, with no specific figures or hints for the viewer to follow. On the one hand, the result is a tightened interaction between the pieces themselves. Massumi claims that Ettinger's "paintings call to one another, call each other forth, across the distance between the first floor and basement, across today and yesterday, light and darkness, visibility and invisibility, in a collective rhythm building from the rhythm of each."[88] The canvases forming the series are thus interconnected, producing together an affective storyline. On the other hand, shaky borders make the

---

88 Massumi, "Afterword. Painting," 205.

images more vulnerable; they do not possess the power — or privilege — to "speak" in a clear manner. For instance, *Eurydice, No. 50*'s boundaries seem not to be found within the frames, due to which the image is prone to any subjective alterations. Simultaneously, this quality may possess an ethical value in matrixial terms. The fragility of the artworks contributes to their openness to the potential observer, who is not obliged to follow the linear story anymore. Thus, they affectively encourage the viewer to enter their realm. Interestingly enough, while the paintings may be claimed to be fragile, this feature is also mirrored in the viewer, who can choose to surrender to the artwork. Therefore, vulnerability, openness, and interaction become *sine qua non* conditions for the encounter with the paintings. Emphatically, just as the paintings invite us to the sphere of reciprocity, we need to prove our readiness to receive the imprints of the Other's experiences since we may not only to be transformed, but also pass the exchanged knowledge on.[89]

In Freudian psychoanalysis, two profound male characters are summoned: Oedipus (with his mythological heritage) and Moses (a religious father figure). Accordingly, we may identify the corresponding females in Ettinger's art and theory, one of them being Eurydice and the other Saint Anne, who appears to be a patroness of not only the matrixial connection but also of the Eurydices themselves. Eurydice is a figure that grasps the complexity of both the matrixial encounter and Ettinger's painting; Judith Butler outlines it as follows: "She is coming toward us, she is fading away from us, and both are true at once, and

---

89 The viewer, as a participant of the encounter, is claimed to transmit the story "to others, present and archaic, cognized and uncognized appealing from the future, from the past or from an unrealized virtuality." Bracha L. Ettinger, "Copoiesis," *Ephemera: Theory and Politics in Organization* 5, no. X (2005): 710. Importantly, however, the matrixial encounter does not happen every time when the subject is ready. We read, "A passage is expected but uncertain, the transport does not happen in each encounter and for every gazing subject, listening subject, touching or moving subject. We can look and observe, but it takes en-duration in con-templation to see." Bracha L. Ettinger, "Fragilization and Resistance," *Studies in the Maternal* 1, no. 2 (2009): 9.

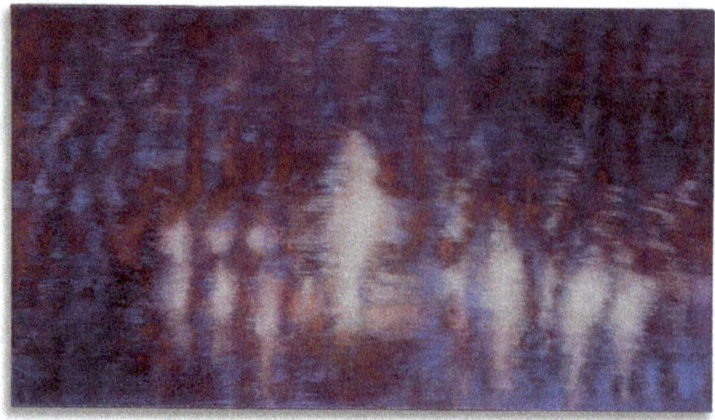

Fig. 5. Bracha L. Ettinger, *No Title Yet*, No. 2 (*Saint Anne*), 2003–2009, oil on canvas, 30 × 54 cm. Private collection, Berlin. © Courtesy of the artist.

there is no resolution of the one movement into the other."[90] A paradoxical encounter with Eurydice is on the verge of impossibility as she is simultaneously present and absent, still alive and already dead, appearing and disappearing. Her act of shattering the dichotomies forms the ground for Ettinger's theoretical assumptions. When it comes to Anne, whose name in Hebrew means favor or grace, she is a patroness of femininity and of the matrix itself. The mother of Mary and a patron saint of unmarried women, housewives, women in labor, mothers, and grandmothers, Anne serves a function as the foremother. As the above list implies, she also becomes a patroness of the women captured in the Mizocz photograph — females of different ages, with children, pregnant, united by not only their gender but also their fate, which in this historical document at the same time belongs to the future and is already met; she is thus a guardian saint of those who have been returning from the dead by means of Ettinger's artistic gesture. Summing up, Anne portrays aspects of the matrix different from those Eurydice stands for, while remaining strictly connected with the other female figure.

---

90 Judith Butler, "Foreword: Bracha's Eurydice," in Ettinger, *The Matrixial Borderspace*, viii.

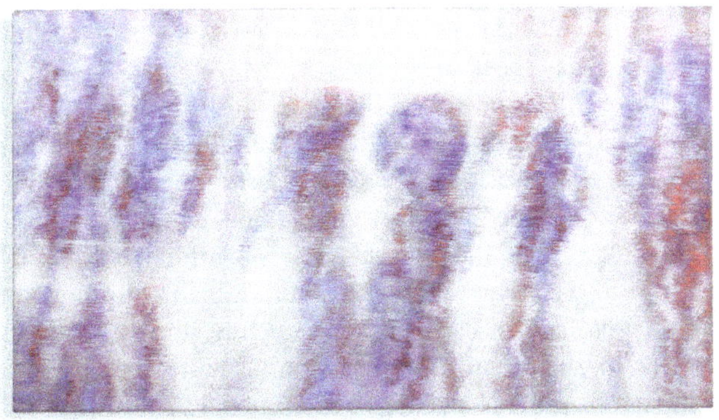

Fig. 6. Bracha L. Ettinger, *No Title Yet,* No. 3 (*Saint Anne*), 2003–2009, oil on canvas, 30 × 54 cm. Private collection, Brussels. © Courtesy of the artist.

Despite the suggestion that the subtitle and the time of creation give us, we may note a number of differences between *No Title Yet,* No. 2 (*Saint Anne*) (2003–2009) (fig. 5) and *No Title Yet,* No. 3 (*Saint Anne*) (2003–2009) (fig. 6), in terms of color and overall impression. No. 2 is noticeably darker than the analyzed *Eurydices,* with its purple-claret surroundings and dispersed vertical light lines. In No. 3, we also observe a "crowd" of vertical stains, but, in contrast, there is an extraordinary amount of light covering most of the canvas, filled with the beige color, and occasional reds and purples mixed in sharp brushstrokes. Color-related bodily connotations are prominent in No. 2, which — when the artworks are collated — emphasizes the unusual character of *Saint Anne,* No. 3; to be precise, in the context of the paintings explored here so far (and, in fact, the pre-2000 period of Ettinger's artistic work), such brightness appears to be transgressive. While the *Eurydices* move in the direction of increasing overlay of the canvas, No. 3 is dazzlingly and disruptively fulgent. Simultaneously, in a broader cultural context, light tends to stand for positive emotions and affects. Such an ambivalence on the level of color makes *Saint Anne,* No. 3 a piece of art immune to binarization. When juxtaposed, No.

2 and No. 3 may leave two distinct impressions, and yet, as I will argue, they may speak together.

In the *Saint Anne* series, the issue of knowledge is thrown further into crisis. In No. 2, there is nothing to be seen — no imprint of an at least semi-present figure to grasp. Therefore, there is no question of an examination in terms of the "plot" or "story." In No. 3, on the other hand, in the middle of the canvas one may find a resurfacing face — does it belong to one of the Eurydices? — as if in a spasm. Consequently, there is an element that possibly strives for the return to visibility, but we cannot identify it or provide a proof of its existence. This brings us to yet another issue — technique. In the discussed series, Ettinger's artistic technique changes. According to Erin Manning, in the *Saint Annes* xeroxing is not used anymore and digital scanning is reduced in favor of the so-called "eye-hand-painting" or "mind-hand-feeling" technique, which, as we read, "brings the machinic tendencies (light, horizontal scanning) to the artwork *through painting itself.* Ettinger's hand-eye becomes the scanner, screening the painting toward the light."[91] Since the chance for grasping at least a remnant of a historical event hidden under the layers of paint is thus eliminated, we are left with affective reading only. The artist's "hand-eye" is able to guide us into the sphere of the painting provided that we are open, ready, and fragile enough for such an encounter with an unknown, unidentifiable non-I.

Ettinger's feminine-bodily paintings support the entanglement of aesthetics in ethics by challenging such notions as knowledge, boundaries, or subjectivity; being in line with Ettinger's theory, these images widen its scope. All the artworks presented connote the womb by means of colors, rhythm, and pulse-like, fluid painting technique. Simultaneously, they transport the womb "from nature to culture," supporting the Ettin-

---

91 Manning, "Vertiginous before the Light," 174n10. Emphasis in original. In this essay, Manning identifies *Eurydice,* No. 50 and the *Saint Annes* discussed in my study as the constituents of the "light-series." See ibid., 173.

gerian notion of the matrix. Not only do they resemble the prenatal encounter, but they also invite one in, making one (re)turn to the maternal. The Other in this meeting is not going to be cognized; instead, the non-I here is forever anonymous. This brings us to the issue of knowledge in this art. Not being mere representations of the historical events, these images produce an affective charge — one to be experienced rather than comprehended. In this sense, they do not so much communicate their content as hospitably communicare with/for the spectator, inviting engagement via transference, communion, and alteration. The paintings also question the stability of boundaries, which is yet another reason why they are related to the maternal sphere understood in the matrixial terms. Their borders seem to be either bendable or inexistent, providing a threshold that the viewer can cross. Yet, what is necessary for such an action is certain willingness on the part of the viewer to give in to the encounter, without which it remains locked. Such an approach undoubtedly has its risks — the said encounter carries the possibility of experiencing pain, traumas, and phantasies that do not originate in the I. Still, it also hides a promise of inducing a change that is impossible for the singular, sole subject: a change that can take place only in togetherness. This issue leads us to the reconsideration of subjectivity in Ettinger's covenant of aesthetics and theory. It is not enough to say that that the experiences arising from the artistic encounters are subjective; rather, they are trans-subjective. They involve the transgression of boundaries of an individual self and an exchange of otherwise impossible information among partial-subjects, while requiring extreme vulnerability that reaches beyond the phallic division into the I and the non-I. Yet, most significantly, the *Eurydice* and *Saint Anne* paintings testify to the ethical dimension in art: to the humanizing and reciprocal linkage with the Other that sends us back to the matrixial space.

Towards the Aesth/ethics

The power of Ettinger's theoretical intervention lies in a new understanding of the subjectivizing process that is based on the womb, pregnancy, and femininity, and that frees womanhood from the burdens of passivity, negativity, and psychosis. Without essentializing the female body, Ettinger affirms its potential for closeness, hospitality, and transmission. The trans-subjective matrixial covenant that she theorizes resurfaces in her art-working. What we witness in the analyzed *Eurydices* and *Saint Annes* is a (re)turn to the ethics of the maternal/matrixial. In these corpo-Real artworks, there is no specified knowledge or story included. In fact, there is no need for it there; what we encounter engrained on the canvases are the affective tropes and traces that can touch the viewer in their willingness to receive and transmit them. Shareability, openness, almost-boundlessness, and the overall womb-like atmosphere not only further portray the notion of trans-subjectivity, but also, more importantly, contribute to the turn towards the ethics of an aesthetic encounter, which supplements and inspires Ettinger's theoretical assumptions.

Having traced bodily origins and ethical connotations in the fundamental concepts of the matrixial theory, we need to proceed with the next question in line: can the body itself — as constructed in Ettinger's *oeuvre* — be a potentially ethical site, or even the origin of ethics?

2

Human(e) Origins

The Female Body as an Ethical Site[1]

The pregnant woman is *meouberet*: she is a transport station, a station of passage for a period of passage, and she herself is a conductor, a conveyer, a transmissible and transitive vector, a transit place, a transition time, a scavenging channel for a transition period.

— Bracha L. Ettinger, "Weaving a Woman Artist
with-in the Matrixial Encounter-Event"[2]

[T]here is always a collectivity, even when you are alone.

— Gilles Deleuze and Félix Guattari, *A Thousand Plateaus*[3]

---

1   Portions of this chapter appeared in Anna Kisiel, "Aesth/Ethical Bodies: Bracha Ettinger's *Eurydices* and the Encounter with the Other's History," in *The Body in History, Culture, and the Arts,* ed. Justyna Jajszczok and Aleksandra Musiał (Routledge, 2019).

2   Bracha L. Ettinger, "Weaving a Woman Artist with-in the Matrixial Encounter-Event," in Bracha L. Ettinger, *The Matrixial Borderspace,* ed. Brian Massumi (University of Minnesota Press, 2006), 185. Emphasis in original.

3   Gilles Deleuze and Félix Guattari, *A Thousand Plateaus: Capitalism and Schizophrenia,* trans. Brian Massumi (University of Minnesota Press, 1987), 177.

> The feminine is that difference, the feminine is that incredible, unheard of thing in the human by which it is affirmed that *without me the world has meaning.*
>
> — Emmanuel Levinas and Bracha L. Ettinger, "What Would Eurydice Say?"[4]

Ettinger's untitled sketch made between 1988 and 1989 invites us to face a crowd of bodies, comprised of two distinct groups — Ettinger's parents on the left and women from the Mizocz ghetto on the right (fig. 7). It calls us to explore the relation arising between them on the canvas. Finally, it points to Ettinger herself: to her human origin — represented by the image of Bluma Fried and Uziel Lichtenberg — and to her humanity, to her compassionate working-through the image of women who are humiliated and sentenced to death.

It is the female body seen as both a human and a humane source that is going to be of interest in this chapter. I will show that in Ettingerian psychoanalysis the body gains a status of a potentially proto-ethical dimension. Referring to Emmanuel Levinas's humanism and Deleuzian–Guattarian schizoanalysis, I will portray the body in Ettinger's psychoanalysis and artworking as an originary site of emergence of meaning beyond linguistic structures and of an encounter during which knowledge and traumas can be passed on and processed; it is because of these very potentialities that the body may be read a source and a site of ethics.

Prototypical Connectedness

From the biological viewpoint, the body is a *sui generis* container for the womb placed within it. This organ is an essential part of the motherly body, but it by no means implies that women are defined by its very presence or possession; still, "anatomy

---

4   Emmanuel Levinas and Bracha L. Ettinger, "What Would Eurydice Say?," trans. Joseph Simas and Carolyne Ducker, *Athena: Philosophical Studies* 2 (2006): 142–43. Emphasis in original.

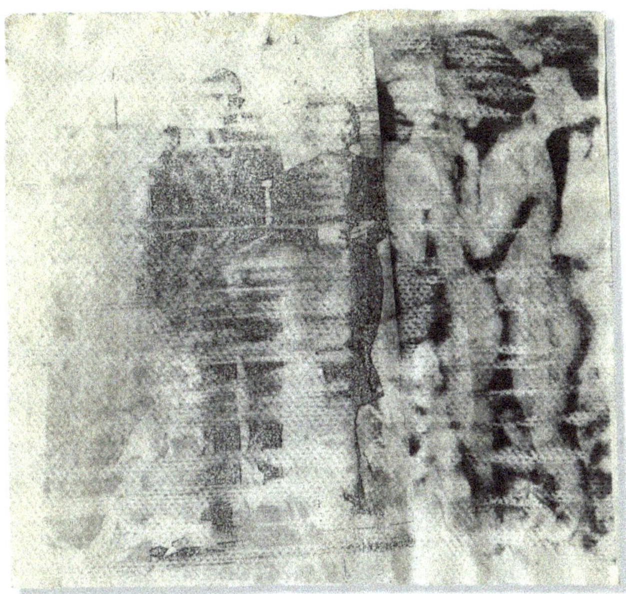

Fig. 7. Bracha L. Ettinger, *No Title — Sketch,* 1988–1989, xerography, photocopic pigment and ashes, graphite, charcoal on paper, 22.3 × 24.9 cm. © Courtesy of the artist.

makes a difference that we should open to conceptualization."[5] The existence of the womb within female corporeality provides us with a possibility of theorizing the body itself. Regarding the questions of "nature," female specificity, and difference, we read:

> The incestuous *in/out-side* relation (*rapport*) between subject-to-be and archaic-m/Other-to-be, by its connection to female corporeal invisible specificity (which is the place where this incest takes place), is the source in the Real for a matrixial stratum. This source should not mislead us into seeking the matrixial encounter in biological nature, any more than the phallic structure stands for the corpo-Real male sexual organ (although it is related to it). [...] In the matrix,

---

5 Ettinger, "Weaving a Woman Artist," 181.

her sex difference in terms of female bodily specificity, and experiencing an affected linking to that specificity (the Real), inscribes a paradoxical sphere on the Symbolic's margins.[6]

In the matrixial context, the notion of incest gains a new meaning. As Ettinger argues, in the prenatal phase, the desire to establish a linkage with the Other — felt by both partners in the encounter — is an ordinary phenomenon, essential to the emergence of life and to the orienting to the matrixial sphere.[7] Therefore, instead of being forbidden, the incestuous relation becomes humanizing and creative. Ettinger makes it clear that even though the meeting between two becoming-subjects is held within the feminine specificity (and thus becomes the origin of the matrixial domain), the matrix itself is no more natural than the phallus. Moreover, female connectedness to her corpo-Reality contributes to the movement towards the peripheries of the Symbolic, the order Ettinger expands in her thought.

As it is the body that becomes a space abundant in linkages, in this respect the matrixial theory connotes Levinas's view on ethics. Bodily tropes gain special relevance in his notion of sensibility, which comprises an affective and sensual encounter without objectification, without the firm division into the I and the non-I, and yet entirely egoistic.[8] The relationship between the body, the Other, and sensibility is solidified as being *for* the Other is absorbed into a greater pre-subjective, corporeal stratum.[9] Because of its precognitive status, this stratum is not necessarily preoccupied with the issue of selfhood; as Levinas

---

6   Bracha L. Ettinger, "The With-In-Visible Screen," in Ettinger, *The Matrixial Borderspace*, 105. Emphasis in original.

7   See Bracha L. Ettinger, "*Fascinance* and the Girl-to-m/Other Matrixial Feminine Difference," in *Psychoanalysis and the Image: Transdisciplinary Perspectives*, ed. Griselda Pollock (Blackwell Publishing, 2006), 88, and Ettinger, "The With-In-Visible Screen," 94.

8   See Emmanuel Levinas, *Totality and Infinity: An Essay on Exteriority*, trans. Alphonso Lingis (Duquesne University Press, 1969), 134–35, 187–88.

9   Emmanuel Levinas, *Otherwise Than Being or Beyond Essence*, trans. Alphonso Lingis (Kluwer Academic Publishers, 1991), 76–77.

writes, "I am bound to others before being tied to my body."[10] He goes on to claim that "subjectivity is sensibility — an exposure to others, a vulnerability and a responsibility in the proximity of the others, the-one-for-the-other."[11] However, the status of the female/motherly body is more complicated here. Analyzing Levinas's *Totality and Infinity*, Kathryn Bevis notes that, "Woman is the precondition for human reflection because she represents [...] a primary human contact and sociality which is not yet the transcendent, shattering presence of the face-to-face relationship with the Other."[12] Simultaneously, she argues, the woman here is neither dialogic nor personalized; rather, she functions as a hospitable envelope for someone else's selfhood.[13] In *Otherwise than Being*, the status of the maternal body undergoes transformation as sensibility becomes strongly connected to the metaphor of maternality. Sensibility is described as "maternity, gestation of the other in the same," where maternity is understood as "responsibility for others, to the point of substitution for others and suffering," and as "bearing par excellence."[14] The maternal metaphors are utilized here to grasp the complexity of the ethical relationship, based on extreme responsibility: responsibility that assumes the option of being affected or even hurt by the Other. Maternity — the site of bearing and the first habitation, by means of which one is originarily "bound to others" — becomes a primary, sensible structure of relations.

Ettinger's affinity to Levinas's understanding of connectedness, encounter, and the maternal body is indisputable, yet when it comes to femininity itself, Ettinger clarifies that for the philosopher it becomes an impassable limit. In *Existence and Existents*, Levinas proclaims that "the other par excellence is the

---

10 Ibid., 76.

11 Ibid., 77.

12 Kathryn Bevis, "'Better Than Metaphors'? Dwelling and the Maternal Body in Emmanuel Levinas," *Literature and Theology* 21, no. 3 (2007): 321. See Levinas, *Totality and Infinity*, 154–55.

13 Bevis, "'Better Than Metaphors'?," 321.

14 Levinas, *Otherwise Than Being*, 75.

feminine,"[15] because of which Ettinger locates Levinas within a wider tendency noticed also in Sigmund Freud and Jacques Lacan: the tendency of identifying the feminine as the Other. She also notices the paradoxical image arising from his early writings — the woman lacks the dialogic quality and is Otherness per se, and yet the originary difference is undoubtedly feminine, as feminine/motherly attributes are ascribed to it. Moreover, femininity is absent in Levinas's late work. Referring to this work, Ettinger puts forward a hypothesis that this notion might have been abandoned not so much because it has ceased to be essential from the ethical viewpoint as, in fact, because the philosopher has started to comprehend the fact that the woman is not an absolute Other, that, instead, the feminine informs the very notion of subjectivity.[16] Ettinger clarifies that the attributes of subjectivity are precisely the traits that used to be identified as feminine.[17] These assumptions are confronted in a conversation between the two theorists, in which Levinas makes a diagnosis that

> Woman is the category of future, the ecstasy of future. It is that human possibility which consists in saying that the life of another human being is more important than my own, that the death of the other is more important to me than my own death, that the Other comes before me, that the Other counts before I do, that the value of the Other is imposed before mine is. [...] The feminine is that difference, the feminine is that incredible, unheard of thing in the human by which it is affirmed that *without me the world has meaning.*[18]

---

15   Emmanuel Levinas, *Existence and Existents,* trans. Alphonso Lingis (Nijhoff, 1978), 85. The issue of feminine otherness reappears in Levinas's work. For instance, in *Time and the Other,* the woman becomes "essentially other." Emmanuel Levinas, *Time and the Other [And Additional Essays],* trans. Richard A. Cohen (Duquesne University Press, 1987), 86.

16   Ettinger, "Weaving a Woman Artist," 190.

17   Ibid.

18   Levinas and Ettinger, "What Would Eurydice Say?," 142–43. Emphasis in original.

In this passage, we can see to what extent Levinas's vision of the feminine coincides with his ethical postulates. Although he claims that femininity is yet to come, the qualities that resurface in this quotation — being for the Other, responsibility, and encounter — prove that the woman is in Levinas's thought persistently present despite her apparent absence.

Ettinger's take on femininity posed in the context of Levinas confirms his position as one of the precursors of the ethics of the matrixial. As Ettinger claims, femininity is responsible for a change in the understanding of the subject, channeled towards a humanizing encounter.[19] The encounter — directly linked to the feminine corporeal specificity — is preceded by and contains an act of self-fragilization, necessary to face the Other openly despite the threat of suffering; such a vulnerable position contributes to the turn towards alterity that Levinas delineates. Most significantly, Ettinger strongly objects to treating the woman as a total Other. She argues that in the matrixial reading of Levinasian femininity, responsibility changes into response-ability, which, while still including the activities of taking care of the Other and answering the Other's calls, also opens up the possibility of responding: dialogue and asymmetrical reciprocity, missing in this philosopher's proposition.[20] Yet, even though the aforementioned postulates and arguments are critical to a degree, they are nevertheless deeply and expressly grounded upon the Levinasian ethics of the Other.

What helps Ettinger establish her position beyond the limitations faced by Levinas is the shift to the border-Other, linked to the notion of severality. Using weaving metaphors, Ettinger describes the woman as a border-Other, with whom relations can be established provided that "we follow upon *her* threads in the texture and the textile of the web."[21] She continues, "She is weaving and being woven. She bears witness in the woven

---

19 See Ettinger, "Weaving a Woman Artist," 190.
20 See ibid.
21 Ibid., 194. Emphasis in original.

textile and texture of psychic transsubjectivity."[22] These excerpts illustrate the matrixial structure of connections, which is active-passive (the subject is simultaneously an addresser and an addressee of processed information), reciprocal, and asymmetrical. Responsive and willing to share, the woman is also a witness. However, what is the condition of her potential response and generosity is eagerness to pursue the traces which belong not to her only, and yet can be found within her psychic space. The imagery employed here distinguishes femininity from the conceptualizations based on fusion or symbiosis: Here femininity is seen not as borderless fluidity, but as a web comprised of threads and strings. Nevertheless, we ought not to ascribe the notion of multitude to this structure since "matrixial subjectivity does not entail an endless multiplicity of singular individuals, but rather a limited multiplicity — a severality — that traverses subjectivity."[23] Modeled upon the motherly specificity and prenatal/pregnancy phase, severality makes any subject a co-subject, or a transject,[24] whereas an Other ceases to be total.

Ettinger transcends Levinasian intersubjectivity, which despite being oriented towards the Other remains immersed in singularity and individual experience. Simultaneously, by no means does she reject the prominence of his proposition, which after all places the female body at the center of his ethical project. Interestingly enough, while for Levinas "the other par excellence is the feminine," for Ettinger it is subjectivity that par excellence is the feminine. Moreover, the originary subjectivity resurfacing in Levinas's writings, described by means of female attributes, corresponds to the matrixial proposition of

---

22 Ibid., 196.

23 Ibid.

24 In her writings, Ettinger introduces the notion of the transject in order to question the boundary between a subject and an object in the matrixial sphere. See Bracha L. Ettinger, "Uncanny Awe, Uncanny Compassion and Matrixial Transjectivity Beyond Uncanny Anxiety," in *Psychoanalysis in French and Francophone Literature and Film*, ed. James Day (Brill, 2011), and Bracha L. Ettinger, "Fragilization and Resistance," *Studies in the Maternal* 1, no. 2 (2009): 1–31.

trans- or co-subjectivity that transcends the pre-mode of subjectivization. What serves the purpose of deconstructing a "lone subject"[25] in Ettingerian sphere is motherhood, the notion that is the common ground for both theories, being a primary structure and source of relations, as well as a mode of responding in vulnerability. All the notions described here reveal their eminent entanglement with corporeality and embodiment. Ettinger's recognition of femininity as the ethical subject itself transports us to the future Levinas has spoken of.

The weaving metaphors direct Ettinger's work towards Deleuze and Guattari. In the matrixial theory, weaving signifies interrelatedness and the possibility of passing fragments of information by virtue of the proximity of threads. "[T]he texture and the textile" that Ettinger writes about imply tangibility and the relation to senses; this sensual structure has no fixed beginning or end and no center or peripheries, as its boundaries are being constantly negotiated, which renders it similar to the rhizome.[26] Deleuze and Guattari share an interest in linkages, incompleteness and (non-linear) continuity, experimentation, and change; inspired by Baruch Spinoza, they argue, "We know nothing about a body until we know what it can do,"[27] which stresses the role of exercising the body and transforming it. Returning to Ettinger's proposition, experimentation can be linked to boundary-shattering openness to the encounter with the anonymous non-I, which becomes a potential path towards change. What seems to be particularly interesting from the perspective of matrixial psychoanalysis is the Body without Organs (BwO). The BwO stands in opposition to the organism, but does not precede it; rather, their relation can be described through adjacency and co-existence.[28] Being "the matrix of intensity," the BwO is occupied by circulating

---

25 Bracha L. Ettinger, "Transcryptum: Memory Tracing in/for/with the Other," in Ettinger, *The Matrixial Borderspace*, 164.

26 See Deleuze and Guattari, *A Thousand Plateaus*, 7–22.

27 Ibid., 300. For Deleuze and Guattari on Spinoza, see ibid., 299.

28 Ibid., 190–91.

"waves and vibrations, migrations, thresholds and gradients,"[29] but also flows and desires.[30] Because of such an abundance within the BwO, one of the assumptions is that "there is always a collectivity, even when you are alone."[31] In order to achieve such excess, Deleuze and Guattari propose to experiment with one's corporeal possibilities, but with moderation and care as this practice poses a danger of emptying the body.[32] The relation between the BwO and the organism may be compared to that between the matrixial and phallic subjectivizing strata, since in both juxtapositions we can speak of a degree of adjacency.[33] What is more, both theories employ an analogous vocabulary, pertaining to alliances, exchange, vibration, flows, boundaries and thresholds, asymmetry, and decentralization. Finally, within the matrixial theory and schizoanalysis, what is at stake is not completeness, but the very endeavor to transgress the imposed limitations: of the body and of the dominant discourse. For these reasons, Deleuzian–Guattarian intervention into psychoanalysis provides an important context and manifests Ettinger's bodily entanglement, which — being straightforward in schizoanalysis — often remains only implied in the matrixial theory.

Despite a number of significant correspondences between the two thoughts, Ettinger reconsiders the need for "opening the body to connections"[34] pronounced by Deleuze and Guattari, and introduces an irreducible ethical aspect of an alliance between several entities. One of the vital discrepancies revolves around multiplicity,[35] instead of which Ettinger pro-

---

29 Ibid., 178.

30 See ibid., 187.

31 Ibid., 177.

32 See ibid., 175. Caution is an underlying principle of this process, for "a body without organs that shatters all the strata, turns immediately into a body of nothingness, pure self-destruction whose only outcome is death." Ibid., 189.

33 We should, however, keep in mind that in Deleuze and Guattari's pair there is an aggressive element — as the organism is called an "enemy" — non-existent in Ettinger. Ibid., 184.

34 Ibid., 186.

35 See ibid., 7.

poses severality. Severality emphasizes the lack of coincidence in an encounter,[36] for its participants ought to fulfil certain conditions such as extreme openness, commitment, or self-fragilization. This fact is directly connected to the issue of caution raised by Deleuze and Guattari. Ettinger notes that while entering the matrixial sphere requires specific qualities, leaving it — and thus putting the encounter to an end — is beyond one's control[37]; hence, the questions of choice and moderation become less relevant. Also, who and what do we encounter in both propositions? Ettinger notes that we can speak of subjectivity in the matrixial encounter, but such subjectivity is partial, as is shared information. To specify, in the matrixial space it is not only intensities that circulate; we can also find traces of residual, affective knowledge originating in the Other. Yet another incongruity can be revealed in the descriptions of the rhizome and the matrixial domain. Even though both have no beginnings or ends, the matrix is always a *border*space — a space moving towards margins rather than focusing on "the middle."[38] The final vital incompatibility between Ettinger and Deleuze and Guattari regards the position of the feminine. It seems that the feminine-motherly aspect underlies some of the concepts elaborated by Deleuze and Guattari; yet, except for the notion of becoming-woman, it is far from being pronounced.[39] As for Ettinger, experimentation and change are not enough, a proof of which is the complex notion of metramorphosis, incorporating transmission, transformation, and communication. Instead, she

---

36 In contrast to the rhizome, which "connects *any* point to *any* other point," the matrixial web is by no means coincidental. Ibid., 21. Emphasis mine.

37 We read, "in the trauma and the phantasy of the other, you can sometimes register your own involvement. And then, from then on, you cannot choose when to terminate the covenant, or how, or to what extent, if at all. Because the phallus cannot master the Matrix." Bracha L. Ettinger, "The With-In-Visible Screen," 118.

38 Deleuze and Guattari, *A Thousand Plateaus*, 22.

39 For an in-depth study of schizoanalysis as a male-oriented system, along with its potentialities and threats for feminist critique, see Elizabeth Grosz's chapter "Intensities and Flows," in *Volatile Bodies: Toward a Corporeal Feminism* (Indiana University Press, 1994), 160–83.

focuses on the body as a prototype for a different mode of connectedness; the encounter in severality theorized in reference to maternity and prenatality both inspires and is inspired by ethics.

Knowledge in/of the Humanizing Specificity

Announcing that "the unconscious is structured like a language,"[40] Lacan frees the unconscious from the bounds of biology and instincts[41]; he also shows it as "Eurydice twice lost,"[42] that is, a kind of structured yet unreachable knowledge. Commenting on the relation between the unconscious, femininity, and language, Jacqueline Rose observes that

> For Lacan [...], there is no pre-discursive reality [...], no place prior to the law *which is available and can be retrieved*. And *there is no feminine outside language*. First, because the unconscious severs the subject from any unmediated relation to the body as such [...], and secondly because the "feminine" is constituted as a division in language, a division which produces the feminine as its negative term.[43]

Can then psychoanalysis conceive of female bodily specificity, the knowledge it might carry, and its ethical dimension?

---

40 Jacques Lacan, "The Freudian Unconscious and Ours," in *The Seminar of Jacques Lacan, Book XI: The Four Fundamental Concepts of Psychoanalysis*, ed. Jacques-Alain Miller, trans. Alan Sheridan (W.W. Norton & Company, 1981), 20. Emphasis in original.

41 Jacques Lacan, "The Instance of the Letter in the Unconscious, or Reason Since Freud," in *Écrits: The First Complete Edition in English*, trans. Bruce Fink, Héloïse Fink, and Russel Grigg (W.W. Norton & Company, 2006), 434.

42 Lacan, "The Freudian Unconscious and Ours," 25. In this excerpt, Lacan compares the relation between the analyst and the unconscious to that between Orpheus and Eurydice.

43 Jacqueline Rose, "Feminine Sexuality: Jacques Lacan and the *école freudienne*," in *Sexuality in the Field of Vision* (Verso, 2020), 80. Emphasis mine.

Ettinger reconsiders the primacy of "the unconscious is structured like a language," pointing to its paternalized undertone and its theoretical insufficiency. She identifies the father as one who,

> "carries" language and the symbolic dimension that establishes this [the paternal] function and that enables the infant to create a distance from the mother, who is at the source of the originary experience. The *Ideal of the I* has a calming influence; it is like a sympathetic paternal representation that helps us to distance ourselves from the phallic, archaic, symbiotic, and incestuous mother, who, in her complicity with the fragmentary body, threatens us with her infinite, engulfing power.[44]

As, according to Ettinger, Freud's and Lacan's readings of the unconscious are insufficient when it comes to the wide range of the subject's not-conscious experiences, she proposes a supplementary mode. What interests Ettinger is a *non-conscious* kind of "knowledge," which can be categorized as neither conscious nor unconscious in Lacan's understanding. What she adds is the matrixial unconscious she names the *sub-non-conscious*: "the connectionist sphere of severality and encounter,"[45] abundant in metramorphic traces of Others and linkages. Such an intervention does not mean that Ettinger rejects the Lacanian unconscious; rather, she fills the empty space Lacan has left with his definition that excludes the potential non-linguistic data.

Ettinger hypothesizes the expanded notion of the Symbolic register, built upon femininity and non-phallic sense. As to the Symbolic, or "the Other's discourse,"[46] Ettinger claims that it does not encompass the non-Oedipal feminine difference she has recognized; she argues that the Symbolic ought to

---

44 Bracha L. Ettinger, "The Matrixial Gaze," in Ettinger, *The Matrixial Borderspace*, 52. Emphasis in original.

45 Ettinger, "The With-In-Visible Screen," 222n38.

46 Jacques Lacan, "Seminar on 'The Purloined Letter,'" in Lacan, *Écrits*, 10. Emphasis in original.

be extended beyond the scope of the phallic signifier and the discourse ruled by it.[47] Pollock adds that the matrixial model assumes "a subjacent, subsymbolic stratum of subjectivization"[48] that challenges the overbearing position of the phallic logic but does not reject it, for it is required both for subjectivizing processes (which prevail in the postnatal phase) and for the acquisition of language. Pollock elucidates that "the Symbolic is shifted or retuned, rather than overturned, by a supplementary co-shaping-not-quite-logic that she [Ettinger] invokes using the term *matrixial*."[49] This "not-quite-logic" is, however, by no means senseless. In the matrixial, the feminine corporeal encounter between several becoming-subjects leaves traces in their psyches, traces which might — or might not — be comprehended. Therefore, the knowledge of and from the feminine as hypothesized here is neither impenetrable nor meaningless even if it is not easily disclosed.[50] Rather, it relies on affectivity and sensibility as its pathways, instead of the phallic +/– paradigm, which rejects the sphere located between its two poles. Ettinger notes that the knowledge escaping both this paradigm and the discourse of signifiers "*not only exists,* but also *can trace itself* and *make sense.*"[51] Although partialized and residing in the sub-symbolic, the meaning is thus carried with-in the web of the matrixial feminine.

Not only is it carried, but also the meaning is constantly woven. Ettinger describes the relationship between the feminine (body), meaning, and weaving as follows:

A feminine difference based on bodily specificity not only occurs as the always-too-early for knowledge and always-

---

47 See Ettinger, "The Matrixial Gaze," 59.
48 Griselda Pollock, "Introduction. Femininity: Aporia or Sexual Difference?," in Ettinger, *The Matrixial Borderspace*, 6.
49 Ibid. Emphasis in original.
50 See Ettinger, "The Matrixial Gaze," 86.
51 See ibid., 61. Emphasis in original.

too-late for access, but it also makes sense, and not by retroactive *significance,* but rather inside a weaving.[52]

Such a difference is located in the domain of pre-knowledge in the phallic sense since the knowledge we speak about in the matrixial is not yet reigned by signifiers and binarized linguistic structures; it is also "too-late for access" because it is grounded upon the intrauterine encounter-event within the female body, which is a "past-side"[53] for the subject. Still, Ettinger claims that it acquires meaning within a web of woven trans-subjective strings. Weaving provides us with the imagery of textiles, textures, and rhizome-like linkages, but it excludes fusion, psychosis, or any other loss of subjectivity. The origins of the woven knowledge are situated in "blanks and holes in the Real,"[54] whereas what makes it resurface is the process of metramorphosis. Knowledge in a weave — non-cognitive, non-linguistic, and yet fragmentarily retrievable — again takes us to the notion of corporeality.

Feminine corporeality theorized by Ettinger is a site and a "transport-station" of knowledge; it calls to mind Levinasian ethics, which renders the maternal body the origin of signification. As Ettinger maintains, the female ought to be open and ready to reconnect with her matrixial realm of severality in order to find meaning in the traces of experiences originating there. To be precise, "She must uncognizantly know her *non-I(s)*."[55] This excerpt emphasizes that the knowledge about the border-Other(s) is not cognitive, and yet it is relevant for the matrixial sphere, being simultaneously its aim and its condition — the subject both strives for it, and needs to be receptive and rendered vulnerable during its acquisition. What is more, it is the female that makes a further transfer of such "subknowledge"[56]

---

52 Ettinger, "Weaving a Woman Artist," 191. Emphasis in original.
53 Bracha L. Ettinger, "Wit(h)nessing Trauma and the Matrixial Gaze," in Ettinger, *The Matrixial Borderspace,* 143.
54 Ettinger, "Weaving a Woman Artist," 194.
55 Ettinger, "Wit(h)nessing Trauma," 142. Emphasis in original.
56 Ibid.

possible as she passes it on to the subjective space, on whose margins it is supposed to reside, challenging the phallic organization but still remaining side by side with it.[57] In his ethical reading, Levinas links the body to signification, posited before language but comprehensible nonetheless. Using the metaphor of motherhood, he describes the workings of signification by means of caretaking activities.[58] Moreover, he points to the interrelatedness of subjectivity, sensibility, and signification as follows: "[S]ubjectivity is sensibility — an exposure to others, a vulnerability and a responsibility in the proximity of the others, the-one-for-the-other, that is, signification."[59] Similarly, the main qualities of the matrixial realm of subjectivization are fragility and fragilization, response-ability, and closeness aiming at opening oneself for the Other and their non-cognitive knowledge. Finally, Levinas notes, "Subjectivity of flesh and blood in matter — the signifyingness of sensibility, the-one-for-the-other itself — is the preoriginal signifyingness that *gives sense, because it gives.*"[60] Hence he establishes the role of maternity and its connection not only to sensibility but also to sense and signification. The maternal-like body becomes the source of meaning precisely because it has the capacity for providing and sharing. Therefore, the intersection of these two approaches depicts the body — be it feminine, maternal, or any body — as an entity that has a number of functions, being an originary locus and a pathway of knowledge beyond the linguistic systems.

Who does this knowledge belong to and what does it cover? Ettinger argues that it is possible to carry and transmit the imprints of memories that do not originate in the I. Ettinger

---

57 The notions of "side-by-sideness" and "besideness" return in Ettinger's descriptions of the matrixial domain, usually describing the relation between the matrixial subjectivizing sphere and phallic subjectivization. They are also used in reference to the artistic encounter; see Ettinger, "Uncanny Awe, Uncanny Compassion," 27.

58 Levinas, *Otherwise Than Being,* 77.

59 Ibid.

60 Ibid., 78. Emphasis mine.

identifies them as "traces of memory of/in/for/with the other,"[61] portraying the intermingled structure of relations that the I and the non-I enter within the matrix. Ettinger emphasizes that the process of metramorphosis can produce "non-symbolic and designified sense,"[62] and thus make one remember what could not have been forgotten because it has not been born within one's psychic apparatus. Furthermore, remembrance is not enough as in the matrix we are confronted with the impossibility of not-sharing, which Ettinger finds profoundly ethical — we are called upon to work-through the Other's memories.[63] Metramorphic processes — based on sharing, togetherness, reciprocity, and mutual transformation — lead to the partialized and affective tracing and (re)cognition of the Other's memories, within which the theorist identifies trauma, suffering, and pain. Interestingly enough, in Ettinger's work we can distinguish two types of trauma, or rather, a twofold trauma, as these types are often interwoven. The first of them, trauma of proximity, characterizes the matrixial sphere itself. It is especially visible in Ettinger's description of self-fragilization, which "is risky and also painful because you are reaching compassion-beyond-empathy and a com-passion that is often hard to tolerate on the level of an individual that seeks mental security and needs to withdraw inside its habits."[64] In general, matrixial processes and encounters are seen as traumatizing per se, for they challenge the subject's boundaries, are transgressive, and are perilously close to symbiosis or fusion. The other type may be identified as the proximity to trauma, in the sense that within the matrixial connection one may find the traces of the Other's traumatic memories. We read:

> Engravings of affected events, of others, and of the world are unknowingly inscribed in me, as mine are inscribed in oth-

---

61 Ettinger, "Transcryptum," 165.

62 Ibid.

63 See Ettinger, "The Matrixial Gaze," 90, and Ettinger, "Weaving a Woman Artist," 182.

64 Ettinger, "Fragilization and Resistance," 9.

ers, known or anonymous, in an asymmetrical exchange that creates and transforms a transsubjective matrixial alliance.[65]

The notion of shared — yet not fully cognized or known — memory carrying the traces of trauma shows that Ettinger makes a step beyond Freud's and Lacan's propositions.[66] As a result of reconceptualizing the feminine body as the sphere of jointness and mutual change, trauma can be witnessed, signified in a non-linguistic manner, and communicated. Thus, it transforms the I and the non-I during the matrixial encounter.

The question of trauma leads us to the Holocaust: an important part of Ettinger's biography and family history, a constantly recurring theme in her art, and a rarely pronounced — but often implied — event contributing to the matrixial theory. As Ettinger suggests, there is a possibility of working-through the Shoah by those who have not gone through it. One of the notions introduced to support such a thesis is based on Dori Laub's assumption that the Holocaust is *an event without a witness* because of not only the scale of this genocide, but also "the inherently incomprehensible and deceptive psychological structure of the

---

65　Ettinger, "Wit(h)nessing Trauma," 145.

66　The double notion of trauma of proximity/proximity to trauma is proposed in my Polish article, "Uraz — bliskość — nie-pamięć." This text explores the changes in and redefines the potential of the psycho-analytically grounded trauma discourse in the context of Ettinger's theory. Namely, it analyzes the main assumptions regarding trauma in Sigmund Freud, Jacques Lacan, Jean Laplanche, Dominick LaCapra, Marianne Hirsch, Shoshana Felman, and Dori Laub in order to introduce Ettinger's proposition and prove that her matrixial theory provides the tools to rethink the possibilities of trauma discourse. See Anna Kisiel, "Uraz — bliskość — nie-pamięć: Psychoanalityczny dyskurs traumy od Freuda do Ettinger," *Narracje o Zagładzie* 2 (2016): 115–32. Another take on trauma and proximity is provided by Ettinger, who writes about "a *triple trauma* of maternity and prematernity: the traumatic proximity to the Other during pregnancy, the traumatic regression to a similar archaic sharing [...] and the traumatic separation from the *non-I* during birth-giving." Bracha L. Ettinger, "From Proto-Ethical Compassion to Responsibility: Besideness and the Three *Primal* Mother-Phantasies of Not-Enoughness, Devouring and Abandonment," *Athena* 2 (2006): 105. Emphasis in original.

event,"[67] which made it impossible to provide any reference or perspective.[68] Ettinger modifies Laub's concept, proposing instead a wit(h)ness with-out an event. To be precise, art in its matrixial understanding reveals the potential to transfer the imprints of traumatic events to those who could not experience them directly. Adding an *h* to "witnessing," Ettinger emphasizes togetherness and shareability with-in the matrix. Wit(h)nessing then becomes a sudden sense of almost unrestricted proximity evoked via the artwork, whose result is an entrance to the matrixial sphere of encounter, in which the artist and the viewer share their affective knowledges and are transformed by each other.[69] To be a wit(h)ness means to process the traces of the Other's trauma, which is deemed particularly significant when speaking of the Other who is not able to work them through within their own psyche. Ettinger elucidates,

> events that deeply concern me, but which I cannot fully handle, are subject to fading-in-transformation […] while my *non-I* becomes wit(h)ness to them and elaborates a memory for them. If, because of the highly traumatic value of events, *I* cannot psychically contain "my" wounds at all, then in the matrixial psychic sphere "my" imprints will be transscribed for potential remembering by the Other. Thus my others will process traumatic events for me, just as my archaic m/Other had metabolized archaic events for my premature and fragile partial-subjectivity.[70]

---

67 Dori Laub, "An Event without a Witness: Truth, Testimony and Survival," in Shoshana Felman and Dori Laub, *Testimony: Crises of Witnessing in Literature, Psychoanalysis, and History* (Routledge, 1992), 80.

68 We read, "it was also the very circumstance of *being inside the event* that made unthinkable the very notion that a witness could exist, that is, someone who could step outside of the coercively totalitarian and dehumanizing frame of reference in which the event was taking place, and provide an independent frame of reference through which the event could be observed." Ibid., 81. Emphasis in original.

69 See Ettinger, "Wit(h)nessing Trauma," 150.

70 Ettinger, "Transcryptum," 167–68. Emphasis in original.

Ettinger simultaneously emphasizes the ethical dimension of wit(h)nessing and points to its bodily origin. Namely, the function of a witness is reconsidered and enriched with the chance of carrying the burden for the sake of someone who could not bear it, which is an expression of utmost care.[71] Such ethical commitment is directly inspired by the intrauterine encounter, in which the becoming-mother in her protective embrace tends to the infant, trying to ease or take over various stimuli it still cannot handle.

Working through the Other's trauma becomes for Ettinger a significant aspect of artworking, which is implied even by the neologism itself.[72] Pollock goes further in her remark regarding the impossibility of the Holocaust in the matrix. She begins with defining the Shoah as an extreme outcome of the phallic logic, which "establishes clear, even phobically defended frontiers between Self and Other,"[73] and identifies difference as a threat that ought to be either incorporated or eliminated; the Other is understood here as dangerous to one's unity. She goes on to claim that because of the redefinition of the notions of boundaries and exchange between subjects, in the matrix "such a catastrophe is unimaginable."[74] This statement may sound counter-intuitive, or even quixotic; however, it has an ethical side — and a political one. In a different text, Pollock casts light on this issue. She notes that since within the matrixial frame a non-oppositional type of relation between subjects has been experienced by all human beings, it can and ought to be used as

---

71 The connection between caring and carrying is grasped in Ettinger's notion of carriance, which embraces caring, being cared for, carrying, and being carried. See Bracha L. Ettinger, "Carriance, Copoiesis and the Subreal," in Bracha L. Ettinger, *And My Heart Wound-Space* (Wild Pansy Press, 2015), 343–51, and Bracha L. Ettinger, "And My Heart, Wound-Space with-in Me: The Space of Carriance," in ibid., 353–66.

72 "Artworking" refers to such psychoanalytical notions as working through, dream work, or work of mourning. See Griselda Pollock, "Aesthetic Wit(h)nessing in the Era of Trauma," *EurAmerica* 40, no. 4 (2010): 865.

73 Pollock, "Introduction. Femininity," 11.

74 Ibid.

an alternative model of approaching difference.[75] In other words, instead of using the phallic view on Otherness, we should keep in mind how the prenatal/prematernal encounter — an encounter characterized by asymmetry, severality, proximity, share-ability, co-emergence, hospitality, and compassion — shapes our becoming-human and becoming-humane. Pollock emphasizes, "*If we are to create peace, it is not through mere tolerance of others. It is in a radical rethinking of how integral a relation of otherness might be to what any 'I' is.*"[76] Going beyond ethics, this statement reaches the political aspect of the matrixial. It is crucial to comprehend firstly how fundamental the Other is in our own process of becoming, and, secondly, that while the Other is hurt, we do not remain unaltered. If, indebted to our shared corporeal origins, we manage to think beyond and before the rejection of the non-I, tragedies such as the Shoah indeed cannot take place.

Aesth/ethical Encounters

In Ettinger's thought, an aesthetic encounter and a late intra-uterine one are closely linked to each other and the traces of the latter may inhabit art. In one of her descriptions of a pre-natal encounter, Ettinger observes that so-called "[m]atrixial awareness"[77] is formed. The becoming-infant has a synesthetic faculty that makes it sensitive to various affective stimuli, reso-nances, and flows, whereas the becoming-mother is capable of "transsubjective inscription,"[78] that is, of registering and re-working the partialized imprints of — and between — herself and the Other that emerge in this relation.[79] Ettinger observes

---

75 Griselda Pollock, "From Horrorism to Compassion: Re-Facing Medusan Otherness in Dialogue with Adriana Caverero and Bracha Ettinger," in *Visual Politics of Psychoanalysis: Art and the Image in Post-Traumatic Cultures,* ed. Griselda Pollock (I.B. Tauris, 2013), 178.

76 Ibid. Emphasis in original.

77 Ettinger, "Weaving a Woman Artist," 187.

78 Ibid.

79 See ibid.

an interesting dynamic in the etymology of the word "pregnant" in Hebrew:

> The pregnant woman is *meouberet:* she is a transport station, a station of passage for a period of passage, and she herself is a conductor, a conveyer, a transmissible and transitive vector, a transit place, a transition time, a scavenging channel for a transition period. To be pregnant, *meouberet,* is to expand the boundaries, to be a ferryboat (*maaboret*).[80]

On the one hand, this excerpt points to the connection between the maternal bodily specificity and the acts of sharing, carrying and imparting information, or challenging borders; it also shows the female's active-passive diversity, being a place, time, and guide for the infant. On the other hand, we cannot deny the artistic connotations here, especially if we keep in mind Ettinger's hypothesis that art is the transport-station of trauma.[81] Returning to the late prenatal encounter, Ettinger claims that one ought not to consider it repressed or foreclosed, but "faded-by-transformation."[82] From the matrixial viewpoint, the dispersed fragments of the intrauterine event are taken to the thresholds of the sub-non-conscious by means of the matrixial encounter, which is made possible by art itself, "impregnate[d]"[83] by the matrix. Art, in turn, is claimed to transfer the shreds of the matrixial encounter-events "into culture"[84] within the process of metramorphosis.

Not only do the traces of the prenatal encounter inhabit the work of art, but also they can be accessed in and through it. Ettinger notes that humans can find themselves in the intimate trans-subjective matrixial borderspace via not only "compas-

---

80 Ibid., 185. Emphasis in original.
81 See Bracha L. Ettinger, "Art as the Transport-station of Trauma," in Bracha L. Ettinger, *Bracha Lichtenberg Ettinger: Artworking 1985–1999* (Ludion, 2000), 91–115.
82 Ettinger, "The With-In-Visible Screen," 108.
83 Ibid., 109. See ibid., 108–9.
84 Ettinger, "Wit(h)nessing Trauma," 144.

sionate joining-in-difference with others in transference rela-tions," but also *"art-objects, art-actions, art-gestures,* such as music, painting, and dance."[85] Artistic activities thus become passageways to the matrix. Referring to Levinas, Ettinger notes that such an access — which is par excellence an access to the Other — has ethical implications, for it requires the vulnerable position; vulnerability here involves becoming and remaining open to the Other despite the traumatizing threat such extreme fragility inevitably brings.[86] Moreover, we ought not to mistake it for sacrificial disappearance as vulnerability covers "a partial disappearing to allow jointness."[87] As we can see, art in the Ettin-gerian frame is inextricably linked to the intrauterine existence since it potentially offers a humanizing pathway to the frag-mented memory of this state.

What is then the position of the artist? The artist is the one who brings the non-consciously inscribed traces to memory and culture by creating the artwork, who "captures/produces/conducts ideas, traumas, and phantasies only inasmuch as s/he is affected by the trauma of the m/Other, of others, and of the world."[88] Such an artist — who discloses the matrixial-feminine qualities, who works through and passes on the traces of the traumas of the Other(s), and who is capable of "conceiving of *a world without me*"[89] — is pronounced the "artist-woman."[90] It is crucial to emphasize that the artist becomes here a part of a bigger structure, which embraces the viewer, the piece of art, and, in general, all the potential Others that can join the covenant. The artist does not occupy the only active position in the encounter — as it would wrongly imply the viewer's pas-

---

85 Ibid., 143. Emphasis mine.

86 Ibid., 145.

87 Ibid.

88 Ibid., 153.

89 Levinas and Ettinger, "What Would Eurydice Say?," 142. Emphasis in original. See Ettinger, "Wit(h)nessing Trauma," 155.

90 Ettinger, "Weaving a Woman Artist," 197. Of course, Ettinger by no means claims that men cannot be artists of this kind. It takes us back to the definition of a difference based on female bodily specificity that is not limited to women.

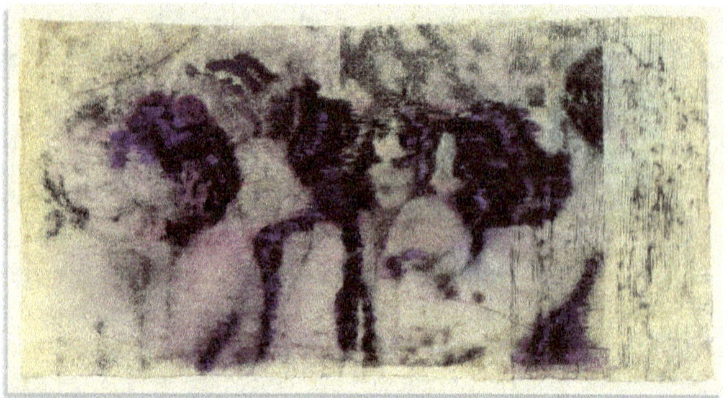

Fig. 8. Bracha L. Ettinger, *Eurydice,* No. 17, 1994–1996, oil, xerography, photocopic pigment and ashes on paper mounted on canvas, 26 × 52 cm. Collection: Pollock, Leeds. © Courtesy of the artist.

sivity — but simultaneously the relationship between the artist and the viewer is by no means symmetrical.[91] Responsive to the Other's call, it is the artist that makes any participation possible; artistic gesture in itself becomes an ethical move, then.[92] However, it does not mean that the artist is aware of the potential ethical charge; when writing about the weaving of aesthetics and ethics in the creative activity, Ettinger maintains that it may happen without the creator's "intentions or conscious control."[93] All in all, the woman-artist is a crucial partner in the matrixial sphere accessible via aesthetics, whereas aesthetics gains an ethical undertone as a result of the woman-artist's activity.

Historically speaking, the women from the Mizocz ghetto are abandoned; yet, are they completely alone? The image they are captured in is a result of the anonymous photographer's action of dubious ethical value; after all, we do not know whether they took it "as witness, as protest, [or] as trophy."[94] The depicted women were murdered in the name of terrible collec-

---

91 See Ettinger, "Wit(h)nessing Trauma," 154.

92 See ibid., 151.

93 Ibid., 148. See also ibid., 151.

94 Griselda Pollock, "Trauma, Time and Painting: Bracha Ettinger and the Matrixial Aesthetic," in *Carnal Aesthetics: Transgressive Imagery and*

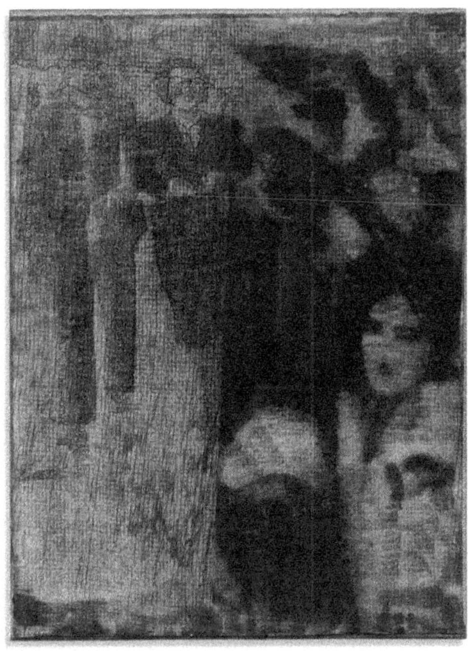

Fig. 9. Bracha L. Ettinger, *Eurydice,* No. 37, 2001, oil, xerography, photocopic pigment and ashes on paper mounted on canvas, 28.3 × 21.4 cm. Private collection, London. © Courtesy of the artist.

tive responsibility — on October 13, 1942, there was a revolt of prisoners in the Mizocz ghetto, Ukraine, the day after which all the men, women, and children were executed. In the picture, the women's bodies are naked: They are exposed to the voyeuristic gaze, left with no chance to defend themselves. Ettinger's art can be claimed to change their hopeless position. *Eurydice,* No. 17 (1994–1996) (fig. 8) is one of Ettinger's early works in the series, in which the women are still discernible. The surface of the piece is blurry and grainy; the bright background merges with black and purple shades. The photographic frame the artist

---

Feminist Politics, ed. Bettina Papenburg and Marta Zarzycka (I.B. Tauris, 2013), 25–26.

works on includes the most characteristic and recurring face of the series, located in the middle of the canvas. We can observe the women with no difficulty, but they are not exposed, being partly clothed by means of Ettinger's artistic gestures as the grain and the color hide their bodies from the voyeur's look. These women are not alone in a threefold sense. At the moment they are captured in the image, they are in "collectivity," supporting and warming each other, waiting for their shared fate. Years later, they encounter the artist, who compassionately wit(h)nesses and works through their pain. Finally, as they are named "Eurydices," they also encounter the viewer, who, like Orpheus, simultaneously sees them dead and keeps them alive.

Not only are the Eurydices not alone, but also they are as if hospitable, occasionally sharing the canvas with Ettinger's mother and father from the prewar photo taken in the street of Łódź in 1936. In *Eurydice, No. 37* (2001), the background determines the border between two temporalities, two fates, two stories, and disparate mental and physical states (fig. 9). The left side reveals the trace of the posed photograph of young, possibly careless, joyful people — Bluma Fried and Uziel Lichtenberg, Ettinger's parents-to-be. We cannot see them clearly because of the technique that employs pigment, ashes, and dust; their shapes remain recognizable, while their faces merge with the canvas. The right side is inhabited by the face known from the previous painting. Even though it is blurry, composed of smears of black paint, we seemingly can read more from it than from Ettinger's parents' almost invisible facial expression. Here, we may discover fear and anguish of this anonymous woman. The right side, therefore, is occupied by the victim — one of anonymous women, who is about to die. On the left, we watch the future survivors, who during the war fled Poland, escaped from several ghettos, camps, and countries, to finally reach Palestine.[95] What we viewers witness is an encounter beyond these differences, an encounter embodied on one canvas.

---

95 See "Bracha Lichtenberg Ettinger: Chronology," in Catherine de Zegher and Griselda Pollock, eds., *Art as Compassion: Bracha L. Ettinger* (ASA

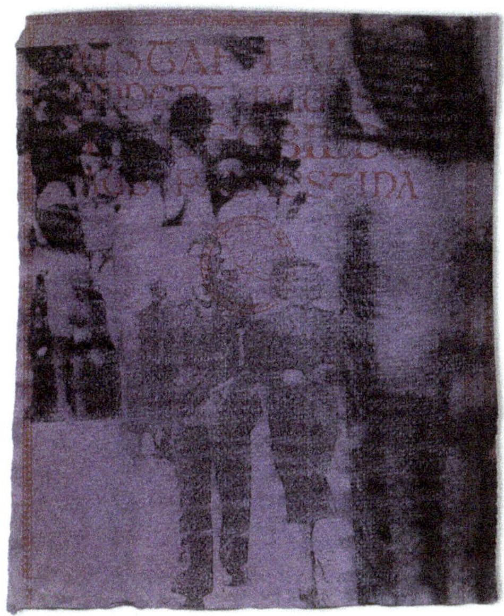

Fig. 10. Bracha L. Ettinger, *No Title — Sketch,* 1985, xerography, photocopic pigment and ashes, charcoal on paper, 27.3 × 23.1 cm. © Courtesy of the artist.

Embodiment takes a more literal form in *No Title — Sketch* (1988–1989), which we can say is "crowded" with bodies (fig. 7). This time, it is not the background that performs the separation; the contrast between the two realities is instead achieved by the juxtaposition of naked bodies of the women standing in a row — using a different photographic frame than in the previous works — with elegantly dressed people. The faces of Bluma Fried and Uziel Lichtenberg are sharper than in *Eurydice,* No. 37, and there is an illusion that they are looking towards the females on the right. Here, the two groups — if we may call them that — are facing each other, unable to turn away. Sentenced by the artist to this co-existence, they are challenged to survive the aesthetically eternalized moment of fragility. The sketch becomes a space of

---

Publishers, 2012), 249.

interweaving, proximity, and blurred borders; because of the unbearably embodied presences it hosts, it opens a lane towards an ethical relation in which Otherness is always already partial.

No Title — Sketch produced in 1985 provides us with yet another manifestation of the analyzed motif (fig. 10). The technique is the same, but the effect appears to be entirely different because of the domination of the purple color in the painting's space. The artwork has three main sets. The upper left part reveals a visible frame from the Mizocz photograph, showing the returning female face. Here, we can observe who surrounds her: behind her there is a woman with a baby in her arms and another woman in front of her — a little girl, who, as we can see in the original, non-manipulated photograph, is holding yet another female, maybe her own mother, tight. This girl appears again in a close-up on the right, just next to Ettinger's parents. They, for one, are standing in the middle of the sketch, as if in the foreground, overlaying the crowd. The mother's smile is hidden from our gaze. Despite dark colors, the image discloses more than the previously described ones. Maybe one of the reasons is that this sketch is made in 1985, thus being one of Ettinger's early works, created seven years before starting the first *Eurydice* painting (1992–1994). Later in her art we can note the nonlinear, yet proceeding disappearance of the origin photo. Still, what we as viewers observe here is more than the Barthesian "return of the dead."[96] It also endeavors to go beyond Susan Sontag's claim that the great number of images of atrocity we encounter makes us as if "anesthetize[d],"[97] more immune to the horror they depict. Ettinger's aim is not to immunize the spectator; on the contrary, by means of hosting the naked bodies — already dead but still alive, depending on the chosen temporality — the image calls us to gaze and to respond, posing an ethical demand in a Levinasian sense.

---

96 Roland Barthes, *Camera Lucida: Reflections on Photography,* trans. Richard Howard (Hill and Wang, 2010), 9.

97 Susan Sontag, *On Photography* (Penguin Books, 1979), 20. See ibid., 19–21.

The artworks have been presented in a non-chronological manner not without purpose; the reason behind such an arrangement was to show that the origin photographs' invisibility fluctuates whether we look at Ettinger's works individually or examine them as a series of interconnected images engaged in a dialogue. When we focus on the bodies of women from Mizocz, we note that they are in no way explicit or straightforward; nor are they easily accessible for the spectator. Ettinger's artistic technique includes the processes of covering the photograph, cropping it, veiling and unveiling certain fragments of bodies or faces, to name a few. All these actions lean towards de-othering and de-objectifying these women, that is, resisting voyeurism, scopophilia, or erotization they may be or might have been subject to. Importantly, it cannot be said that they are disappearing as a sacrifice for the Other. Rather, in an Ettingerian manner, they are "partial[ly] disappearing to allow jointness," becoming vulnerable so as to let the Other approach them. As a result, when we reach the space they occupy, we are called not to leave, but to remain and coexist with them. We are drawn to face that which is unintelligible and potentially unbearable, and to carry the burden. Through their partial invisibility, the female bodies — of daughters, mothers, grandmothers, girls, pregnant women — invite us to become one of them, without appropriation or objectification, but in terms of being interwoven. They invite us to join their affective web in a struggle towards humanity.

When it comes to the alliance of the Mizocz Eurydices with Bluma Fried and Uziel Lichtenberg, we might choose to follow the interpretation that what we witness in these works is the meeting of personal and historical trajectories; after all, a picture from Ettinger's family album and a drastic photographic document of the genocide coinhabit the canvas. Yet, the artist's position is more complex than that. Born to a Jewish family, Ettinger was never able to meet the majority of her relatives, which is far from being a marginal issue for her. In one of her notebooks, we read about the photograph from Mizocz:

> I want her to look at me! That woman, her back turned to me. The image haunts me. It's my aunt, I say, not, my aunt's the other one, with the baby. The baby! It could be mine. What are they looking at? What do they see? I want them to turn toward me. Once, just once. I want to see their faces.[98]

Another excerpt goes as follows:

> Please look at me once. You are my dead aunt, or you are my living aunt or you are someone I [have] known. [...] Mother-I, my aunt could have been my daughter.[99]

I do not — and do not have the right to — know whether Ettinger's relatives were in the Mizocz ghetto, and whether one of the women might have been Ettinger's aunt. These passages shatter the binary opposition between the private and public spheres; in other words, they disturb the simplicity of the meeting that seemed to take place between two groups of people anonymous to each other, having different fates, but linked by the fact of being victims of the Holocaust. However, as I would like to argue, these excerpts are not aimed at revealing the historical connection between Ettinger and the Mizocz women, which would somehow explain why she has been returning to this particular photograph. Instead, from an Ettingerian viewpoint, historical knowledge does not play a role once one enters the matrixial domain. When evoking these lines, Pollock comments that there occurs a paradoxical structure of identification there, having its source in maternity itself. Namely,

> As the woman becomes a mother, she is at once her own mother and her own child precisely because any mother was also once child and daughter and now lends her own uncon-

---

98 Bracha L. Ettinger, *Matrix Halal(a): Lapsus: Notes on Painting*, trans. Joseph Sims (Museum of Modern Art, 1993), 67, quoted in Pollock, "Trauma, Time and Painting," 27.

99 Ibid.

scious history to this event [...] that is at once a repetition for her and a novelty for the child she now holds.[100]

I would add that such a feminine connection is made possible thanks to the maternal-female bodily specificity. Hence, in Ettinger's painting — which relentlessly interlaces with her theory — corporeality is significant not per se, but because it takes one to the level of the matrixial sphere of an almost-boundless proximity. An encounter with the bodies of Eurydices becomes trans-historically ethical, notwithstanding the anonymity of the I(s) and the non-I(s).

Human(e) Origins

Ettinger's theoretical and artistic interventions allow us to take a closer look at our human — and humane — origins. Here, the body is taken out of the biological frame and becomes a source of proto-ethics; to specify, matrixially understood female bodily specificity becomes a site of the emergence and a dwelling-space of humanizing closeness. The matrixial ethics relies on prenatal/prematernal encounter-events that all human beings have gone through and by which they have been non-consciously affected. The matrix, a sphere related to the sub-non-conscious and grounded upon the mother–infant prenatal rapport, is argued to be capable of carrying and transmitting the imprints of the non-cognitive — but by no means meaningless — knowledge originating in the Other, which may include the traumatic memory the Other could not bear. Finally, since the aesthetic experience and the intrauterine encounter-event are directly linked, art itself can provoke and testify to non-historical, corporeal, painful yet deeply humanizing connections between the I(s) and the non-I(s).

---

100 Pollock, "Trauma, Time and Painting," 28. Pollock also suggests that Ettinger identifies with these women as a result of her own experience of becoming a mother, but in my opinion that suggestion means that we remain in the historical reading, which — keeping Ettinger's theoretical remarks in mind — is not necessarily the most relevant one.

The question that may be posed in reference to the above remarks is whether the pronouncement of humane — and hence universal — origins is not far-fetched. In other words, does the Ettingerian notion of corporeality truly evade gender distinctions?

3

Femininity and Universality

Gender(lessness) of the Matrixial Body

[A]natomy makes a difference that we should open to
conceptualization.

> — Bracha L. Ettinger, "Weaving a Woman Artist
> with-in the Matrixial Encounter-Event"[1]

This theory is not just about women for women, but for all of
us, for we are all born of woman.

> — Griselda Pollock, "Introduction. Femininity:
> Aporia or Sexual Difference?"[2]

It doesn't matter if the image contains representation of
"woman" or "womb" or not. For me it usually does, though.

> — Bracha L. Ettinger, "And My Heart, Wound-Space
> with-in Me: The Space of Carriance"[3]

---

1   Bracha L. Ettinger, "Weaving a Woman Artist with-in the Matrixial
Encounter-Event," in Bracha L. Ettinger, *The Matrixial Borderspace*, ed.
Brian Massumi (University of Minnesota Press, 2006), 181.

2   Griselda Pollock, "Introduction. Femininity: Aporia or Sexual
Difference?," in ibid., 29.

3   Bracha L. Ettinger, "And My Heart, Wound-Space with-in Me: The Space
of Carriance," in Bracha L. Ettinger, *And My Heart Wound-Space* (Wild
Pansy Press, 2015), 357–58.

As implied in Ettinger's remark on "representation of 'woman' or 'womb'" in art, her paintings indeed teem with feminine motifs, starting from the choice of colors and ending with the presence of women on numerous canvases. Similarly, her theoretical reflections refer mainly to women and to female corporeality itself. Such strong feminization evokes a plethora of questions concerning applicability and the universal character of the matrixial theory, but also a possible privileging of women.

The aim of this chapter is to address the questions that have surfaced in my study of Ettinger's theoretical and artistic oeuvre and that are crucial in providing a fuller picture of the matrixial feminine difference and the ethics of the body, including their possible limitations. How can we theorize the neutrality, universality, or genderlessness of the matrix if it is inspired by the workings of the female body? What is the status of men and women[4] when it comes to accessing the matrix? Does overt

---

4   While I refer to "men" and "women" here, I am fully aware of the reductive nature of these two categories as they fail to recognize transmen, transwomen, non-binary people, and other genders. Ettinger refers to these two categories specifically in her writings, and the chapter is devoted to an analysis of her take on gender and universality in reference to the matrix and this take's potential shortcomings. Ettinger does not directly address the issues of, for instance, transness or non-binary people; this is so because — I would venture to assume — matrixial theory is devoted mainly to the non-Oedipal, pre-gendered, prenatal, beyond-phallic formation of subjectivity, which resurfaces, but is not dominant, in the postnatal phase, and as a consequence categories related to gender are of lesser relevance to Ettinger's theorization of the matrix. In fairness, the scarcity of references to other categories than "men" and "women" is a huge challenge matrixial theory faces. The closest Ettinger gets to considering transness is in her text "Transgressing With-In-To the Feminine" that refers to the mythological figure of Tiresias to theorize the eponymous transgression. See Bracha L. Ettinger, "Transgressing With-In-To the Feminine," in *Differential Aesthetics: Art Practices, Philosophy and Feminist Understandings,* ed. Penny Florence and Nicola Foster (Routledge, 2018). Sheila L. Cavanagh effectively links transgender theorizing and matrixial theory. For instance, in "Tiresias," Cavanagh explores in detail the potential of Ettinger's theorizing of Tiresias to transgender studies. We read: "Although Ettinger is not a transgender studies scholar and, to the best of my knowledge, has not worked analytically with transgender clients, her conception of the transgression

focus on motherhood and intrauterine encounter make potential essentialist, biologically determinist, or right-wing readings of Ettinger's work viable? Finally, what are the implications of Ettinger's use of female and male figures — be they biblical, mythological, or familial — in her theory and art?

Femininity, Neutrality, and Universality

The theory of the matrix proposes a feminine supplement to Freudian–Lacanian psychoanalysis; the body Ettinger refers to is, therefore, by no means neutral. The matrix and matrix-related concepts (such as co-naissance, severality, communicaring, and subjectivity-as-encounter) are modeled specifically on the female body. Such a decision is not made in order to provide an antithesis to Freud's and Lacan's ideas; on the contrary, Ettinger tries to supplement the psychoanalytic system with the feminine element, which she considers to have been abandoned. When reflecting on the use of the female body, Ettinger clarifies:

> I believe that to avoid dealing with any aspect that touches on the female body and bodily experience, to avoid the conceptual potentiality that can be abstracted from the female body or has consequences with regard to it and its history — the agglomeration of its traumatic or pleasurable experiences,

---

with-in to the Feminine gives us a template to think about Tiresian-like transitions. A Tiresian-like transition is not the same as a transsexual transition (but the later may involve the former). It is, in Ettingerian terms, an entry into the matrixial whereby we co-emerge, transmutate and change with Others in unconscious and asymmetrical." Sheila L. Cavanagh, "Tiresias: Bracha L. Ettinger and the Transgression With-In-To the Feminine," in *Femininity and Psychoanalysis: Cinema, Culture, Theory*, ed. Agnieszka Piotrowska and Ben Tyrer (Routledge, 2019), 205. Cavanagh's "Transsexuality as Sinthome" rethinks the position of transsexuality in psychoanalysis through matrixial feminine difference, metramorphosis, and the matrix. See Sheila L. Cavanagh, "Transsexuality as Sinthome: Bracha L. Ettinger and the Other (Feminine) Sexual Difference," *Studies in Gender and Sexuality* 17, no. 1 (2016): 27–44. See also Sheila L. Cavanagh, "Transgender, Hysteria, and the Other Sexual Difference: An Ettingerian Approach," *Studies in Gender and Sexuality* 20, no. 1 (2019): 36–50.

its potentiality, the phantasies that link to its inscriptions — I believe that this amounts to an unconditional surrender to the dominant, seemingly neutral, symbolic filter that censures both women and men and molds them in its phallic frame.[5]

Ettinger argues that the conceptual application of female corporeality cannot be considered a threat or rejected straightaway as a form of essentialism since that would mean falling back into the phallic logic one might want to escape. This statement may find an ally in Elizabeth Grosz's analysis of the "universal" body in the works of selected theorists (including Sigmund Freud, Jacques Lacan, Maurice Merleau-Ponty, and Gilles Deleuze and Félix Guattari). As she observes, "a corporeal 'universal'" that these theorists endeavor to grasp is grounded upon the "implicitly white, male, youthful, heterosexual, middle-class"[6] body. However, when the female flesh is used, it is subject to another mechanism, described in the example of Deleuze and Guattari's becoming-woman and the figure of the girl. These philosophers are argued to "deterritorialize women's bodies and subjectivities only to reterritorialize them as part of a more universalist movement of becoming."[7] Ettinger's theory, in contrast, seems to smuggle neither the male nor the female body under the guise of the neutral/universal one. Instead, female corporeality is shown here as a sphere everyone can relate to — as an archaic site of the first encounter.

Rather than theorizing the neutrality of the female body, Ettinger puts forward a thesis that it is a site everyone has experienced. Ettinger states that "we have all, men and women, been prenatal once upon a time."[8] Yet, "once upon a time" — or "before," often used by Ettinger in descriptions of the matrixial

---

5 Ettinger, "Weaving a Woman Artist," 179–80.

6 Elizabeth Grosz, *Volatile Bodies: Toward a Corporeal Feminism* (Indiana University Press, 1994), 188.

7 Ibid., 182. See ibid., 173–80.

8 Bracha L. Ettinger, "Diotima and the Matrixial Transference: Psychoanalytical Encounter-Event as Pregnancy in Beauty," in *Beyond the*

borderspace — is by no means a diachronic point of reference.[9] Instead, Ettinger defines "before" as a "pole in the structure of the human subject," or "time before time, literally signifying even from before my face."[10] Matrixially, "before" belongs to an archaic time in which the becoming-subject has not yet recognized its borders. It is in this time that the "first corporeal-psychic connection"[11] takes place — the encounter with-in the motherly-feminine body which contributes to one's becoming as a subject.[12] Ettinger names such becoming-subjects "first matrixial partial-subjects,"[13] who, characterized by not the phallic but the matrixial difference, participate in sharing and transforming with and in the non-I.

Reading the feminine matrixial difference through the prism of a man/woman dichotomy is not fully adequate since this notion does not relate to women exclusively. As Ettinger notes, such difference is not concerned with biology, which would enact the male *versus* female division based on the principle of having or not having particular organs. Nor is it grounded upon the notion of identity, which utilizes the masculine/feminine binary.[14] Ettinger endeavors to escape such dichotomous structuring, as the main focus in this theory is not the "feminine" posited in opposition to the "masculine" but the woman-

---

Threshold: Explorations of Liminality in Literature, ed. Hein Viljoen and Chris N. van der Merwe (Peter Lang, 2007), 107.

9   Bracha L. Ettinger, "Carriance, Copoiesis and the Subreal," in Ettinger, *And My Heart Wound-Space,* 344.

10 Ibid.

11 See Bracha L. Ettinger, "Fascinance and the Girl-to-m/Other Matrixial Feminine Difference," in *Psychoanalysis and the Image: Transdisciplinary Perspectives,* ed. Griselda Pollock (Blackwell Publishing, 2006), 70.

12 Pollock considers it "the unique form of human becoming" and describes it as follows: "[A]ll human life shares an encounter with a woman-subject, who is herself being changed by what is becoming *with/in-side/with-in* her." Griselda Pollock, "Between Painting and the Digital: Matrixial Aesthetics Creates Matrixial Thought-Forms," in Ettinger, *And My Heart Wound-Space,* 263–64. Emphasis in original.

13 Bracha L. Ettinger, "The Matrixial Gaze," in Ettinger, *The Matrixial Borderspace,* 71.

14 Ibid., 56.

mother herself along with the meaning of her contact with the becoming-infant. Pollock puts it bluntly: "This theory is not just about women for women, but for all of us, for we are all born of woman."[15]

The word "feminine" in the matrixial feminine difference has a twofold origin. First, instead of being understood as a part of the "masculine/feminine" binary pair, the "feminine" here stands for the first, originary contact that the subject experiences — the contact with and in the mother's female body. Ettinger writes:

> The matrixial designates a difference located, in its originary formation, in the linkage to female corporeal invisible specificity, to the archaic enveloping outside that is also an inside: the womb. However, by matrix I do not mean the organ but a complex apparatus modeled on this site of feminine/prenatal encounter — not fusion — that places any human becoming-subject-to-be, male or female, in relation with female bodily specificity and her encounters, trauma, *jouissance,* passion, phantasy, and desire. [...] Female bodily specificity is thus the site, physically, imaginatively, and symbolically, where a feminine difference emerges, and through which a "woman" is interlaced as a figure that is not confined to one-body, but is rather a hybrid "webbing" of links between several subjectivities, who by virtue of that webbing become partial.[16]

The difference is feminine in the sense that it refers to and is modeled upon the womb, the experience of pregnancy, and, most importantly, the prenatal encounter, which encompasses both male and female becomings. Moreover, the "woman" here is not a separate "one-body," but a partial-subject, similar in this respect to the prenatal subject; this is why the feminine specificity makes it possible to theorize trans-connectedness and shareability of affective knowledge. The other origin of the

---

15 Pollock, "Introduction. Femininity," 29.

16 Bracha L. Ettinger, "Wit(h)nessing Trauma and the Matrixial Gaze," in Ettinger, *The Matrixial Borderspace,* 141. Emphasis in original.

"feminine" difference is related to its quality of going beyond the phallus, and its subjectivity and difference formation.[17] We may conclude, on the one hand, that Ettinger utilizes the binary nature of language here to distinguish between these two supplementary types of difference; this might be problematic as binarization is what Ettinger usually endeavors to avoid, or even to challenge. On the other, it is the matrixial "woman" that transcends the phallic frames of symbiosis and cut, which renders the "feminine" an adequate name.

Calling the matrixial sexual difference "feminine," Ettinger simultaneously declares it non-gendered. As Ettinger proposes, the matrixial difference ought not to be placed within the dichotomy of "gendered individuals (male versus female)," but it should instead be perceived in terms of "borderspacing with-in a female affective-mental corporeality (for example; the difference between a male differentiating from female-m/Other and a female differentiating from female-m/Other)."[18] How does the genderlessness of the difference apply to the female body referred to in this theory? First of all, the feminine body is not a social construct here; it is not anchored in the Symbolic or performed. Nor is it embedded in language as a set of binary terms; rather, the matrix — and thus the matrixially understood body — ceaselessly moves to the affective margins of language and cognition. When biology is considered, the position of female corporeality becomes more complex. One cannot easily reject Ettinger's indebtedness to the biological notion of the body. Namely, as it relates to intrauterine and pregnancy experiences, not to mention the inter-generational transmission occurring in the womb, the matrixial feminine specificity is to an extent biological; however, instead of remaining within the realm of anatomy, Ettinger treats these issues as inspirations, utilizing the female flesh as a model of relations and difference,

---

17　Bracha L. Ettinger, "Art as the Transport-Station of Trauma," in Bracha L. Ettinger, *Bracha Lichtenberg Ettinger: Artworking 1985–1999* (Ludion, 2000), 114.

18　Ettinger, "Diotima and the Matrixial Transference," 116.

and not placing it at any side of the sex/gender dichotomy. In this respect, Pollock proposes that female-maternal bodily specificity is a *"thinking apparatus* for human subjectivity."[19] Thus, while in part the Ettingerian body eludes the above categorizations, it becomes hardly possible to conceive of the notion of the body entirely outside of these frames.

Despite its apparent femininity, Ettinger's notion of the body becomes the source of universal experience. It ought not to be mistaken for a form of essentialism — Ettinger strongly opposes such an approach, emphasizing that she does not make any claims about women having to experience motherhood in order to grasp the matrixial sphere.[20] She does not define the womb as a "natural" basis of man/woman difference; nor is it an "origin, [...] a passive receptivity or passive internal container."[21] As a psychoanalyst indebted to Lacan, Ettinger focuses on the correspondence between the matrixial difference and the phallic one as both are available to men and women, and not to one of the genders exclusively.[22] Importantly, the matrixial difference deals with being with-in the female-maternal body, which is a phase that each emerging human being necessarily goes through. The female body, as a result, becomes a universal site which all the subjects have experienced and may experience again, but by no means is it a universalized body.

In part, Ettinger's reading of the female body as a site of humanizing encounter responds to Grosz's postulate to rethink feminine corporeality. Having uncovered the hidden male agenda of the so-called universal body in the philosophers listed above, Grosz enumerates possible directions that may contribute

---

19 Griselda Pollock, "Mother Trouble: The Maternal-Feminine in Phallic and Feminist Theory in Relation to Bracha Ettinger's Elaboration of Matrixial Ethics/Aesthetics," *Studies in the Maternal* 1, no. 1 (2009): 13. Emphasis mine.

20 Ettinger, "Weaving a Woman Artist," 180.

21 Ibid.

22 See Ettinger, "Wit(h)nessing Trauma," 140.

to affirmative, non-patriarchal "women's self-representations."[23] One of such directions is the liberation of the female flesh from the biologically determined frame, which considerably narrows and simplifies its potentialities. She also hints at the advantages of utilizing "the psychical or interior dimensions of subjectivity and the surface corporeal exposures of the subject to social inscription and training."[24] Next to biological determinism, dualism as well as monism are other perspectives that Grosz suggests ought to be eluded; simultaneously, she advocates a theorization of the woman which relies on "(at least) two surfaces"[25] that do not necessarily fuse. Independently, Ettinger is guided by similar motivations. Since the matrixial theory is a psychoanalytic system, biological determinism is not an issue here. Turning to the interior/exterior relation in reference to matrixial subjectivity, one can observe that both elements reappear in Ettinger's theory, but what gains significance is the internal aspect; also, the matrixial subjectivizing sphere is not focused on the social, and Ettinger herself seldom tackles this question. Finally, Grosz's study of dualism and related issues corresponds with Ettinger's theoretical proposition of severality, which assumes the presence of two or more becoming-subjects within the matrix; matrixial subjects that do not merge into one another, enter a symbiotic relation, or turn into a multitude, and these qualities coincide with Grosz's postulate. To sum up: While Grosz's postulates are rather guidelines than conditions of a "successful" reading of the female flesh, the correspondence between Grosz and Ettinger is meaningful since both thinkers identify the need to escape phallic and patriarchal paradigms by means of a supplementary mode and not a binary opposition. What seems to be implied in their postulates is the usefulness of

---

23 Grosz, *Volatile Bodies*, 188. I aim at discussing just several propositions — the most relevant ones with regard to Ettinger's theory. For all postulates, see ibid., 188–89.

24 Ibid., 188.

25 Ibid., 189. What she seems to propose is a multilayered theorization of femininity and female corporeality, but she does not recognize or strictly define the abovementioned "surfaces."

a new perspective on female corporeality for women. However, to what extent can such a reading be relatable not only to women, but also to men?

Female Privilege

Although Ettinger makes it clear that the matrixial domain is open to both men and women, she simultaneously notes that they do not have equal access to it. As has been mentioned, the womb is "an archaic *out-site* and *past-side*" for both men and women; women exclusively are subject to the womb's other spectrum: an "*in-site/future-side.*"[26] Ettinger does not deny this difference; she goes as far as to describe women's access to the matrixial sphere as "double" and thus their position regarding it — "privileged."[27] Yet, Ettinger adds right away that the privilege ought not to be understood in the basic sense of the word, but as "access to *surplus-of-fragility*,"[28] which by no means is safe, satisfactory, or comfortable. Ettinger also states that the differentiation occurring between a girl-infant and a woman-mother during the prenatal period reveals the insufficiency of lack as a marker of difference. We read:

> If each female differs from a woman first, a subject doesn't desire only lacking objects (*objet a*), as Lacan would have it. There is a languishing beating by com-passionate connecting and by fascinance [...]. This kind of yearning for binding-in-difference is healed by new vibrations of a com-passionate non-sexual love in future cross- and trans-connectedness (also interwoven inside sexual love).[29]

---

26 Ettinger, "Wit(h)nessing Trauma," 143. Emphasis mine.
27 Ettinger, "Weaving a Woman Artist," 182.
28 Ibid. Emphasis mine.
29 Bracha L. Ettinger, "Antigone With(out) Jocaste," in *Interrogating Antigone in Postmodern Philosophy and Criticism,* ed. S.E. Wilmer and Audronė Žukauskaitė (Oxford University Press, 2010), 221. Emphasis in original.

What the girl-infant brings to the notion of difference is a desire for com-passion — understood as a transubjective effect that exceeds empathy, breaches the Symbolic order, and contributes to matrixial care for and involvement with the Other[30] — and linkages while the minimal separation between her and the mother is maintained. Such "yearning," or "languishing," is considered to be crucial for the girl's postnatal development, but it also carries more universal implications for all the matrixially understood subjects. Still, pronouncing the becoming prenatal subject as a female is not a coincidence as Ettinger differentiates between "the female and male *daughter*"[31] in the matrix. Even though the subject can be both male and female, the implication about the predominant gender becomes obvious here — they are a "*daughter.*" We cannot ignore the intensity with which the woman occupies this realm and the seeming inexistence — or irrelevance — of the masculine reference.

The matrixial difference is claimed not to be grounded upon gender distinctions or the "essentialistic raw data"[32] of human anatomy; still, it has varying resonances depending on the type of body that encounters female-motherly corporeality in the subjectivizing process. That is to say, while women are "privileged" when accessing the matrix, male corporeality itself poses a certain limit. After the prenatal period, men are permanently separated from the womb, it being an outside space for them, accessed in the past with no future potentiality.[33] Ettinger puts it bluntly: "The adult male will not experience pregnancy and therefore will not coemerge again matrixially in that primary and radical real sense."[34] This shows how expressly men are deprived of the access to the Real of the "in-site/future-side." What is more, Ettinger claims that the male body has a special

---

30 The notion of com-passion will be discussed in detail in Chapter 4.

31 Ibid., 215. Emphasis in original. Later in the article, Ettinger states that, matrixially, "each son is *also* a daughter." Ibid., 227. Emphasis in original.

32 Ettinger, "Art as the Transport-Station of Trauma," 112.

33 See Ettinger, "Diotima and the Matrixial Transference," 126, and Ettinger, "Wit(h)nessing Trauma," 143.

34 Ettinger, "Diotima and the Matrixial Transference," 126.

resonance with the phallic type of difference as the opposition between having and not having a sexual organ becomes an instant reference point, or "a corporeal self-evidence."[35] Nevertheless, Ettinger finds the possibilities for men of returning postnatally to the matrixial sphere in participation in various aesthetic activities — for instance "music, painting, and dance"[36] — and in transference, which in the matrixial theory is seen through the prism of com-passion and creation of linkages between the I and the non-I[37]; these two aspects are applicable to both men and women. In a sense, therefore, the matrixial experience becomes a challenge for men — it is accessible, but to a lesser extent as a result of their corporeality. Indeed, matrixial psychoanalysis is highly "feminized." Still, Ettinger does not try to hide the discrepancies between male and female access to the matrix; despite these disparities, she considers the matrix to be an originary subjectivizing space that is necessary for one's further development as a human(e) being.

Even though the matrixial theory has its source in the female body, pregnancy, and motherhood, Ettinger draws a line between these encounter-events and any restrictions concerning women's reproductive rights. Ettinger emphasizes that she is a feminist and a supporter of women's rights.[38] She also notes that there are two radical poles of treating female corporeality. One of them is the essentialist claim that a woman's main role is that of a mother; the other immediately rejects any theoretical uses of the feminine body, identifying them as perilous. Not positing herself on any of the sides, Ettinger claims they can be equally dangerous.[39] She stresses that the matrixial frame can by no means be interpreted as restricting women's rights since the matrix is founded on response-ability, a notion different from — and broader than — responsibility and including "women's full response-ability for any event occurring with-in

---

35 Ettinger, "Weaving a Woman Artist," 195.
36 Ettinger, "Wit(h)nessing Trauma," 143.
37 See Ettinger, "Diotima and the Matrixial Transference," 105–32.
38 Ettinger, "Weaving a Woman Artist," 179.
39 Ibid.

their own not-One corpo-Reality."[40] Less an argument than a confirmation of Ettinger's position, this quotation may not be sufficient in a debate regarding women's rights.[41] One ought to bear in mind, however, that even though this theory encourages certain social or political readings, it is still a psychoanalytic system, and its theses concerned with pregnancy and relations with-in the female body are not congruent with any social, political, or medical discourse concerning reproduction and reproductive rights. As a result, while it is a challenge to use the matrixial theory as an argument for women's reproductive rights, this system poses no threat to them.

Is there any possibility of an essentialist, biologically determined, or right-wing interpretation of the matrixial theory, then? Before we focus on the matrixial take on motherhood, let us take a look at the figure of the father in psychoanalysis. In his discussion on right-wing readings of Lacan, Jan Potkański refers to Bruce Fink's reflections on the contemporary position of the father. As Fink claims, the father who "does not believe fathers should wield authority over their children, believes children are rational creatures and can understand adult explanations, [...] wants to be loved not feared"[42] poses a threat recognized

---

40 Bracha L. Ettinger, "The With-In-Visible Screen," in Ettinger, *The Matrixial Borderspace*, 221n9.

41 In this context, Pollock writes, "the exploration of the prenatal does not in any way prejudice the woman's right to choose. In fact, the ethics of this asymmetry enhance the adult subject's rights over her shared body and support the choice positions of the maternal partner who is the only adult who can choose for this profound partnership in difference." Pollock, "Mother Trouble," 25. Although it utilizes a number of matrixial concepts, this excerpt generates more questions than answers, for instance: What is the ethics of asymmetry? In what sense is the statement that the adult is the only one to make a decision in the encounter matrixially grounded? Does it not diminish the role of the becoming-infant in the encounter? I believe, however, that this statement does not aim at being part of the discussion on women's rights; rather, it intends to assure the potential reader that this theory will not try to appropriate and essentialize women's bodies. In this sense, it agrees with Ettinger's intention.

42 Bruce Fink, *A Clinical Introduction to Lacanian Psychoanalysis: Theory and Technique* (Harvard University Press, 1997), 180.

by Lacan — a threat to the symbolic paternal function, whose rejection can eventuate, for instance, in perversion or psychosis.[43] However, as Potkański argues, Lacan "does not ascribe practical-pedagogical or socio-political interpretation"[44] to the *nom du père* and its rejection. Potkański goes on to claim that the paternal function, which itself is an abstract term, and the father's role in society ought not to be coupled as there is no adequate link between them.[45] Similarly, Ettinger's depictions of the encounter-event in pregnancy, of the mother–child relations, or of trans-connectedness and affective communication in the womb may appeal to theorists and philosophers who attempt to derive the social function and reproductive rights of the woman from essentialism and biological determinism. Yet, as we immerse deeper into Ettinger's thought, we can notice that such readings — as well as those which seek to translate the psychoanalytic model directly into social relations without recognizing the gap between the two spheres — are tenuous. First, the difference between hospitality (towards a becoming subject co-inhabiting one's body) and duty (to privilege the infant's well-being) needs to be recognized. Matrixial hospitality embraces vulnerability, rejection of narcissism, willingness to co-transform, and openness to one's non-I's despite the risk they pose, but simultaneously, as a concept, it is based on decision and readiness; an ideological orientation of the reproductive rights at the a priori moral obligation of the woman-mother can be hardly combined with such a stance as it challenges the question of choice. Also — and this mirrors Potkański's position — the matrixial abstract of motherhood cannot simply be placed in the social or political contexts and legitimize a cultural role for every woman. What one, however, cannot deny is the metaphorical or rhetorical strength of Ettinger's portrayals of the pregnancy-, intrauterine-, and motherhood-related notions.

---

43 Ibid., 111.

44 "nie nadaje interpretacji ani praktyczno-wychowawczej, ani społeczno-politycznej." Jan Potkański, "Przeciw lacanowskiej prawicy," *Śląskie Studia Polonistyczne*, no. 1 (2013): 54. Translation mine.

45 Ibid.

To summarize, just as the father in Lacanian psychoanalysis does not necessarily reflect the father's social role, the matrixial woman-mother cannot be taken for a particular woman; instead, she is a psychoanalytic figure of relations between subjects. Nevertheless, elements of this theory may be of use for fundamentally different discourses, but mainly as rhetorical tools.

Ettingerian Mythos

We might say that Ettinger's thought is "crowded" with characters — mostly women — from various fields. Ettinger refers to literary examples, such as Lol Stein from Marguerite Duras's novel or literary personas from Sylvia Plath's poems,[46] and to cinematography (*Hiroshima mon amour*, written also by Duras[47]). With regard to ancient philosophy, Ettinger considers Diotima, but she also comments upon psychoanalytic cases, notably Freud's Dora and Donald Winnicott's Margaret Little.[48] Nevertheless, Ettinger's two main sources of inspiration are the Bible and Greek mythology, with Saint Anne and Eurydice functioning as patronesses of the matrix. Ettinger also refers to Moses, identifying him — in a Levinasian manner — as "*Father* precisely because he carries like the mother caries infants."[49]

---

46 For the analysis of Lol Stein, See Ettinger, "Fascinance and the Girl-to-m/ Other Matrixial Feminine Difference," 60–93. For the reflections on Sylvia Plath's poems, see, for instance, Bracha L. Ettinger, "Demeter–Persephone Complex, Entangled Aerials of the Psyche, and Sylvia Plath," *ESC: English Studies in Canada* 40, no. 1 (2014): 123–54.

47 See Bracha L. Ettinger and Kyoko Gardiner, "Affectuous Encounters: Feminine-Matrixial Encounters in Duras/Resnais' *Hiroshima Mon Amour*," in *PostGender: Gender, Sexuality and Performativity in Japanese Culture*, ed. Ayelet Zohar (Cambridge Scholars, 2009), 251–75.

48 See Ettinger, "Diotima and the Matrixial Transference," 105–32; Dora is discussed in a number of texts, including "*Fascinance* and the Girl-to-m/Other Matrixial Feminine Difference," and "Demeter–Persephone Complex," while Margaret Little is mentioned, for instance, in the latter.

49 Bracha L. Ettinger, "Laius Complex and Shocks of Maternality: With Franz Kafka and Sylvia Plath," in *Interdisciplinary Handbook of Trauma and Culture*, ed. Yochai Ataria et al. (Springer, 2016), 282. Emphasis in original. For an analysis of Moses as a maternal figure in Levinas, see

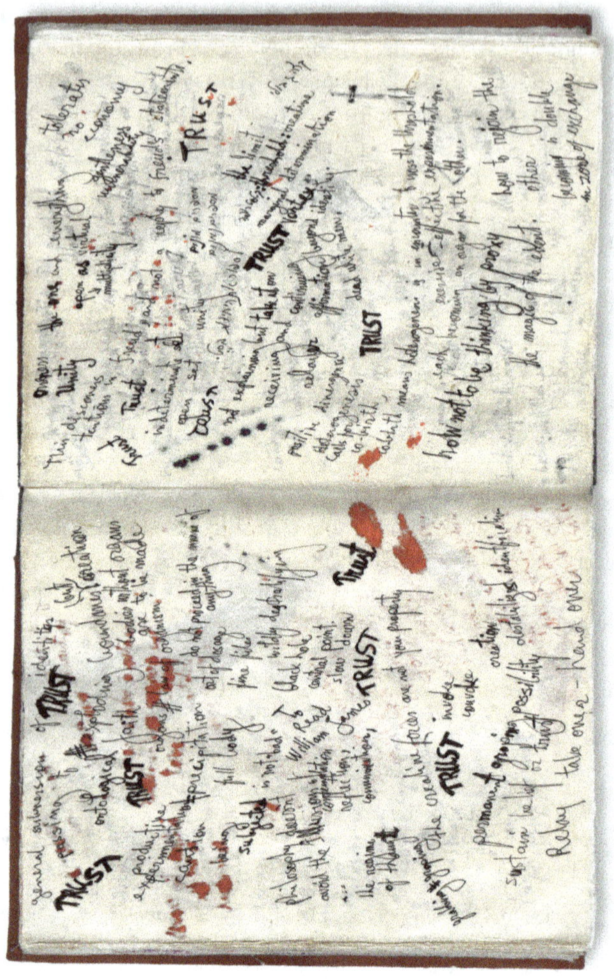

Fig. 11. Bracha L. Ettinger, *Notebook,* 2005. © Courtesy of the artist.

Yet, there are many more biblical and mythological figures that are worthy of further exploration as they prove to be valuable contributions to the matrixial take on corporeality and ethics; together, they constitute what I propose to call the "Ettingerian mythos."

Maternity as a site of pain and trust is identified in the figure of the primary biblical woman-mother, Eve. Having gone through the tragedy of one of her sons killing another, Eve decides to trust: in Ettinger's reading, "she trusted life to carry *again.*"[50] She gives birth to her third son, Seth,[51] who is a father of Enosh — whose name signifies "human being" and "humankind" — and a direct ancestor of Noah, the forefather of the whole post-flood humanity. Eve's motherly body thus becomes the originary site of all human beings; she hospitably allows her body to be inhabited despite the pain she has experienced and the fear that presumably accompanies her choice.[52] This position contributes to Ettinger's concept of carriance, in which carrying, being and having been carried (within the mother's body), caring, and being cared for are intertwined, as the very name suggests, but which goes even further in its ethical implications. Ettinger specifies: "Carriance = care+response-ability+wit(h)-nessing in self-fragilization is a direct path to ethics: witnessing and responsibility to the vulnerable other."[53] Carriance grasps the matrixial relation which involves the ability to respond

---

Lisa Guenther, "'Like a Maternal Body': Emmanuel Levinas and the Motherhood of Moses," *Hypatia* 21, no. 1 (2006): 119–36.

50 Ettinger, "Carriance, Copoiesis and the Subreal," 344. Emphasis in original. The question of trust also returns in Ettinger's art, most explicitly in one of her notebooks — two pages are covered mostly with the repetition of this word. Fig. 11.

51 Ettinger argues that this name in Hebrew has the root "N.Sh.A," and that it "means *carry.*" See Brigit M. Kaiser and Kathrin Thiele, "If You Do Well, Carry! The Difference of the Humane: An Interview with Bracha L. Ettinger," *philoSOPHIA: A Journal of Continental Feminism* 8, no. 1 (2018): 107.

52 In terms of suffering connected to the death of son, Eve bears similarities to yet another significant mother figure of the Bible, Virgin Mary; this figure, however, resurfaces not in Ettinger's theoretical reflections but in her aesthetic oeuvre — in the motif of Pietà.

53 Ettinger, "Carriance, Copoiesis and the Subreal," 344.

compassionately, to be attentive, and to tend to the intimate yet unknown Other, ignoring the potential danger that comes with such a fragilizing encounter. "[T]rust[ing]" and "carr[ying] *again*," Eve embodies carriance as she opens herself to a new human life with all its threats and promises.

Eve's trust can be linked to Ettinger's study of Isaac and his relation with Abraham. Referring to Caravaggio's painting *Sacrifice of Isaac* (1603), Pollock describes the situation as an "act of paternal violence against his [Abraham's] *vulnerable, trusting* son," whom she portrays further as "the helpless child [...] crying out in protest and terror."[54] Despite the fact that Isaac's trust is betrayed — after all, his father seems to be ready to sacrifice him and is interrupted just before committing this act — Ettinger asks the reader to try to "imagine Isaac's compassion for his father."[55] Here, compassion is not supposed to mean one's ability to understand or forgive the Other, for it is prior to mere empathy in terms of both chronology and significance.[56] The source of such primary compassion is argued to be found, again, in the maternal-matrixial mode:

Isaac was compassionate toward his father, because, as Infant, he had already been compassionate toward his mother, apprehending her compassionate hospitality uncognizingly, and emotionally feel-knowing the trauma he had been to her in her bringing him to life.[57]

Choosing Isaac ought not to be read as a pretext to explore the specificity of the matrixial space. On the contrary, this child's

54 Griselda Pollock, "From Horrorism to Compassion: Re-Facing Medusan Otherness in Dialogue with Adriana Caverero and Bracha Ettinger," in *Visual Politics of Psychoanalysis: Art and the Image in Post-Traumatic Cultures*, ed. Griselda Pollock (I.B. Tauris, 2013), 180. Emphasis mine.

55 Bracha L. Ettinger, "From Proto-Ethical Compassion to Responsibility: Besideness and the Three *Primal* Mother-Phantasies of Not-Enoughness, Devouring and Abandonment," *Athena* 2 (2006): 100.

56 Ibid., 124.

57 Ibid. Emphasis in original.

extreme and incomprehensible situation is necessary here to understand that compassion theorized by Ettinger goes beyond and before the phallic logic since it is a direct result of the matrixial encounter. Compassion, hospitality, and trauma accompany the prenatal becoming-subject and influence its development, including the postnatal one. Ettinger goes even further, stating that a "perpetrator can kill the subject, but it has no hold on its archaic compassionate potentiality."[58] Isaac's trust, therefore, may have been violated, but this does not take away his originary capability for compassion.

In one of her articles, Ettinger reflects on Abraham, biblical figures directly related to him (Sarah, Hagar, Isaac, Ishmael), and common condemnation of his action; these reflections do not constitute a complete theoretical stance, but the family relations discussed reveal the structuring of the matrix and bear an ethical charge. Ettinger begins with a critique of "the denial of our human potentiality to become an Abraham who might abandon and kill."[59] Even though such deeds belong to the catalogue of human actions, they are treated as unimaginable and appalling; coping mechanisms activated in this respect are grounded upon identifying Abraham as the Other, and separating him from both his family members (especially Isaac) and ourselves as humans.[60] Establishing definite distance, these mechanisms solidify the denial of the idea that we may be capable of committing comparable wrongs. Further on, Ettinger portrays matrixial connectedness, alluding to Abraham's relatives:

A child is being abandoned. [...] If you are opened to the matrixial horizon you know that an individual might be unconsciously *metramorphosing* traces of the trauma of someone else, who belongs to the same matrixial web. You might suddenly realise that the child that had been aban-

---

58 Ibid., 125.

59 Bracha L. Ettinger, "Uncanny Awe, Uncanny Compassion and Matrixial Transjectivity Beyond Uncanny Anxiety," in *Psychoanalysis in French and Francophone Literature and Film,* ed. James Day (Brill, 2011), 16.

60 Ibid.

doned is another child, perhaps even one that is unknown to you, another child of your own father [...], an unknown half-brother, someone else who had been abandoned by a parent, sent to some kind of desert, like the Biblical son of Hagar. Perhaps even, *a mother is being abandoned* — this mother is not your own one, but still, she is someone who belongs to the fabric of your matrixial webs [...], and she reveals for you the capacity of the other to abandon, and your own capacity to abandon too. [...] We carry traces of the trauma and of the joy of others who belong to our past and present webs. When you realise this possibility — another dimension for dream interpretations opens. If you are Abraham's child, sometimes you are the son of Sara[h], sometimes you are the son of Hagar.[61]

Within the matrix, the subject may encounter and affectively work through the fragments of memory, pain, and trauma which belong to the subject's intimate Other. The Other and the subject share the matrixial rhizome-like web even though they do not have to know each other. Still, in such a web, information is transferred, through which the subject learns also about abandonment. Importantly, matrixial connectedness goes further than the bloodline — it is not transmitted merely between one generation and the next. In the matrix, one may have access to the traces belonging not only to one's "immediate" Others, such as parents, but also to those one does not recognize, which does not diminish the significance of such a relation.

The issue of abandonment takes us to the mythical figures of Antigone and Jocaste.[62] In Ettinger's reading, some actions of Jocaste are encrypted in Antigone even if they have taken place before Antigone's birth. The surface level is that of incestuous marriage with Oedipus, her son who becomes Antigone's

---

61 Ibid., 22–23. Emphasis in original.

62 For the sake of consistency, I will use the name Jocaste — instead of Jocasta — after Ettinger, who introduces the Jocaste complex and tends to use this spelling.

father and brother simultaneously. Yet, when one goes further, a "much earlier offence"[63] of Jocaste can be found. This offence it threefold. Firstly, she abandoned Oedipus (which actually saved him from death) and then her other children by committing suicide. Secondly, she collaborated with Laius, passively accepting his "paternal paranoid jealousy and an envy of the infant's fate."[64] Finally, she is identified as a survivor — she survived her own act of abandonment. Antigone, thus, is raised in the shadow of her mother, who is capable of abandonment, and of her abandoned father-brother. As a result, two complexes function within her: the Oedipus complex and the Jocaste complex, the latter one corresponding to one of three primal phantasies proposed by Ettinger — the primal mother-phantasy of abandonment.[65] Why is the Jocaste complex significant? Ettinger argues that the situation here is similar to that of the Oedipus complex. The Oedipus complex frees actual fathers from responsibility for that which "surpasses individual fathering and touches a human suffering," and actual mothers are in need of a corresponding complex, which can "humanize" their "place/position."[66] This theoretical intervention indirectly responds to Jacqueline Rose's diagnosis that,

---

63 Ettinger, "Antigone With(out) Jocaste," 216.

64 Ibid., 217.

65 Ettinger argues that in the clinical analyst-patient situation the analyst frequently employs the *ready-made mother-monster* figure, according to which the mother becomes a reason for the majority of the patient's problems. Ettinger notes that the frequency of using this figure points to a blank spot in psychoanalysis necessary to be filled, and what she proposes instead of shifting the guilt upon the mother are three primal mother-phantasies, expanding the basic list. These are the phantasies of not-enoughness, devouring, and abandonment. Ettinger, "From Proto-ethical Compassion to Responsibility," 100–135. See also Ettinger, "Demeter–Persephone Complex," 123–54.

66 Ettinger, "Antigone with(out) Jocaste," 216. For Pollock's reading of Antigone (and Oedipus), See Griselda Pollock, "Beyond Oedipus: Feminist Thought, Psychoanalysis, and Mythical Figurations of the Feminine," in *Laughing with Medusa: Classical Myth and Feminist Thought*, ed. Vanda Zajko and Miriam Leonard (Oxford University Press, 2006), 67–117.

motherhood is, in Western discourse, the place in our culture where we lodge, or rather bury, the reality of our own conflicts, of what it means to be fully human. It is the ultimate scapegoat for our personal and political failings, for everything that is wrong with the world, which it becomes the task — unrealisable, of course — of mothers to repair.[67]

In the matrixial theory, mothers are freed from this impossible burden. And so, Antigone and Jocaste's difficult relation becomes a model of a universal psychological experience.[68] Ettinger's reading of Laius points to the necessity of a new take on the feminine from the male perspective. In one of her articles, Ettinger briefly hints at the existence of the "feminine man-to-man difference."[69] This issue is further developed in the context of the mythical figure of Laius, who is governed by, above all, two impulses. The former is related to his rape of Chrysippus, which leads to the boy's suicide; Ettinger identifies it as the "envious erotic-aggressive"[70] impulse. The latter concerns his own son: Laius wishes to sacrifice — that is, kill — Oedipus. Ettinger finds an equivalent of the myth in the clinical situation in which the analyst conceals a Laius complex[71]; this poses a

---

67 Jacqueline Rose, *Mothers: An Essay on Love and Cruelty* (Faber & Faber, 2019), 1.

68 Juliet Mitchell provides a thought-provoking perspective on abandonment and mother–children relations. She argues that prior to the Law of the Father, the Law of the Mother is in effect: the mother "insists that there must be no incest or murder *between* her children," and these "prohibitions […] constitute an absolute 'law'"; what is more, the mother threatens "she will desert her utterly dependent toddler if it does not obey," which turns out to be traumatic for the child. Juliet Mitchell, *Fratriarchy: The Sibling Trauma and the Law of the Mother* (Routledge, 2023), 4–5. Emphasis in original.

69 Ettinger, "Antigone with(out) Jocaste," 220.

70 Ettinger, "Laius Complex and Shocks of Maternality," 280.

71 Ettinger summarizes the difference between the Oedipus complex and the Laius complex as follows: "The Oedipus complex is a child-version of what *does the father want.* In the Oedipus complex the Father is viewed from the infant's eyes. Yet other paternal possibilities are born with the arrival of

danger of pathologizing "the son's creativity."[72] Also, this results in rejecting and de-subjectifying the mother in the name of the dyadic relation. Ettinger postulates that these "pervert father-son relations"[73] may and should be resisted and even mended by means of the matrixial difference. Compassionate carriance and self-fragilization are believed to hamper Laius's impulse and to lead to "an ethical position of paternality where to have more power will mean to have more responsibility, not tyranny."[74] Characterized by the act of "carrying" his people, Moses is presented as a paternal figure informed by the matrix[75] and thus a potential alternative to destructive Laius.

All the above figures are burdened with loss, pain, and trauma, or themselves impose such burdens on others; Demeter and Persephone's case is no different in this respect, but this time Ettinger proposes an affirmative reading of the notion of a complex. Ettinger bases her considerations on the version of the myth in which Persephone makes it possible for Orpheus to enter the Underworld in his search for Eurydice because his endeavor reminds her of Demeter's search for her. "Identification," as Ettinger notes, "takes place here with the *primordial mother* as Love, an Eros beyond sexuality," later called "the maternal-matrixial Eros of borderlinking."[76] Non-sexual and non-narcissistic but originary and compassionate, such love is not governed by the Oedipal logic of separation; it contributes to one's process of becoming, which within the matrix always entails *becoming-together*. That is why Ettinger asks, "With Demeter so abased, her scars bleeding in the sky and on earth, does not Persephone, too, secretly bleed from her wounds?"[77] In this context, Ettinger

---

    parentality. Laius is one of the figures that mark a father-version of what a father wants." Ibid., 282. Emphasis in original.

72 Ibid., 281.

73 This is an excerpt from private email correspondence with Ettinger, who has granted me permission to quote her directly.

74 Ettinger, "Laius Complex and Shocks of Maternality," 283.

75 See ibid., 282–83.

76 Ettinger, "Demeter–Persephone Complex," 124. Emphasis in original.

77 Ibid., 128.

postulates the recognition of the Demeter–Persephone complex. What such recognition results in is subjectivization of both the mother and the daughter, and respect for the mother and her desire.[78] Transsubjective linkages affirmed via this complex embrace sharing, compassion, and self-fragilization, and thus they lead to a deeper understanding of the mother-subject's own traumas instead of alienating or blaming her (which frequently is, according to Ettinger, an unwanted outcome of clinical treatment).

The Ettingerian mythos is dominated by women, particularly mothers and daughters; yet, even though male figures are out-numbered, they serve important functions here. Not only phallic counterparts, men can also be matrixial partners-in-difference. The example of such "matrixial masculinity" is Isaac; however, his compassion, argues Ettinger, originates in the female body-space. The features that the women portrayed above share are maternity and mother–child relations, which usually imply pain and trauma, but also require trust to take a risk. What their female bodies offer is the prospect of humanizing connectivity, even if such connectedness burdens the daughter. Alongside linkages, trust, compassion, and distress, there is also humanity, which includes the persistently denied human capability to take away someone's life or abandon someone, even one's own son or daughter. Still, what holds a unique position in this theoretical pantheon is non-sexual love that informs subjectivization, mutual respect, and understanding.

Gendered Family Album

Is Ettinger's artistic oeuvre as feminized as her theoretical work? Ettinger points out that the theme of the artistic piece is not decisive in terms of the entrance to the matrixial borderspace; in other words, feminine motifs are by no means essential for art to be "matrixial." However, she bluntly adds that while in gen-

---

78 See ibid., 124, 125–26, 129–30.

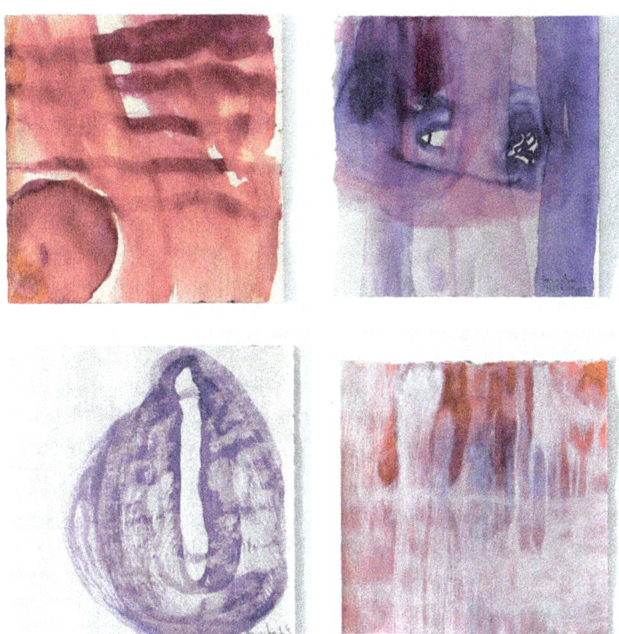

Figs. 12a–d. Selection of works on paper, featured at the exhibition *Bracha Lichtenberg Ettinger: Eurydice — Pieta* in Muzeum Śląskie (Silesian Museum), Katowice, July 7–September 2, 2017. Top left: *And my heart space-wound with-in me,* No. 14, 2012–2013, India ink on paper, 15 × 15 cm. Top right: India ink on paper, 2014–2016, 22 × 22 cm. Bottom left: India ink on paper, 2014–2016, 15 × 15 cm. Bottom right: India ink on paper, 2015–2016, 22 × 22 cm. © Courtesy of the artist.

eral "it doesn't matter," in her case "it usually does."[79] It is hard not to agree with this statement. Womb-like imagery, deployed in the late period of the *Eurydice* series, is intensified in some of Ettinger's works on paper, in which various elements are associated with the womb (figs. 12a–d). Although such connota-

---

79 Ettinger, "And My Heart, Wound-Space with-in Me," 357–58.

tions are often related to the red color (which recalls blood and thus carries the womb–wound pair within itself), the shape is an equally significant trope. The shapes are frequently circular, but with gaps and breaches; the strokes of color are watery and inconsistent. Like intimate envelopes, these images may also connote dangerous and incomprehensible spaces. Moreover, some of her works renegotiate the inside/outside dichotomy, as it is difficult to decide whether the image may be read as the female body interior or the entrance to it. As a result, the womb experience is elevated in this series.

While the womb indisputably is a feminine theme, we will now face family relations, turning from the mythical and biblical figures to Ettinger's mother, father, and brother. Bluma and Uziel Lichtenberg have already been introduced; Mordechai, Ettinger's brother, was born in Palestine in 1945.[80] The three relatives inhabit Ettinger's art, but one can spot differences between the representations of the mother and the male family members, including the quantity of their appearances; in this category, Bluma Lichtenberg outruns Uziel and Mordechai. The Mizocz women also have to be evoked here — they may be claimed to belong to the category of historical figures, but there is something relentlessly private and intimate in them for Ettinger. The abundance of female representations is not the only feature that may suggest the highly feminine character of this oeuvre; gender issues may also be revealed in artistic techniques and strategies.[81] The discussion will feature artworks based on at least

---

80 See "Bracha Lichtenberg Ettinger: Chronology," in *Art as Compassion: Bracha L. Ettinger,* ed. Catherine de Zegher and Griselda Pollock (ASA Publishers, 2012), 249.

81 Paintings and works on paper are not the only types of artistic practice Ettinger has been interested in. In 2009, Ettinger created an installation in the Freud Museum, London, entitled *Resonance. Overlay. Interweave. Bracha L. Ettinger in the Freudian Space of Memory and Migration.* In short, it was based on various additions and interventions, such as private photographs and other items, notebooks, and artworks, arranged in three museum rooms. I discuss the part of the installation placed in Freud's consulting room in my article "Dis-Obedience to the Father." In the article, I show how, in her theory and installation, Ettinger finds the place for the

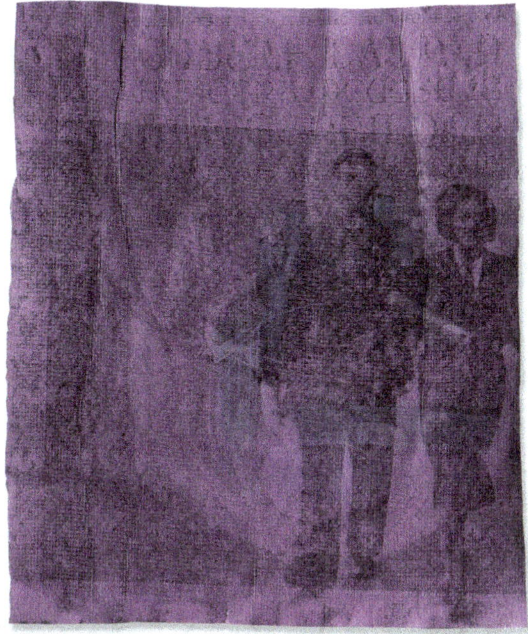

Fig. 13. Bracha L. Ettinger, *The Eye of the Compass–Lapsus,* ensemble I, drawing 4, 1990, India ink, xerography, photocopic pigment and ashes on paper, 18.2 × 15.8 cm. Collection: Israel Museum, Jerusalem. © Courtesy of the artist.

---

mother in the space of the Law of the Father. I conclude that, "[i]nstead of trying to veil Freud's room, Ettinger actively interacts with it, engaging in the dialogue and sharing experiences. She questions the Father and his rules, but in a creative way, as she notes the blind spots and ambiguities of his seemingly unquestionable laws. Yet, most importantly — she introduces the mother. [… T]he woman-mother is given well-deserved and longed-for sphere, yet instead of replacing the figure of the Law, she productively co-exists with it." This installation has various gender connotations and male/female relations to explore, but the results of such explorations would coincide with those I propose basing on the works of art chosen for this chapter. Anna Kisiel, "Dis-Obedience to the Father: Bracha L. Ettinger's Theory and Installation Confronted with Freud and Lacan," *Romanica Silesiana* 12 (2017): 61–62.

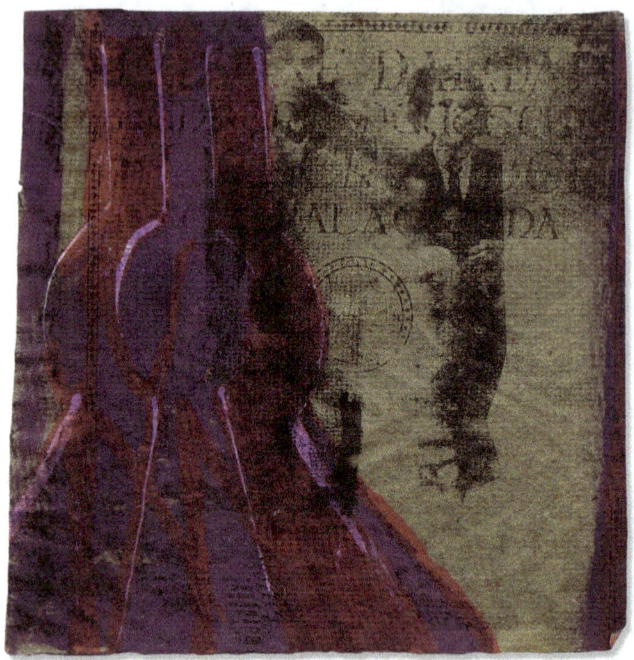

Fig. 14. Bracha L. Ettinger, *No Title*, 1987–1989, India ink, xerography, photocopic pigment and ashes, color pencil and graphite on paper, 24 × 24.3 cm. © Courtesy of the artist.

one of the three following photographs: the picture of Ettinger's parents-to-be taken in 1936 in Łódź, the picture of Ettinger's mother taken in Slovakia in 1941, and the family shot of Bluma with her both children from 1950, taken in Tel Aviv.[82]

When exploring the images with the prewar photo of Ettinger's parents as a background, one may note the unceasingly present pattern of blur and coverage, and wonder whether and how it is related to the figures of mother and father. In the image

---

82 See Griselda Pollock, "A Matrixial Installation: Artworking in the Freudian Space of Memory and Migration," in *Art as Compassion,* ed. Zegher and Pollock, 199–200.

from the *The Eye of the Compass–Lapsus* series (ensemble I, drawing 4, 1990), we can see both parents in purple surroundings moved towards the right side of the piece (fig. 13). They are juxtaposed with another reappearing motif, Gustaf Dalman's book *Hundert Deutsche Fliegerbilder aus Palaestina* published in 1925, filled with aerial photographs of Palestine.[83] In the artwork, the parents are not cropped, but the intensity of the purple color makes them less visible. Uziel's face seems to be less clear than Bluma's, but simultaneously it is he who occupies a more central position in the image. However, this does not form a consistent theme; for instance, in the *No Title — Sketch* (1988–1989), it is the mother who stands centrally and whose face is vaguer (fig. 7). In an untitled piece from 1987–1989, sharing the same motifs (the photograph and the cover of *Hundert Deutsche Fliegerbilder...*), Bluma and Uziel are posited near the center of the image, but this time their bodies are cropped (fig. 14). Moreover, their faces appear to fight for dominance with the letters comprising the title of the mentioned book, because of which it is difficult to grasp their expressions, while the mixture of red and purple form a pattern that partially covers the father's body. The distortion goes in a peculiar direction in the untitled piece made in 1989 (fig. 15). In this meeting of survivors with victims, Bluma and Uziel are hardly discernible while the bodies of women from Mizocz are unusually distinct (if one keeps in mind the later progress of the *Eurydice* series). The father's face becomes almost invisible as it merges with the purple surroundings, while the mother's face is as if obliterated with white smudges. It produces a paradoxical impression — even though Uziel's face is less dim, it is the mother who attracts more attention. Blur is, then, not a reliable trope in the case of Bluma and Uziel's photograph, for it is not permanently assigned to any of the figures.

---

83 Rosi Huhn writes more about this book and its implications; See Rosi Huhn, "The Folly of Reason," in *Art as Compassion*, ed. Zegher and Pollock, 43–55.

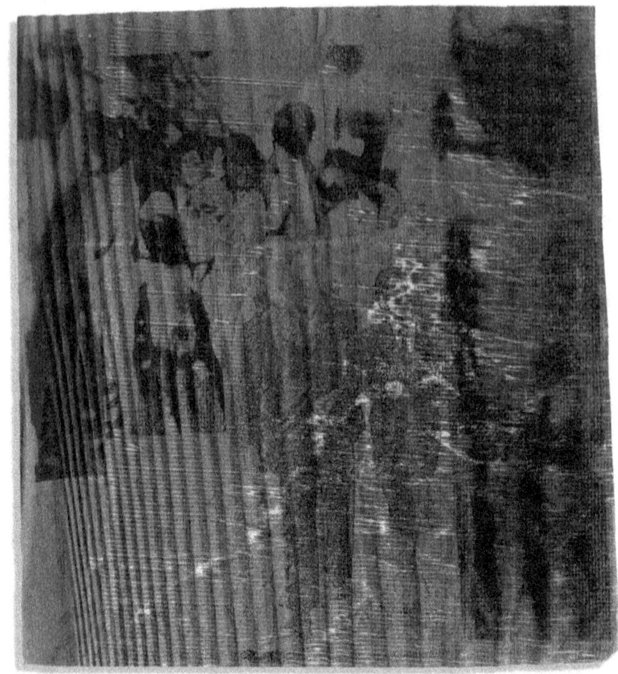

Fig. 15. Bracha L. Ettinger, *No Title,* 1989, pastel crayon, xerography, photocopic pigment and ashes on paper, 30.3 × 28.1 cm. © Courtesy of the artist.

Another artistic strategy that affects both parents in Ettinger's pieces is that of coverage initiated by the paint. In an untitled piece from 1986 — in which the interplay of the photograph, the purple color, and *Hundert Deutsche Fliegerbilder…* can be spotted again — Bluma and Uziel appear to be pushed to the left side by the expanding black surface (fig. 16). Their eyes and lips are made unavailable for the viewer, who can grasp only smears in their place. In *Eurydice,* No. 4 (1992–1994), the same happens again (fig. 17). The parents share the canvas with a page from a French–Hebrew dictionary; matrixial connotations of such entries as *langage maternelle, vivante/morte,* or *languir*

Fig. 16. Bracha L. Ettinger, *No Title*, 1986, xerography, photocopic pigment and ashes on paper, 23 × 23.5 cm. © Courtesy of the artist.

are apparent. Frozen, purple, and red machine-like movements have almost managed to cover Bluma and Uziel; their resistance has not been futile this time, but the spectator may be left with an impression that next time they may lose the battle. In both artworks, the bodies of Ettinger's parents are under the threat of disappearance, and this threat may be considered equal for both of them. Hand in hand, they resist being removed from the canvas, arresting the painter's gestures midway.

Although Bluma and Uziel's resistance is shared, it is indisputable that the father is never alone in the paintings — he seems to appear either with his wife or not at all — while the mother becomes a recurring motif on her own. One of the photographs that function as the basis for this motif is that of Bluma during the war, in which she is captured while drinking from a ves-

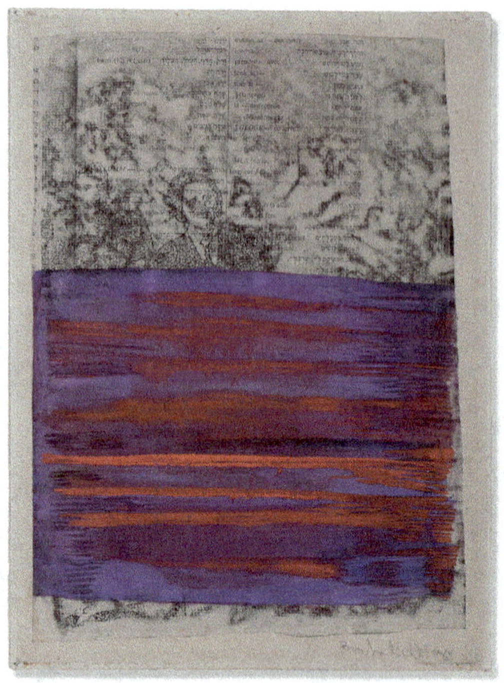

Fig. 17. Bracha L. Ettinger, *Eurydice,* No. 4, 1992–1994, oil, xerography, photocopic pigment and ashes on paper mounted on canvas, 36.8 × 27 cm. © Courtesy of the artist.

sel. According to Pollock, this image was supposed to let Uziel know she was alive.[84] Ettinger repeats this gesture of affirming Bluma's existence in, among other projects, her works on paper. In the images where she resurfaces, the future mother is a sole motif, not accompanied by the Eurydices or by her family members. In one of the works, she is as if sketched, almost invisible; we can recognize the shape of her body, but perhaps such an

---

84 Griselda Pollock, "Resonance: The Consulting Room," in *Art in the Time-Space of Memory and Migration: Sigmund Freud, Anna Freud, and Bracha L. Ettinger in the Freud Museum, Artwriting after the Event* (Wild Pansy Press, 2015), 68.

Fig. 18. Bracha L. Ettinger, *Untitled,* 1985, xerography, photocopic pigment and ashes, India ink and chalk on paper, 25.2 × 22 cm, featured at the exhibition *Bracha Lichtenberg Ettinger: Eurydice — Pieta* in Muzeum Śląskie (Silesian Museum), Katowice, July 7–September 2, 2017. © Courtesy of the artist.

identification would not be easy if we knew nothing about the original photograph (fig. 18). This artwork is bright and delicate in contrast to another one, dominated by the purple color (fig. 19). Here, the figure is even less clear: The landscape of the photo is a combination of black and red spots with which the lower part of her body merges, whereas the upper part belongs to the purple background of the work on paper. The mother's body thus becomes a hybrid of two surfaces, but it is hard to decide whether it exists on its own. Nevertheless, even if Bluma has almost disappeared from the examined works, a trace of her occupies them and brings her back to visibility.

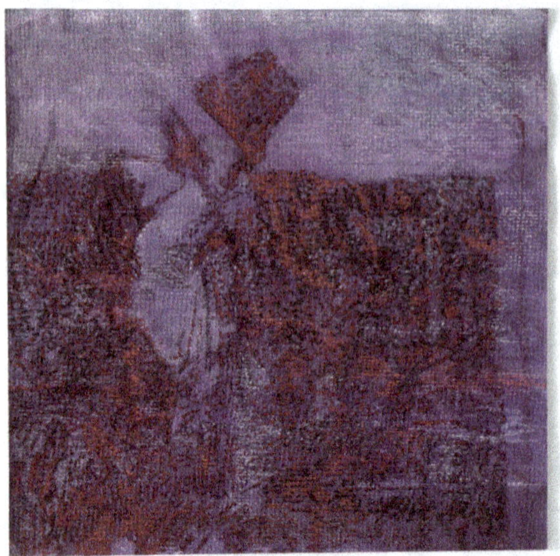

Fig. 19. Bracha L. Ettinger, *Family Album* (series), 1985, xerography, photocopic pigment and ashes, India ink and chalk on paper, 23.5 × 24.5 cm, featured at the exhibition *Bracha Lichtenberg Ettinger: Eurydice — Pieta* in Muzeum Śląskie (Silesian Museum), Katowice, July 7–September 2, 2017. © Courtesy of the artist.

Reworking the photo of Ettinger's mother, the above images may connote Roland Barthes's *Winter Garden Photograph,* extensively studied in his *Camera Lucida.* The image of the author's mother as a child becomes a vehicle for truth, long sought by him.[85] This photograph is claimed to grasp the essence of the mother even though it is not his mother yet — she is "the mother-as-child,"[86] a child who "does not look 'like' her,"

---

85 Roland Barthes, *Camera Lucida: Reflections on Photography,* trans. Richard Howard (Hill and Wang, 2010), 67–71.

86 Ibid., 71.

and whom Barthes "never knew."[87] This image evokes in Barthes a desire of exploring it further. We read,

> I look at it, I scrutinize it, as if I wanted to know more about the thing or the person it represents. Lost in the depths of the Winter Garden, my mother's face is vague, faded. [...] I want to outline the loved face by thought, to make it into the unique field of an intense observation; I want to enlarge this face in order to see it better, to understand it better, to know its truth [....] I decompose, I enlarge, and, so to speak, I *retard,* in order to have time to *know* at last. The Photograph justifies this desire, even if it does not satisfy it.[88]

Barthes, however, concludes bitterly that whatever actions he undertakes, in the end they are worthless since the photographic image is unable to communicate knowledge — it only shows the captured content.[89] Ettinger's relation with the mother — as read through the prism of her works on paper based on the image from 1941 — may be similar to that described by Barthes. Ettinger repeatedly works through the image that grasps her mother before maternity. No matter to what extent Ettinger manipulates the base picture, the figure of Bluma persistently remains on the verge of sight, revealing sometimes less and sometimes more; what is revealed, however, is hardly tangible to the viewer. What distinguishes the matrixial perspective from Barthes's final remark on the nature of the image is the possibility of communicating information beyond the sole ability to see a captured object even if this kind of content is not linguistic or fully comprehensible.

What fragments of information do we receive when observing images based on the photo of Ettinger as a child with her mother and brother? Although the trope of blur and disappearance seems to be a dead end when we consider Uziel Lichten-

---

87 Ibid., 103.
88 Ibid., 99–100. Emphasis in original.
89 Ibid., 100.

Fig. 20. Bracha L. Ettinger, *Eurydice,* No. 3, 1992–1994, oil, xerography, photocopic pigment and ashes on paper mounted on canvas, 28.7 × 23.4 cm. Collection: Museum of Puri, Finland. © Courtesy of the artist.

berg, in the case of Mordechai it arguably is more reliable. One of the early *Eurydices — Eurydice,* No. 3 (1992–1994) — is fully devoted to the maternal triad (fig. 20). All three persons occupy the frame; below them, one can find the already mentioned excerpt from the dictionary, with the central position of phrases *langage maternelle* and *vivante/morte.* Even though Bracha, Bluma, and Mordechai are graspable, their faces are distorted or even deformed, which makes their expressions unnatural and ghostly. Still, it may be claimed that they are treated equally, all being arrested in the moment of vanishing. The situation changes in an untitled piece from 1984/1986 (fig. 21). Here, gradual disappearance is performed differently: The faces are not deformed, but instead they become more and more invisible,

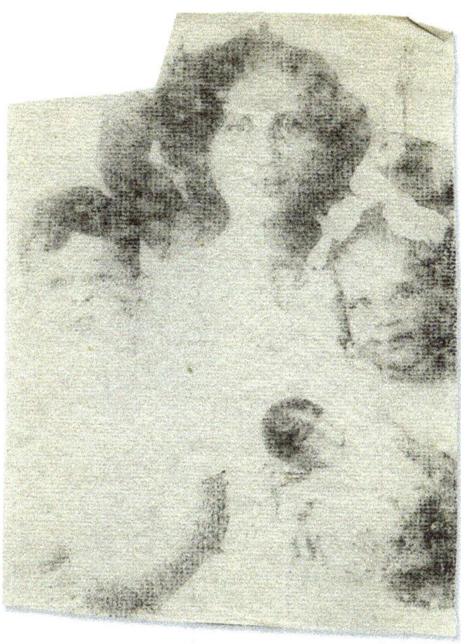

Fig. 21. Bracha L. Ettinger, *No Title,* 1984/1986, xerography, photocopic pigment and ashes on paper, 23.9 × 18.5 cm. © Courtesy of the artist.

merging with the paper background. What is still distinctive are hair and elements of faces, including those of Ettinger's doll held in her hands. Importantly, Bluma Lichtenberg's and her daughter's faces are notably clearer than Mordechai's. He accompanies them, but the process of disappearance is more advanced in his case. *Matrix–Family Album,* No. 3 (2003–2005) is the image that reduces the family unit to two figures (fig. 22). Even though the space for him is still kept, the brother is no longer there. The mother remains in the central position, and her face is the most visible: We still see a delicate smile and shapes of her eyes, whereas her skin merges with the background covered in mainly Hebrew words. Finally, her daughter is partly hidden by lines of purple paint; her mouth is covered, but her eyes are still focused on the viewer. As we can see, it is impossible to ignore

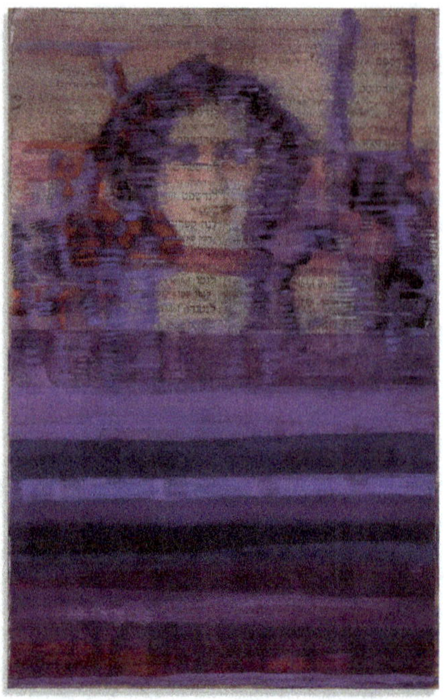

Fig. 22. Bracha L. Ettinger, *Matrix — Family Album,* No. 3, 2003–2005, oil, xerography, photocopic pigment and ashes on paper mounted on canvas, 39.5 × 26 cm. Collection: Haifa Museum. © Courtesy of the artist.

the brother figure's tendency to fade away from the view; nevertheless, although the mother–daughter connection is the main issue here, it seems to wend its way towards a breakdown.

Let us explore the relationship between the mother and daughter further. Grainy and fuzzy, *Eurydice,* No. 10 (1994–1996) draws attention to Bluma, who is as if full of comfort and peace of mind (fig. 23). When we seek Ettinger, we find her forehead and a ribbon, but the rest of her face seems to be gone. Yet, if we watch the painting closely, we discover her left eye, sharper than the rest of this figure. Not abandoning the image, Ettinger appears to keep it guarded against paint and other tools

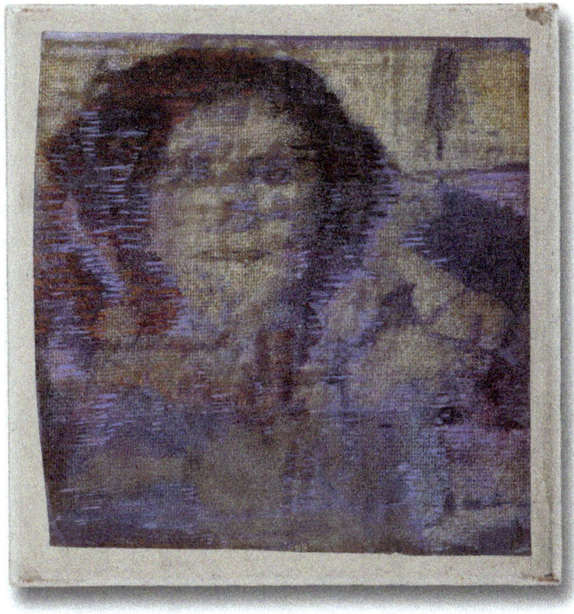

Fig. 23. Bracha L. Ettinger, *Eurydice,* No. 10, 1994–1996, oil, xerography, photocopic pigment and ashes on paper mounted on canvas, 27.8 × 28.1 cm. © Courtesy of the artist.

of distortion. Perhaps, she is also guarding the mother, shifting the usual roles. The question of protection — but also its connection with speech and its lack — becomes more significant if we take a look at an untitled artwork made between 1998 and 1999 (fig. 24). This time, the daughter's eyes are smeared, and thus she is deprived of the ability to observe the viewer. Since we can still recognize fragments of Ettinger's face, the mother is not left alone on the canvas. Bluma, too, is made incomplete here: Her lips are covered with the purple line of paint. As a result of the painter's gesture, she becomes a mother who cannot speak. This situation corresponds to Ettinger's account of her parents' refusal to talk about the Holocaust. She notes, "My parents are proud of their silence. It was their way of sparing others and their children from suffering. But *in this silence all was transmit-*

Fig. 24. Bracha L. Ettinger, *Untitled*, No. 2, 1998–1999, oil, xerography, photocopic pigment and ashes on paper mounted on canvas, 29.7 × 23.1 cm. © Courtesy of the artist.

ted except the narrative. In silence nothing can be changed in the narrative which hides itself."[90] The mother's silence is associated with the wish to protect the children, that is, with the decision to try to limit their pain by not telling them stories of the war. The mother may have locked the "narrative," but the traumatic information is shared nonetheless. Even if unconsciously, the mother delivers fragments of the hurtful message. The communication between the mother and her daughter may be marked by silence, but this act does not cease to carry a meaning.

---

90 Bracha L. Ettinger, *Matrix Halal(a): Lapsus: Notes on Painting,* trans. Joseph Sims (Museum of Modern Art, 1993), quoted in Ettinger, *Artworking 1985–1999,* 98. Emphasis mine.

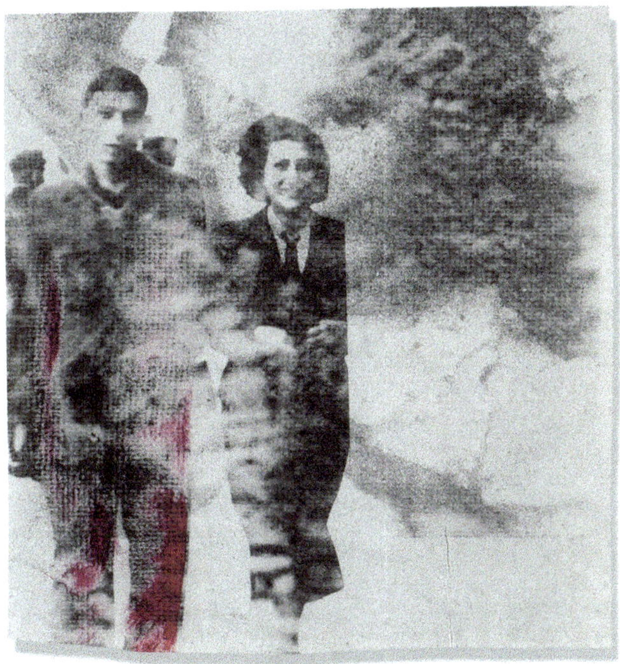

Fig. 25. Bracha L. Ettinger, *Mamalangue — Borderline Conditions and Pathological Narcissism,* Ensemble V, No. 3, 1989–1990, India ink, xerography, photocopic pigment and ashes, watercolour and chalk on paper, 22 × 21.7 cm. © Courtesy of the artist.

Another meaningful encounter takes place in the works of art that merge the postwar photograph with the prewar one. In the foreground of *Mamalangue — Borderline Conditions and Pathological Narcissism,* Ensemble V, No. 3 (1989–1990), Bluma and Uziel walk a street in Łódź (fig. 25).[91] If we compare them to other figures from photo-based images, they are rather visible and clear since we easily see their face expressions, postures, and clothes; we can even spot anonymous men standing behind

---

91 The same theme is used, for instance, in an untitled piece made between 1987 and 1989 (fig. 26).

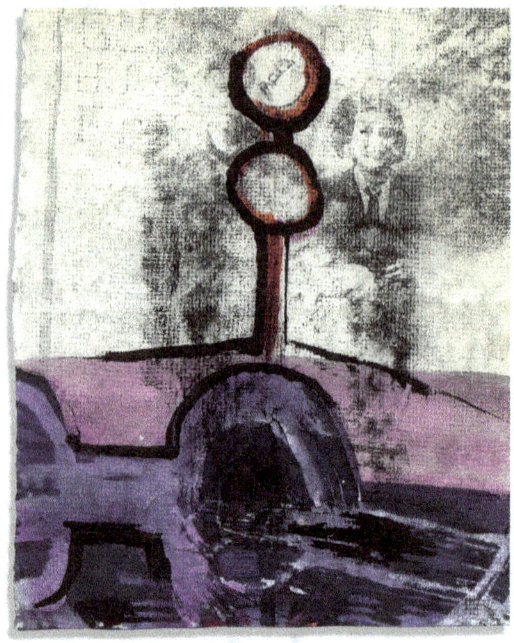

Fig. 26. Bracha L. Ettinger, *No Title*, 1987–1989, India ink, xerography, photocopic pigment and ashes on paper, 25.7 × 22 cm. © Courtesy of the artist.

them in the original photograph. Yet, what is most interesting is the background as it interacts with the described figures. We can spot Ettinger's faded face from the family photo here. The face is posited in such a way that it converges with Bluma, whose head goes between the girl's eyes and whose shoulders cover her smile. The mother–daughter line of communication appears to become the major theme of the piece; undeniably, the father does keep them company, but it is their bodies that intermingle whereas his is more radically separated.

Gender(lessness) of the Body

Grounded upon female corporeality, the matrixial theory may appear to boldly reduce the male element. That is, however, an overly simplistic judgment as this system is promising not only from the female perspective. Ettinger by no means suggests that the matrixial body is universal or neutral; what she offers instead is a theorization of an experience originating in the female body, an experience everyone has gone through. Although necessarily gendered, the matrixial feminine difference proposed by the theorist is applicable to both men and women. Women have a privileged position in this respect, but this does not mean that the matrix is closed for men; their access may be impossible "in that primary and radical real sense," but they still have other paths, kept open because of the originary experience of being in the woman-mother's body. Importantly, even though in this theory the emphasis is put on the female flesh and events within it, the matrix is far from being an essentialist concept, and Ettinger stresses that elements of this thought ought not to be used against women's reproductive rights.

Men and women appearing in Ettinger's oeuvre provide a crucial context in the discussion about gender, the matrix, and corporeal ethics. When the use of female and male figures in the matrixial theory is concerned, it is easy to assess who prevails: biblical and mythological women. Linked by their maternality, trust, and burdens they share with Others, these women provide a possibility of proto-ethical conjoining launched in their corporeality. Simultaneously, such male figures as Isaac and Moses take the understanding of matrixial connectedness further. They show that while the origin of their matrixial structuring is a female body, such structuring goes beyond (having) it. When we turn to Ettinger's artistic activity, we may note certain aesthetic strategies open to gender-based readings. The figures of her father and brother tend to occasionally haunt the paintings whereas the mother resides there on more permanent terms. All the family members equally struggle against gradual disappearance, but it is the mother who most frequently survives the strokes of paint and other artistic techniques. However, it seems that it is not a mere question of Bluma being a woman, and of Uziel and Mordechai being men. Rather, what proves to be most engaging is the very mother–daughter relation, intimate and convoluted, painful and intense. Almost borderless and inherently corporeal, the humanizing encounter between two becoming-I's does not cease to be the defining event of the matrixial subjectivizing domain.

PART II

ENCOUNTERS IN COM-PASSION

4

Through/With/In the Body

Theological Resonances of the Matrixial Specificity

[A] virgin shall be with child, and shall bring forth a son.

— Matthew 1:23 (KJV)[1]

Take, eat; this is my body.

— Matthew 26:26 (KJV)

[God] is "himself" the among: he is the with or the between of us.

—Jean-Luc Nancy, "In the Midst of the World"[2]

Eve, Isaac, Abraham, Sarah, Hagar, Moses, Saint Anne — these biblical figures testify to humanity, trust, compassion, and complexities of maternity. These women and men are not merely theological points of reference in the matrixial theory, and yet it would be hasty to omit religious and theological connotations they evoke. It seems that both registers are significant elements of Ettinger's theory and artistic imagination. This chapter is by no means an exhaustive account of theological traces in Ettinger's

---

1   All the biblical quotes are taken from the King James Version; unless stated otherwise, the emphases are in the original.

2   Jean-Luc Nancy, "In the Midst of the World," in Jean-Luc Nancy, *Adoration: The Deconstruction of Christianity II,* trans. John McKeane (Fordham University Press, 2013), 30. Emphasis in original.

oeuvre[3]; instead, it aims at exploring theological resonances of matrixial corporeality and the position of ethics at the intersection of the matrixial body and theology. Although strictly theological interpretations of Ettinger's thought are possible,[4] I do not aspire to take part in theological debates. Rather than theologians, philosophers engaged in theological reflections will be referenced for the sake of examining potential theological openings of matrixial corporeality. I will focus on two religious traditions, Christianity and Judaism, as they form the two pillars of Ettinger's theological entanglement. The questions that will reverberate through this chapter are: What are the interrelations between the matrixial logic and theological patterns and modes, and how do these interrelations complement our understanding of corporeality? How can religious notions of covenant, compassion and passion, and sacrifice inform the matrixial ethics of the body? Finally, can we treat an artistic encounter — including an encounter with Ettinger's *Eurydices* — as a (quasi-)religious event?

From Word to Flesh

One of theologically defined events that bears a striking resemblance to the matrixial logic is incarnation. In Christianity, Jesus Christ is simultaneously a human being and God. He descends to the earth and takes up a human form, but without abandoning his deific nature since "it please[s] *the Father* that in him should all fulness dwell."[5] When clarifying his relation

---

3   Ettinger herself turns to biblical tropes, taking a special interest in Hebrew phrases and words: their etymology and potentially matrixial implications. See, for instance, Brigit M. Kaiser and Kathrin Thiele, "If You Do Well, Carry! The Difference of the Humane: An Interview with Bracha L. Ettinger," *philoSOPHIA: A Journal of Continental Feminism* 8, no. 1 (2018): 101–25.

4   See Mary Condren, "Relational Theology in the Work of the Artist, Psychoanalyst and Theorist Bracha Lichtenberg Ettinger," in *Through Us, with Us, in Us: Relational Theologies in the Twenty-First Century,* ed. Lisa Isherwood and Elaine Bellchambers (SCM Press, 2010).

5   Colossians 1:19 (KJV).

with God the Father, Christ argues that they ought not to be conceived of as separate entities[6]; he emphasizes the strength of their trans-connectedness by saying, "he that hath seen me hath seen the Father."[7] Also, he claims that it is only *through* him that one can reach God.[8] The stable dichotomy of a divine being versus a human being is, therefore, challenged here; what is offered instead is the logic of both/and similar to that proposed by Ettinger. Christ embodies the possibility of shattering binaries; he opposes ascribing the phallic logic of cut to his almost-complete affinity to the Father. Their interdependence is revealed in the access to the transcendent: One can access God only through his son, and one can cognize God only if one cognizes his son. The metaphor of dwelling — with its homely or maternal connotations — is another accurate description of the matrixial structure of relations between the two persons; we can, however, assume that this structure goes in both directions, that is, not only does God dwell within Christ, but also the Son inhabits the Father. Nevertheless, incarnation transcends the Father–Son relation as it also applies to that between humanity and God. As Matthew the Apostle reminds us, another name ascribed to Jesus is "Emmanuel," meaning "God with us."[9] Apparently, Christ invites humankind to a realm of inclusion and togetherness instead of rejection and separation; matrixial subjectivity is modeled on the same logic.

Incarnation and matrixial subjectivity also share their root: the body. In the incarnation of Christ, the notion of corporeality has two meanings. First, one of the attributes of "the mystery of godliness" in Christ is that he "was manifest in the *flesh*."[10] Likewise, the etymology of *incarnation* sends us to Late Latin

---

6   "I and *my* Father are one." John 10:30 (KJV).

7   John 14:9 (KJV).

8   "[N]o man cometh unto the Father, but by me." John 14:6 (KJV). In the New American Standard Bible, among other bibles, "through" is used instead of "by" in this passage.

9   Matthew 1:23 (KJV). See Isaiah 7:14 (KJV).

10 1 Timothy 3:16 (KJV). Emphasis mine.

incarnari, "be made flesh."[11] Christ's paradoxical status of an entity that is both divine and human is, therefore, tied to the question of him having a body, or even coming into possession of a body. In other words, the act of materializing himself in a mortal corporeal form is what makes Christ truly human. Second, since Christ took the same path as all the people, the beginning of it was marked in the female body. As announced by Isaiah and repeated by Matthew, "a virgin shall be with child, and shall bring forth a son."[12] Mary's womb is thus the site where Christ's human life commences: his first earthly home. The root of Christ's humanity, Mary's corporeal space resembles that of the matrix. "[W]e are all born of woman,"[13] and so is the Son of God; in both cases, this results in the formation of a new paradigm, which above all emphasizes an encounter between subjects, proximity, and togetherness, instead of distance or non-availability of a transcendent divinity.

Such a new paradigm corresponds to Jean-Luc Nancy's reflections on tenderness and the logic of (corporeal) opening. Nancy characterizes the Son of God by means of "the force and tenderness necessary to salute [*saluer*] another life in the midst of this one."[14] From the matrixial angle, the juxtaposition of tenderness and force becomes quintessential as it refers us back to the notion of self-fragilization. One needs a sufficient amount of agency, strength, and decisiveness to fragilize oneself for the sake of entering a relation with the matrixial border-Other; simultaneously, fragilization incorporates the notion of tenderness — gentleness and compassion in tending to one's non-I. However, the notion of saluting is where Nancy and Ettinger diverge. While affirming and facing the Other — implied in saluting — are crucial for both theorists, Nancy keeps his dis-

---

11   *Online Etymology Dictionary,* s.v. "incarnation," https://www.etymonline.com/word/incarnation.

12   Matthew 1:23 (KJV); compare: Isaiah 7:14 (KJV).

13   Griselda Pollock, "Introduction. Femininity: Aporia or Sexual Difference?," in Bracha L. Ettinger, *The Matrixial Borderspace,* ed. Brian Massumi (University of Minnesota Press, 2006), 29.

14   Nancy, "In the Midst of the World," 28. Emphasis in original.

tance from the potentiality of "sav[ing]"[15] the Other. Ettingerian psychoanalysis, however, outlines the possibilities of an encounter with the Other in broader terms. The matrixial encounter operates on reciprocity, which includes also working through the Others' traumas when these wounds are too deep to be handled on their own.[16] This act cannot be identified as saving yet; however, what the matrixial encounter certainly offers is more than pure affirmation implied in Nancean saluting. Next, in Nancy's reading, Christ's tenderness and his act of saluting embody the new type of logic — the logic of (corporeal) opening. We read,

> the outside of the world *in* the world is not "outside" according to the logic of a divorce, a rift, but according to that of an opening that belongs to the world, as the mouth belongs to the body. Better still: the mouth is, or is what makes, the eating and speaking body, just as the other openings are what make it the breathing, listening, seeing, eliminating body. The outside traverses the body in all these ways, and this is how it becomes *a body:* the exposure of a soul. Our bodies are thus entirely, in their turn, openings of the world, and so are other open bodies, those of animals and plants. They can all salute.[17]

The openings of human corporeality challenge the inside/outside dichotomy and contribute to the capabilities of the body itself. Drawing a line between these openings and the flesh is irrelevant as they become borderspaces of the flesh, mediating between the inside and outside "worlds." The logic of cuts is revealed as insufficient, for there is a necessity to explore other, more tender modes of relation between the I and the non-I.

---

15 Ibid.

16 See Bracha L. Ettinger, "Transcryptum: Memory Tracing in/for/with the Other," in Ettinger, *The Matrixial Borderspace,* 167–68.

17 Nancy, "In the Midst of the World," 28. Emphasis in original.

It is exactly through this relation that — in Nancy's proposition of Christian atheism[18] — we should perceive God. As he observes, Christianity is not concerned with God that is remote but with one that is "the *among*: he is the *with* or the *between* of us."[19] Nancy defines the world by means of relations between its inhabitants; such relations between ones that "are near or neighboring one another"[20] are claimed to be the only relations that exist and matter. The question of relations is omnipresent in the matrixial theory as well. Most and first of all, however, it is the woman that breaks the impassable distance and thus escapes the logic of remoteness and cut. As opposed to the phallic understanding of the woman as "*either* a subject in the masculine format *or* an object patterned on masculine desire" and as that "which can be reduced to nothing," within the matrixial domain she oscillates "*between* subject and object and *between* center and nothingness, on the axis of heterogeneous severality."[21] A figure of in-between, the woman is not finite; rather, she stands for change and proximity. Since the very model of the matrixial encounter is the prenatal/pregnancy mother–child union commencing in motherly-feminine corporeality, the woman opens the path of connectedness and severality. Just as in Nancy "God is relation,"[22] the matrixial female body is the site and the origin of (primary) relation.

Both in Ettinger's psychoanalysis and in the Bible, the relation is necessarily embodied despite its entanglement in language. In the gospel of John, we are informed that "the Word was made flesh."[23] Christ is presented here as *logos* — the message of God. In order to be passed to the people, the Word became a corporeal entity: God "dwelt among us,"[24] continuing

---

18 For the clarification of the notion of Christian atheism, See ibid., 28–33.
19 Ibid., 30. Emphasis in original.
20 Ibid.
21 Bracha L. Ettinger, "The With-In-Visible Screen," in Ettinger, *The Matrixial Borderspace*, 113. Emphasis in original.
22 Nancy, "In the Midst of the World," 30.
23 John 1:14 (KJV).
24 Ibid.

to develop a relation with the believers. For this connection to gain in strength and significance, embodiment was necessary: God had to take a human form to transcend the limitations of language. The relation between body and word is tackled by Ettinger in a twofold manner. First, principles of binarized language do not apply (yet) to the matrixial subjectivizing sphere; linguistic structures are inexistent here and what reigns are bodily sensations and experiences. The other issue is connected not so much to the theory as to Ettinger's writing itself. Ettinger's style is exhaustively playful: abundant in loops, neologisms, and descriptive vocabulary. Noting that "[i]t involves shifts, moves, repetitions, circlings and a poetic language of created terms,"[25] Pollock links this kind of writing to Hélène Cixous's proposition of *écriture féminine.* In a sense, Ettinger's texts share several similarities with her artistic technique since her style seeks new modes of expression while trying to transcend inherent insufficiencies of the act of writing. Via its vocabulary and structures, this language constantly deconstructs and exercises itself. As a result, Ettinger's écriture carries affect-oriented, performative, and corporeal aspirations; because of its preoccupation with rhythms and pulses of bodily articulations, it is placed near the margins of conventions imposed by the binary structure of language. As for Ettinger *logos* is an insufficient figure, her writing also endeavors to be "made flesh" — to materialize itself and thus grasp the complexities of relationships between embodied beings.

Com-Passionate Covenants

Ettinger notes that in the matrixial borderspace, an encounter with the non-I — occasioned by metramorphosis — is considered

---

25 Griselda Pollock, "Mother Trouble: The Maternal-Feminine in Phallic and Feminist Theory in Relation to Bracha Ettinger's Elaboration of Matrixial Ethics/Aesthetics," *Studies in the Maternal* 1, no. 1 (2009): 13. See Hélène Cixous, "The Laugh of the Medusa," trans. Keith Cohen and Paula Cohen, *Signs: Journal of Women in Culture and Society* 1, no. 4 (1976): 875–93.

a covenant.[26] Although she does not explain how the two notions are connected, the link between them is more evident once we turn to the etymology of the word. In Old French, *covenant* embraces an "agreement, pact, promise," and originally it points to the Latin verb *convenire*, of which one meaning is to "come together" (*com-*, "together," and *venire*, "come"), to "unite," and to "agree."[27] A matrixial covenant is, therefore, a union or a pact agreed upon between at least two becoming-subjects. Described as "an alliance" and "an anonymous intimacy,"[28] this encounter is necessarily based on decisiveness. Such an arrangement does not have to be symmetrical; it can be based on a need or request and a compassionate response to it — a promise of a kind. Can this promise be broken, or can we decide to dissolve the union? Ettinger asserts that the answer is negative: If one commits oneself to the matrixial connection, one "cannot choose when to terminate the covenant, or how, or to what extent, if at all. Because the phallus cannot master the Matrix."[29] Ettinger raises the question of the covenant in the context of aesthetics as well. In her proposition, traces of the prenatal-intrauterine encounter are shared by means of "matrixial covenant(s) assembled by art."[30] Art thus becomes the space hospitable for a covenant to occur, and even perhaps the privileged space in terms of its possibility to unfold such an encounter. What is also unmasked here is the close relation between the intrauterine, aesthetic, and matrixial spheres. Still, apart from Ettinger's hints and the etymological insight into the covenant, one cannot deny the biblical connotations of this figure.

The Last Supper, followed by the death and resurrection of Christ, marks the new covenant between God and humankind, grounded upon promise and reconciliation, and not upon reg-

---

26 Ettinger, "The With-In-Visible Screen," 102–3.

27 *Online Etymology Dictionary*, s.v. "covenant," https://www.etymonline.com/word/covenant.

28 Bracha L. Ettinger, "Wit(h)nessing Trauma and the Matrixial Gaze," in Ettinger, *The Matrixial Borderspace*, 150.

29 Ettinger, "The With-In-Visible Screen," 118.

30 Ibid., 108.

ulations or restrictions. During the Supper, Christ first offers his apostles the bread: "Take, eat; this is my body."[31] Then he proceeds to the wine; he hands it around, saying: "Drink ye all of it; For this is my blood of the new testament" — or "covenant" — "which is shed for many for the remission of sins."[32] These two gestures of sharing are supposed to seal the contract between the Son of God and his disciples, but the deal is also extended to humanity in general; Christ makes a promise that people's sins will be forgiven as a result of his sacrifice. The Supper also stands for reconciliation. On the one hand, Christ reconciles with Peter, who is bound to deny knowing him, and with Judas, who has betrayed him; on the other, the Son of God appears to accept the painful task he has been given. Yet, the covenant is not merely a promise or a union, but also a pact: a codified agreement. When the question of laws is concerned, the covenant Christ agrees upon with his disciples is interpreted by Paul as "the new testament; not of the letter, but of the spirit."[33] Giorgio Agamben observes that it is not a covenant based on regulations and prohibitions, like the Mosaic law. The new covenant invalidates that of the commandments, for it is, instead, "written with the breath of God on the hearts of the flesh."[34] Grounded upon hope that Messiah will keep his word rather than a set of rules to follow in "servitude,"[35] the covenant of Christ in a sense refreshes the I–Other relationship.

How can the logic of covenant apply to the encounter between the becoming-I and the becoming-non-I? To begin with the question of a promise, Ettinger makes it clear that what the matrixial borderspace cannot offer are "peace and

---

31 Matthew 26:26 (KJV).

32 Matthew 26:27–28 (KJV). "Covenant" is used instead of "testament" in this passage in the New American Standard Bible and other versions of the bible.

33 2 Corinthians 3:6 (KJV).

34 Giorgio Agamben, *The Time That Remains: A Commentary on the Letter to the Romans,* trans. Patricia Dailey (Stanford University Press, 2005), 122. See ibid., 121–22.

35 Ibid., 122.

harmony"[36]; these two constitute a wish impossible to fulfill in such an utterly traumatic space. This sphere carries a different promise:

> When metramorphosing with the artwork, you may unexpectedly find yourself in proximity to an event, as if you had always been potentially sliding on its margins. You are threatened by this potential proximity, yet at the same time compelled by a mysterious […] promise to refind in jointness what had faded away and been dispersed, but on the condition of accepting matrixial vulnerability to the *non-I,* since your own desire is the effect of borderlinking to others' trauma.[37]

If in severality, the subject may grasp partialized and non-cognitive knowledge, which was reachable once. Simultaneously, the covenant is by no means one-sided; the terms are set for both partners, one of whom is made a promise but needs to get ready to become vulnerable and open. Similarly to the covenant of Christ, the act of reaching the mutual agreement is linked to the ability to share: food and wine in the biblical sense, and traces of information in the matrixial one. Although not directly, the matrixial covenant also embraces reconciliation; after all, Latin *reconcilare* means "to bring together again" and to "regain."[38] What is regained here is the intimate relation grounded upon that between the becoming-I and the mother within her corporeality: the space where the law of the Father is not yet observed. The matrixial sphere is not preoccupied with regulations or commandments of any kind as it only upholds affective shareability and extreme togetherness. However, the major discrepancy between Christ's covenant and the matrixial one regards varying temporalities. The covenant of the New

---

36 Ettinger, "Wit(h)nessing Trauma," 147.

37 Ibid., 148. Emphasis in original.

38 *Online Etymology Dictionary,* s.v. "reconcile," https://www.etymonline.com/word/reconcile.

Testament is viewed as a universal one, applying to the whole of humanity. The matrixial covenants, however, are "temporary, unpredictable, and unique," but "[e]ven in the process of dissolving"[39] they still influence ones involved in them. Still, the dialogue between these two types of covenant proves to be constructive.

It is the body that lays the ground for both the covenant of Christ and Ettingerian covenant. In this respect, the biblical covenant occupies a paradoxical position. On the one hand, the corporeal entanglement of the Last Supper is evident — the Son of God invites his disciples to consume his body and blood, which is meant to solidify their arrangement. The apostles agree to let Christ's body inside their organisms in order to enter the most intimate union that goes beyond them: the union that embraces humanity as a whole. Consequently, the success of the covenant depends on one's ability to open oneself to the Other, and such an opening is utterly corporeal. On the other hand, this is a covenant of "the Spirit," and not — as Paul notes — of "the flesh."[40] Paul reminds us of Abraham, who has a son with Hagar, a slave, and another son with Sarah, his wife. The slave's son is "born after the flesh," whereas Sarah's child — "by promise."[41] Agamben points out that while the former, Mosaic covenant corresponds to Hagar's status and is built on abiding by the law in "servitude," the new covenant — as has been discussed — is governed by a different set of values. As can be seen, the covenant of Christ is viewed as simultaneously bodily — since it requires a corporeal union and an act of sharing — and non-bodily — because it breaks the previous covenant symbolized by Hagar. The matrixial encounter is bodily in a more straightforward manner. Still, the body's shareability and its openness to the non-I are the qualities that unite both kinds of covenants.

The qualities mentioned above are also components of the matrixial notions revolving around compassion; Ettinger makes

---

39 Ettinger, "The With-In-Visible Screen," 111.
40 Galatians 4:29 (KJV).
41 Galatians 4:23 (KJV).

a distinction between primary compassion and com-passion. Com-passion is defined as "an effect within the transubjective sphere."[42] This effect goes beyond and before the scope of sensorial perception; since it belongs to the matrixial realm, it is not restricted to the Symbolic, constantly breaching the boundaries of this order.[43] Most importantly, it is comprised of transformational affects; Ettinger enumerates three of them: primary fascinance, primary awe, and primary compassion.[44] Primary compassion functions prior to the notions of abjection and abandonment, which are necessary in the subjectivizing process from the phallic viewpoint; what is more, it may "counter-balance"[45] their workings. It does so because it "links the non-strangeness-in-anonymous-intimacy of the other and the Cosmos to the subject."[46] The Other thus occupies the position of a non-stranger, unknown and yet close. Such a structure refers us back to homeliness and hospitality of the prenatal/pregnancy encounter between the subjects that are becoming-together. That is why Ettinger argues that this transformational affect, arousing and influencing com-passion, is "a Home-affect — Heimlich."[47] Finally, Ettinger stresses that neither compassion nor compassion equals empathy, the involvement of which appears to be less extensive. Ettinger goes as far as to claim that if one is empathetic to the non-I but not compassionate and respectful towards the non-I's intimate Other(s), such

---

42 Bracha L. Ettinger, "Fragilization and Resistance," *Studies in the Maternal* 1, no. 2 (2009): 1.

43 Ibid., 3.

44 Ibid., 1.

45 Ibid.

46 Ibid., 2.

47 Ibid. See also Bracha L. Ettinger, "The *Heimlich*," in Ettinger, *The Matrixial Borderspace*, 157–61. Since primary compassion and other enlisted affects belong to the category of Home-affects, they also provoke anxiety. We read, "Anxiety accompanies their emergence into the surface, and thus, as we receive the same signal as that evoked by the frightening, we are 'tricked' by our own unconscious and conscious associations to believe that we are in contact with some horrible instances from an unremembered past." Ettinger, "Fragilization and Resistance," 10.

"empathy-without-compassion" is not so much insufficient as even "malignant."[48] Now, the terms rooted in "compassion" are portrayed as homely, hospitable, and beyond-empathetic, but how specifically are they ethical?

Ettinger links compassion with ethics by means of the notions of wit(h)nessing, sharing, and non-objectifying. She writes:

> The effects of com-passion and the affects of primary compassion and primary awe are the proto-ethical edges of the aesthetic sphere [...]. They might be sublimated and embodied in artistic artifact; they can also be transformed into mature ethics. They inform Ethics from a very particular angle. They announce wit(h)nessing since they signal the impossibility of non-sharing. The ethical implications of wit(h)nessing are accessed if a subject that reverberates "its" I — non-I transubjective strings takes responsibility for them.[49]

Ettinger observes the potential of art as a site of ethics provided that it involves com-passion and primary compassion: an effect and an affect that carry the possibility to go further than proto-ethical aesthetics and reach the ethical mode. The two types of compassion are the harbingers of wit(h)nessing,[50] which incorporates opening oneself to the non-I and — as a result — facing unremembered traces of the non-I's trauma in the sphere where one cannot choose not to share. It is also the sphere of responsibility: One needs to be responsible for the traces one carries in order to reach the ethical potential of the matrix; responsibility also entails not turning the Other into an object, but instead treating the Other as one's co-subject, or a "transubject."[51] Moreover, the mode in which com-passion and wit(h)nessing conjoin their forces in a struggle towards ethics can be accessed

---

48 Ettinger, "Fragilization and Resistance," 19.

49 Ibid., 2.

50 Ettinger goes as far as to note that in the circumstances when, "fascinance meets primary compassion, com-passion leads to wit(h)nessing and wit(h)nessing is already also a com-passion." Ibid., 16.

51 Ibid., 2.

only in so far as one is able to restrain oneself from the acts of shaming or abandoning the Other and from other "paranoid tendencies."[52] If one cannot achieve that, a retreat to one's "own paranoid abjectivity and narcissistic passive-aggressivity"[53] is inevitable. Only when willing to share and com-passionately open to Otherness can one take part in a deeply humanizing covenant.

Although it is not mentioned by Ettinger directly, a theological reference in com-passion is apparent. The prefix com- is certainly one of the reasons for dividing the term, but the very word "passion" — signifying Christ's final days, which reach their climax in agony and crucifixion leading in Christian thought to the salvation of humanity — carries interesting implications. Etymologically, *passion* is based on Late Latin *passionem* — "suffering" and "enduring" — and Latin *pati*, which adds the activity of experiencing to the overall meaning of the term.[54] The meaning added later is that of a "predilection," or fondness. All these elements are to a greater or lesser degree reflected in Ettingerian com-passion. Taking responsibility for the people, Christ dies on the cross for them. Similarly, com-passion is tightly linked to the responsible act of caring for the Other, and such an act includes tending to the fragmentary and non-remembered trauma — trauma that originates in the Other, yet is transferred in the matrixial connection. Such a gesture of taking care is necessarily perilous for the subject in a twofold manner — because of the weight of partial knowledge conveyed in the encounter and because of the inherently traumatic value of the matrixial sphere itself — but the Other is partly unburdened as a result of it. Com-passion is, then, a state in which suffering and love *for* the Other are conjoined; it is an ethical act in which pain and trauma are shared in a way that is beneficial for the non-I, who

---

52 Ibid., 3.

53 Ibid., 4.

54 *Online Etymology Dictionary,* s.v. "passion," https://www.etymonline.com/word/passion.

is not turned into an object or an abject, and who is not left to suffer alone.

It is impossible to think passion outside of the notion of *sacrifice,* which in the matrixial theory resurfaces in Ettinger's critique of Jacques Derrida. Derrida develops his understanding of sacrifice on the example of Abraham and Isaac, with a special emphasis put on Abraham and his relation with God. In Derrida's reading, Abraham's God is the radical Other who does not allow his worshipper to grasp his plans; despite that, Abraham responds with allegiance. Abraham is trapped between two notions: "responsibility in *general* and *absolute* responsibility."[55] While he ought to put Isaac's security and well-being first (which is an obvious and right position from the ethical perspective of a father), he instead answers to God, who is, therefore, higher in the hierarchy than familial bonds. "[B]eyond ethics, beyond duty qua duty," Abraham testifies to "the absolute relationship to the absolute,"[56] to use John D. Caputo's words. It does not mean, however, that he does not love his son:

> If I put to death or grant death to what I hate it is not a sacrifice. I must sacrifice what I love. I must come to hate what I love, in the same moment, at the instant of granting death. I must hate and betray my own, that is to say offer them the gift of death by means of the sacrifice, not insofar as I hate them, that would be too easy, but insofar as I love them. [...] Hate wouldn't be hate if it only hated the hateful [...]. It must hate and betray what is most lovable. Hate cannot be hate, it can only be the sacrifice of love to love.[57]

---

55 Jacques Derrida, *The Gift of Death*, trans. David Wills (University of Chicago Press, 1995), 61. Emphasis in original. On Derrida's notion of sacrifice, see also Jacques Derrida, "Faith and Knowledge: The Two Sources of 'Religion' at the Limits of Reason Alone," trans. Samuel Weber, in *Religion,* ed. Jacques Derrida and Gianni Vattimo (Polity Press, 1998), 50–51.

56 John D. Caputo, *The Prayers and Tears of Jacques Derrida: Religion without Religion* (Indiana University Press, 1997), 200.

57 Derrida, *The Gift of Death*, 64.

Only if Abraham loves Isaac can he give the boy the *gift of death;* simultaneously, only then can such a gift be bestowed upon God. In this "story of father and son, of masculine figures, of hierarchies among men,"[58] sacrifice becomes an inconceivable mixture of affection, cruelty, and twisted paternal ir-responsibility.

Ettinger finds Derrida's notion of sacrifice — and sacrifice in general — problematic in several ways. She identifies Abraham's action as *sacrifice without sacrifice:* a situation in which "a son is lost then saved by the father."[59] It is the father who condemns the son to death and then spares his life; the father, thus, takes up a domineering subject position in which he can decide on the Other's existence. Ettinger notes that such a sacrifice is not so much "a *men's only* affair" (which is Derrida's suggestion) as a "kind of *père*-version (*father*-version),"[60] in the sense that the non-I is deprived of their subjectivity and treated as the I's object. Another *père*-verse sacrifice discussed by Ettinger — similar to the Abrahamic one, yet more extreme in its execution and consequences — is that of Laius. Compared to Abraham's choice, which in the end leads to the rescue of the son, Laius's deeds are described as "a *secret sacrifice per se:* the perfect crime,"[61] for the child is doomed never to be saved even if he survives, that is, he will never be able to cope with the father's betrayal. It is precisely betrayal — inherent in paternal sacrifice — that Ettinger postulates to resist. In order to do so, one needs to become self-aware of one's possibility of betraying the Other. Such awareness, however, does not come over time; instead, it can be "awaken[ed]"[62] from the deeply encrypted residues of matrixial subjectivity. Ettinger explicates it by means of referring to motherhood; mothers are claimed to be

---

58 Ibid., 75.
59 Bracha L. Ettinger, "Laius Complex and Shocks of Maternality: With Franz Kafka and Sylvia Plath," in *Interdisciplinary Handbook of Trauma and Culture,* ed. Yochai Ataria et al. (Springer, 2016), 279.
60 Ibid. Emphasis in original.
61 Ibid., 280. Emphasis in original.
62 Ibid., 284.

fragilized by the force of a sudden unexpected love, by sudden and irremediable response-ability and responsibility, by the enormous *trust* directed toward them by the infant, by the shock, sorrow, and jouissance of their *care-carry mode of com-passion*. Vulnerable, they are facing a new reality, realizing their deep transconnectedness to the vulnerable other. The weight of this *carriance-and-trust* estranges them in a world lacking the language to account for it [...]; a world where trust already expects a betrayal.[63]

Motherhood is a position via which one can acknowledge one's potential to sacrifice the Other and then resist it. Having embraced the Other's fragility and reliance, one can follow the ethical path paved with rediscovered carriance and response-ability, and thus restrain oneself from *père*-verse betrayal and objectification engrained in sacrifice.

Derridean sacrifice and Laius's impulse to kill his son — these are the types of sacrifice Ettinger considers *père*-verse. Can we also think of a *mère*-version of sacrifice in the matrixial domain? As I believe, we can if we rethink the very meaning of the term and focus not on offering the (loved) Other to the more radical and transcendent Other, but on self-sacrificing for the sake of the close — even if unknown — non-I. The primary matrixial self-sacrifice we can take into consideration is that of bodily boundaries in the prenatal/late pregnancy encounter. What follows is partial relinquishment of integrity and self-security: Once one partly surrenders one's boundaries in order to engage in an encounter with the Other, one's defenses operating in accordance with phallic rules recede. Matrixially understood sacrifice does not equal loss. Rather, it encompasses partial losing whose result is the prospect of gaining knowledge of and from the Other. Nevertheless, even though the matrixial sacrifice is partial and is not based on the logic of loss, it is still an offering directed at the Other. Risky and potentially painful for the subject involved, such an offering has ethical resonances.

---

63 Ibid., 283–84. Emphasis mine.

Namely, it forces us to rethink the notion of Otherness and the I–non-I covenant. The matrixially informed subject needs to recognize and bear responsibility for the Other. Moreover, the subject has to resist the possibility of breaching the gained trust, prioritizing the now-intimate Other. It is the capability to perform partial self-sacrifice that places the Other in the position of a co-subject. Only when the subject's boundaries and safety are sacrificed can the Other co-occupy the shareable space, and — as a consequence — only then can the ethical I–non-I relation which involves becoming-in-togetherness take place.

Revelation, Messianism, and the Artistic Encounter

We can claim that if one's boundaries and safety are sacrificed, one is revealed before the Other. Although appearing infrequently in matrixial psychoanalysis, the notion of revelation casts light on Ettinger's theoretical reflections and artistic activity. Revelation can be defined as a singular divine act of disclosure of knowledge usually related to humans; this act of communication tends to take place between God and one person, a prophet. A secret pertaining to human existence is thus revealed, from Latin *revelare:* "reveal, uncover, disclose," and "unveil."[64] In Jewish philosophy, as Adam Lipszyc argues, the uniqueness of the human–God relationship can be portrayed precisely by revelation, which temporarily suspends the transcendence of the divine being:

> The aspect of God's absence in the world, inscribed in the idea of creation, is balanced here by means of the aspect of presence, of God's conditional exposure in front of the human being. The whole Jewish philosophy is grounded upon the paradox hidden in this idea. The exposure that takes place

---

64 *Online Etymology Dictionary,* s.v. "reveal," https://www.etymonline.com/word/reveal.

in revelation cannot annul separation. Presence needs to be incomplete, marked by absence.[65]

Revelation, then, is accompanied by the partial suspension of an otherwise impassable border; still, even though the Other appears, this presence is conditional. The status of absence remains unchanged: It neither recedes nor loses relevance in the whole occurrence. What we witness here is a play of *pres-absence,* traceable also in Ettinger's thought. While metramorphosing, the becoming-subjects are argued to participate in an exchange of linkages "on the borders of presence and absence, in the in-between sphere of matrixial *pres-absence.*"[66] The very condition of being in-between is what connotes revelation. The subject's Other is simultaneously absent and partially — or almost — present, suspended between these two states; despite that, communication of a kind occurs, which results in mutual transformation and in formation of trans-subjectivity. We may conclude that the matrixial female body is a space of revelation; namely, within feminine-motherly corporeality, binaries such as I/non-I, inside/outside, and presence/absence are temporarily arrested. Suspension is, therefore, the condition for the matrixial flow of traces of knowledge to be shared.

Nancy proposes a different approach to revelation than that suggested by Lipszyc, but his reading may prove to be valid in the context of an encounter with art, including an encounter with

---

65 "Aspekt nieobecności Boga w świecie, wpisany w ideę stworzenia, zrównoważony jest tutaj przez aspekt obecności, warunkowego odsłonięcia się Boga przed człowiekiem. Cała filozofia żydowska stoi paradoksem, jaki kryje się w tej idei. Odsłonięcie, do jakiego dochodzi w objawieniu, nie może anulować separacji. Obecność musi być niepełna, naznaczona nieobecnością." Adam Lipszyc, *Ślad judaizmu w filozofii XX wieku* (Fundacja im. Prof. Mojżesza Schorra, 2009), 15. Translation mine.

66 Bracha L. Ettinger, "Weaving a Woman Artist with-in the Matrixial Encounter-Event," in Ettinger, *The Matrixial Borderspace,* 181. Emphasis mine. As Ettinger points out in the footnote to this excerpt, the term has originated in conversations with Ghislaine Szpeker-Benat and is related to, among other ideas, "the between-presence-and-absence status of the matrixial partial-subject." Ettinger, "Weaving a Woman Artist," 225n12.

Ettinger's Eurydices. Nancy summarizes revelation succinctly as "[c]all and response" and adds that it embraces "the responsibility to respond"[67] as well. The Other necessarily utters a call, for without it a response is virtually impossible. If there is, however, no response to the call, the call remains empty and meaningless: No relation is established, and nothing is revealed. To take place, revelation needs (at least) two responsive — or rather *responsible* — subjects; only then can they become involved, that is, only then can something be shared, perhaps forwarded. For Nancy, it is the very response that is imparted via revelation: "What is revealed is not concerned with content-based principles, articles of faith, and revelation does not unveil anything that is hidden: it reveals insofar as it addresses, and this address constitutes what is revealed."[68] Normativity and implementation of rules are not the points of interest of Nancean revelation[69]; instead, he focuses on the value of the act of addressing the Other. A few aspects of Nancy's reading of revelation apply to Ettinger's understanding of an artistic experience. As Pollock observes, "Ettinger directs us aesthetically away from content towards *gesture*."[70] Indeed, in her oeuvre it is not precisely content that plays the most important role but rather an encounter in togetherness and compassion made possible by the artistic activity. Moreover, from the matrixial angle, art can be safely considered a call; such a call originates in the artist, but also in the artist's Others, the latter possibility being especially relevant when Ettinger's aesthetic practice is read through the prism of her experiences as a daughter of Holocaust survivors. The viewer's function then is to affectively answer such a call. Still, in the matrix, carrying

---

67 Nancy, "In the Midst of the World," 41.

68 Ibid.

69 At this point Nancy is in dissonance with Lipszyc's view on revelation. As Lipszyc observes, Jewish theology focuses on the dualism of revelation, which embraces both the truth and the law; of these two, the law is claimed to be a more significant aspect of revelation. See Lipszyc, *Ślad judaizmu w filozofii XX wieku*, 16.

70 Griselda Pollock, *After-Affects/After-Images: Trauma and Aesthetic Transformation in the Virtual Feminist Museum* (Manchester University Press, 2013), 3. Emphasis in original.

and (re)distributing a certain kind of knowledge is theorized. Not "content-based" per se, such knowledge does surpass the gesture of "salut[ing] one another"[71] Nancy advocates. Nevertheless, what unites the two approaches is the recognition of revelation — after all, an exposure — as never a one-sided deal: While one of the subjects addresses the other, the other needs to accept the invitation and become exposed, too.

Ettinger's *Eurydice* series can be characterized by means of the "[c]all and response" dualism, especially if one takes the images with the woman who looks away in the viewer's direction into account. While the whole series may be considered a call of the Mizocz women, it is the mentioned woman who addresses the viewer almost directly. The original photograph captured, as we can assume, a desperate plea for her life to be spared. Looking away, the woman seemed to be trying to find anyone who could stop the injustice — these women were going to die in the name of collective responsibility, and not because of their own actions. The injustice, however, did not cease. The woman returns in Ettinger's paintings over and over again, as if haunting these canvases. *Eurydice,* No. 17 (1994–1996) is crowded with female bodies, but the woman who looks away somehow attracts our attention as her gaze is hard to be ignored (fig. 8). In this artwork, she is striving to come to the surface and to find the potential viewer: she wishes to be *seen* and *heard*. The need to be acknowledged can be also identified in *Eurydice,* No. 37 (2001), but in this image her call goes in two directions (fig. 9). Her primary addressees are Ettinger's parents, whom she faces in the space of the canvas. Since they are the survivors, it is as if she asks them to remember for her, or rather *instead* of her. The other potential interlocutors are, again, viewers, who are asked to shelter the knowledge of these women's history; they are asked not to remain indifferent to their pain, fear, and imminent fate. What used to be a call for mercy is now a call for attentiveness to the memory that cannot be carried by its own-

---

71 Nancy, "In the Midst of the World," 41.

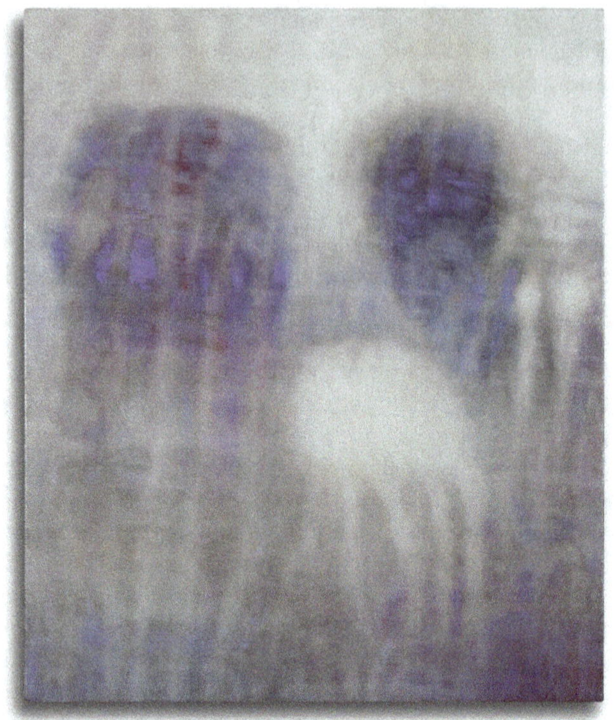

Fig. 27. Bracha L. Ettinger, *Eurydice, The Graces, Demeter,* 2006–2012, oil on canvas, 50 × 41 cm. Collection: Fiorucci, Monaco, featured at the exhibition *Bracha Lichtenberg Ettinger: Eurydice — Pieta* in Muzeum Śląskie (Silesian Museum), Katowice, July 7–September 2, 2017. © Courtesy of the artist.

ers anymore. It is the viewers' ethical duty to respond once they experience such a call.

The acceptance of the invitation and the response that follows need to be marked by involvement for the aesthetic revelation to occur. Created between 2006 and 2012, *Eurydice, The Graces, Demeter* (fig. 27) is dominated by the bright grey color, which is occasionally disturbed by purple shades. The painting can be easily distinguished from the early *Eurydice* artworks as the Mizocz women seem to be absent from it. Also, because of its brightness, the image does not directly recall the late *Eurydices,* which usually oscillate between red and purple. At first glance, the painting appears to be an abstract combination of non-specific shapes. However, every now and then, a face may appear on the canvas. Perhaps the purple shades constitute two women standing in a row before the execution; perhaps there is a female face just beneath the darkest shade on the right, or just above the brightest, elliptical smear of paint. Perhaps there are more faces waiting to be noticed between the strokes of paint. In the image, there is severality — and not multiplicity — of potential faces, yet their existence is not dependent on the painting per se but on the viewer. When and if such a face emerges (or a few of them do), the viewer is captured in a "momentary revelation"[72] — a sudden instance of connectedness and communication. When it happens, one "cannot choose when to terminate the covenant,"[73] for one necessarily becomes deeply involved. Otherwise inaccessible or absent from one's perception, these faces are now temporarily and *conditionally* present; Massumi notes, "The 'feminine' [...] is accessible to any body — on the condition that it surrender itself to the several."[74] One has to make oneself vulnerable and give in to the severality encountered in the image, no matter whether this severality includes one face or more of them. The aesthetic revelation can thus be experienced only in so far as one becomes fully committed to the artwork.

The response in revelation is inextricably linked both to the im-possibility of rejection and to the impossibility of not-sharing. From the phallic perspective, one can easily ignore the Other's call, the Other being an entirely separate, inaccessible entity; furthermore, even if one does not, the matrixial type of connectedness and involvement is still an aspiration that cannot

---

72 Ettinger, "The With-In-Visible Screen," 118.

73 Ibid.

74 Brian Massumi, "Afterword. Painting: The Voice of the Grain," in Ettinger, *The Matrixial Borderspace,* 212.

be satisfied. In this set of paradigms, one is doomed to reject the Other and, as a result, to remain within the seemingly impassable borders of one's individual self. Within the matrixial realm, one struggles with, as I propose, the im-possibility of rejection. The potential of ignoring or even abandoning the Other is constantly present in one's psyche, and it is one's responsibility to fight such a tendency. Only if one prevails can the ethical encounter take place, and then rejection becomes indeed impossible. Revelation, however, comes with not only the impossibility of rejection, but also the impossibility of not-sharing. Ettinger contrasts the phallic realm and the matrixial one as follows: "In the phallus, we confront the impossibility of sharing trauma and phantasy, whereas in the matrix, to a certain extent, there is *an impossibility of not sharing* them."[75] One of the consequences of the matrixial understanding of shareability is that art is no longer seen as strictly individual, for it may be informed by the artist's Others. This claim can be applied to Ettinger's usage of the historical document as the background resurfacing in her oeuvre. Her artistic gesture, then, is not that of appropriating someone else's work, but that of welcoming the Other's contribution. Ettinger observes, "It is art that leads us to discover our share of response-ability in transmissible events whose source is not inside One-self."[76] Response to the Other's call, also — or perhaps especially — in art, necessarily embraces the act of sharing the transferred knowledge. When one hears the call of the women from Mizocz, it is not enough to just listen; one is ethically obliged, on the one hand, not to turn one's back on these women and their message, and, on the other hand, to transmit the painful knowledge further.

In order to be answered, the women from Mizocz need to be seen, and this is not always a simple task since in Ettinger's artworks they are engaged in the play of pres-absence. In some of the paintings the female bodies are easily found. Sometimes

---

75 Bracha L. Ettinger, "The Matrixial Gaze," in Ettinger, *The Matrixial Borderspace*, 90. Emphasis in original.
76 Ibid.

Fig. 28. Bracha L. Ettinger, *Eurydice,* No. 14, 1994–1996, oil, xerography, photocopic pigment and ashes on paper mounted on canvas, 25 × 52 cm. Private collection. © Courtesy of the artist.

it is the original photograph that remains largely unaltered, just as in Ettinger's *No Title — Sketch* (1988–1989), where the parents are juxtaposed with the Eurydices, but both parts of the work of art remain rather photography-like instead of being covered by multiple layers of paint (fig. 7). The other way to maintain the women's visibility is that of highlighting their shapes with strokes of paint, the example of which is *Eurydice,* No. 17, where the original photograph is hidden by means of the artist's painterly gestures. In both cases, the women occupy the canvas with persistence. In other images, such as *Eurydice,* No. 14 (1994–1996), their presence — or indeed existence — is more dependent on the viewer (fig. 28). The women are visible provided that the spectator is already acquainted with the series or with the background for most images and thus is able to identify otherwise unclear shapes. Their presence becomes conditional: They are striving towards it but may nevertheless remain unseen. Finally, paintings from the late *Eurydice* series leave the viewer defenseless, with no visible clues to follow, but it does not mean that the Mizocz women are absent there. Images such as *Eurydice,* No. 47 (2001–2006) (fig. 1) or *Eurydice,* No. 50 (2006–2007) (fig. 4) testify to the ongoing struggle of pres-absence:

Even though the original photograph is no longer traceable, the women tirelessly endeavor to enter the domain of visibility, shades of their faces resurfacing on the canvas every now and then. This complexity of Ettinger's *Eurydice* series connotes the mythical situation of the eponymous woman. At the precise moment Orpheus looks back, Eurydice simultaneously appears and vaporizes: She affirms her presence and becomes absent. By that, she shatters the presence/absence binary opposition, oscillating between the two poles and not being reducible to one of them during the momentary encounter with her beloved. Similarly, the women in Ettinger's artworks are lost and found at the same time. Already dead, the Eurydices become conditionally present only to disappear again; even though they reveal themselves and call the viewer, they are never complete or fully available, for they are forever stuck between presence and absence.

Keeping in mind such recurring issues as the bodily space, the matrixial stratum, boundaries, and presence/absence of women and their representations on the canvas, the matrixial theory and art seem to be preoccupied with spatiality. What is, then, the status of time in Ettinger's art? As I believe, it may prove to be messianic in the sense that corresponds to Agamben's understanding of the term. Although it neither contradicts nor is outside of chronological time, messianic time is posited as that of exception; here, the logic of exception suspends and opens the law, completing rather than overthrowing the prevailing order. Messianic time is, in Agamben's words, "the time that contracts itself and begins to end," or "the time that remains between time and its end."[77] Just as an abstract and momentary albeit real *operational time* is needed so that one can "translate" the actual flow of time into its mental representation, as Agamben reminds us after Gustave Guillaume, messianic time breaches and occurs in chronological time even though this instant is hardly graspable.[78] Hence, *kairos* meets *chronos*: it seizes and contracts the flow of the latter, opening it to its poten-

---

77 Agamben, *The Time That Remains*, 62.
78 Ibid., 66.

tiality and affirming the chance within it.[79] If we apply Ettinger's understanding of subjectivity found in her theoretical writings and Agamben's messianism to the question of an encounter with art, the relation between the two philosophical systems becomes most apparent. A meeting with the Mizocz Eurydices can happen by chance, and if it does, it is sudden and irruptive. This encounter is hard to conceive of in linear terms for it punctures chronology and suspends one between one's present and the Eurydices's paradoxical temporality. The momentariness of the meeting makes it almost ungraspable. Still, the messianic-like encounter with the Mizocz women remains a valuable ethical potentiality, for it may result in humanizing transmission and transformation.

Alliances Between the Matrix and Theology

The matrixial aesth/ethics and the matrixial concepts indebted to corporeality are abundant in biblical echoes. These widen the scope of Ettinger's oeuvre and, perhaps more importantly, open new potentialities for both strata — that of the matrix and that of theology. The matrixial turn towards the Other becomes equipped with new ways of contemplating and articulating responsibility and co-dependence: The embodied status of the matrixial relation is solidified as it finds an ally in the gospel of John; the matrixial covenant carries the echoes of Christ's covenant, defined by promise, reconciliation, and corporeality; and the theological aspect of com-passion complements it with a valuable combination of love and suffering. Theological reflections might benefit from envisioning corporeal dimensions that do not focus on contained individuals but rather open us up to incarnated communities. Incarnation turns out to be an event following the matrixial logic — it is derived from corporeality, it challenges separation, and it directs us towards togetherness

---

79 Ibid., 69. Agamben also makes a clear distinction between messianism and prophecy, the former being directed towards disciples and the present time, the latter belonging to prophets and the future. See ibid., 60–61.

and (trans)connectedness; when informed by the matrixial logic, Nancean tender relation with the Other goes beyond pure affirmation; and as sacrifice becomes more *mère*-verse, it simultaneously becomes more humanizing since it can result in helping assuage the Other's pain. Finally, turning to the field of aesthetics, Ettinger's artworks can be read through the prisms of revelation and messianism: Com-passionate viewers may be called upon to respond to the forever pres-absent Eurydices.

Some of the issues addressed here will return in the final chapter, devoted to the Holocaust in the context of Ettinger's work. Sacrifice, violence, the (female) body, embodied encounter, and a few other concepts will help investigate the very possibility of ethics in the post-Holocaust reality.

5

In-Appropriate(d)

Art, Humanism, and the Body after Auschwitz[1]

We are carrying, at the beginning of the twenty-first century, enormous traumatic weight, and aesthetic wit(h)nessing in art brings it to culture's surface.

— Bracha L. Ettinger, "Wit(h)nessing Trauma
and the Matrixial Gaze"[2]

Too late to help, utterly impotent, we nevertheless search for ways to take responsibility for what we are seeing, to experience, from a remove, even as we try to redefine, if not repair, these ruptures.

—Marianne Hirsch, "Nazi Photographs in Post-Holocaust Art"[3]

---

1   Portions of this chapter appeared in: Anna Kisiel, "Gazing at Eurydice: Authorship and Otherness in Bracha L. Ettinger," *Analyses/Rereadings/Theories: A Journal Devoted to Literature, Film and Theatre* 6, no. 1 (2020): 7–17.

2   Bracha L. Ettinger, "Wit(h)nessing Trauma and the Matrixial Gaze," in Bracha L. Ettinger, *The Matrixial Borderspace,* ed. Brian Massumi (University of Minnesota Press, 2006), 147.

3   Marianne Hirsch, "Nazi Photographs in Post-Holocaust Art," in *The Generation of Postmemory: Writing and Visual Culture after the Holocaust* (Columbia University Press, 2012), 138.

> To write poetry after Auschwitz is barbaric.
> —Theodor W. Adorno, "Cultural Criticism and Society"[4]

Is it appropriate to gaze at the bare bodies of women from the Mizocz ghetto just before their imminent execution? Or is it inappropriate to look away once we face them? If we respond to this image by becoming vulnerable and experiencing something of the pain (en)crypted within its frame, then do we not appropriate the suffering of the women observed? In other words, do we not usurp what should belong exclusively to them? Can we break this chain of inappropriateness/appropriation, or — perhaps — can we try instead to conceive of an ethics of encountering these women, but in the borderspace where "such a catastrophe is unimaginable"[5]?

This chapter aims at exploring the interrelations between humanism, (female) corporeality, and Ettinger's artistic activity in the context of the Shoah. What I wish to address is not only the potential of Ettinger's oeuvre, including its possibility of changing the Nazi gaze, but also ethical objections and doubts that might be raised when the viewer is confronted with it. As I will show, even though Ettinger's art may be perceived as ethically risky to a degree in the context of the Shoah, the combination of her artwork and theoretical considerations can, without appropriation, delineate a path towards humanism based on compassion, response-ability, attentiveness, trust, tenderness, and capacity to be deeply affected.

It is not accidental that certain notions and categories hinted at above have already appeared in the previous chapters. The final chapter returns to the chosen artistic and theoretical tropes in Ettinger's oeuvre in order to confront them with Holocaust-related issues. The Shoah is inherent in Ettinger's work; not only does it pose a recurring theme in her artworks, but it is also

---

4   Theodor W. Adorno, "Cultural Criticism and Society," in *Prisms*, trans. Samuel Weber and Shierry Weber (MIT Press, 1983), 34.

5   Griselda Pollock, "Introduction. Femininity: Aporia or Sexual Difference?," in Ettinger, *The Matrixial Borderspace*, 11.

implicit in her matrixial psychoanalysis. The Shoah remains one of the foundations of matrixial theory, yet Ettinger seldom tackles it directly, which is why her artistic and theoretical activity benefits from being juxtaposed with Giorgio Agamben, Emmanuel Levinas, Jacques Derrida, and other selected Holocaust scholars. Then, I would like to propose treating this chapter as a space for a meeting, or a juncture of tropes and themes united by the Shoah, a tragedy impossible to be passed over in silence when speaking of Ettinger and her massive, multi-layered oeuvre.

Feminine Experiences of the Shoah

In her scrutiny of popular Holocaust images and their artistic post-productions, Hirsch notes that femininity and the representation of victimhood tend to go side by side. Even though such an association should not be thought to reflect the death toll of the actual war victims,[6] Hirsch observes the mechanisms of feminization, infantilization, and masculinization in depictions of the Second World War. Her reflections are especially important in the context of Ettinger's art, whose most common background photo is that presenting precisely women and children as victims. As Hirsch notes, children — who are figures of innocence — frequently appear in widespread Holocaust photographs, but in various artistic reworkings they are taken out of their original context: Their surroundings and perpetrators are often absent, which leads to universalization of the child

---

6   While it was not the Jewish people's gender that was a decisive factor in the context of their extermination, we should nevertheless take into account, for instance, different strategies, treatments, or power mechanisms of the perpetrators that contributed to differing Holocaust experiences and testimonies of men and women. See, for instance, Myrna Goldenberg and Amy H. Shapiro, eds., *Different Horrors, Same Hell: Gender and the Holocaust* (University of Washington Press, 2013); Nechama Tec, *Resilience and Courage: Women, Men, and the Holocaust* (Yale University Press, 2003); and Lisa Pine, "Gender and Holocaust Victims: A Reappraisal," *Journal of Jewish Identities* 1, no. 2 (2008): 121–41.

victims.[7] Universalization makes it possible to identify with the victims, particularly if they turn out to be "the only [subject] position available"[8] as the actual perpetrator has been erased from the image. The same children are also subject to feminization in a twofold sense: On the one hand, they are portrayed as vulnerable and fragile, and on the other they are sometimes contrasted with newly added "hyper-masculinized" figures of perpetrators, who are "represented as the ultimate in phallic, mechanized, supra-human evil."[9] As a result of their hyper-masculine representation, perpetrators are depersonalized and devoid of agency, which, as mentioned above, renders their perspective and subject position inaccessible.[10] Of course, the Holocaust imagery is also abundant in depictions of women, an example of which is the picture from the Mizocz ghetto. As Hirsch argues, women tend to be eroticized in artistic remakes of historical photographs in order to draw the viewer's attention to "sexual humiliation"[11] inflicted by the perpetrators. Yet, during the war "the opposite seems to have been the case: the victims were dehumanized precisely by being *desexualized*"[12]; this strategy of the perpetrators is in accordance with, among other strategies, Nazi propaganda's endeavor to ascribe animal features to the Jewish people. All in all, in the Holocaust representations, women and children — culturally associated with defenselessness — become as if transparent figures, comfortable to identify with and prone to projection.

Aleksandra Ubertowska postulates that the feminine perspective on the Shoah needs to be highlighted and developed within Holocaust studies because of the specificity of the women's experience (marked by, among other factors, appropriation of

---

7   Hirsch, "Nazi Photographs," 140.

8   Ibid., 144.

9   Ibid.

10 Ibid.

11 Ibid., 148.

12 Ibid. Emphasis mine.

the female body) and its divergence from that of men.[13] This

---

13   In the feminist context, I believe we should not ignore the situation
     of prewar Nazi Germany women, whose status was also biologically
     determined as a result of the workings of Nazi ideology and policy.
     Although it would be superfluous for my book to provide an all-embracing
     study of women in Nazi Germany and I am aware of the ethical doubt
     that may arise when discussing Jewish and German women next to each
     other, I believe that German women's situation provides a significant
     context without which it is hard to discuss women's bodies, the Holocaust,
     and ethics. As Leila J. Rupp demonstrates, the position of women in Nazi
     Germany was by no means unequivocal. Most of all, they were praised
     as potential mothers and encouraged to bear more children, which was
     arguably not supposed to render them inferior to men but biologically
     different from them and, thus, destined to have a different role in the
     society. See Leila J. Rupp, "Mother of the *Volk*: The Image of Women in
     Nazi Ideology," *Signs: Journal of Women in Culture and Society* 3, no. 2
     (1977): 364. Giving birth to — but also raising and educating — children
     was portrayed as an important and estimable duty serving the common
     good. It was also reflected in Nazi policies: On the one hand, women were
     persuaded by propaganda and social programs to leave their jobs and
     concentrate on the household tasks, on the other, there were more and
     more restrictions and prohibitions that made it almost impossible for
     women to pursue a professional career, including a career in the National
     Socialist party. For Nazi strategies and policies in this respect, see ibid.,
     370–71. As Rupp notes on pages 364–69, also among Nazi supporters there
     were women who opposed such a treatment; they postulated equality
     and significance of women in politics and in structures of the National
     Socialist party but were not successful in their endeavors. It does not
     mean, however, that women ceased to work, especially working-class
     women, who often had no other choice; also, when it was necessary for
     economic reasons, the policy was adjusted in order for women to be
     re-employed, which was read as "a woman's sacrifice for her people" (ibid.,
     374). It is crucial not to forget that numerous women were not forced into
     such thinking but were instead attracted to it, for example by the vision
     of a woman who is appreciated for her domestic life and for devotion to
     her children, that is, a woman who fulfils her "natural" destiny (see ibid.,
     379). As we can see, the status of women in Nazi Germany was formed
     in accordance with the principles of biological determinism: Recognized
     primarily for achievements related to childbearing and maternity, German
     women faced the reality in which they were defined through their bodily
     capacities. For more insightful analyses of the position of women in Nazi
     society, see, for instance, Jill Stephenson's thorough and all-embracing
     study, *Women in Nazi Germany* (Pearson Education, 2001). For the concise
     characteristics of the ideal woman in Nazi society, see ibid., 18.

issue has begun to gather scholarly attention, but, as Ubertowska notes, gendered perspectives on the war and the Shoah are still a relatively recent phenomenon, emerging around the mid-seventies; before that, "women were not perceived as a separate group of victims, as a specific historical subject,"[14] which resulted in a universalized, homogenous portrayal of men's and women's suffering. Following Joan Wallach Scott, Ubertowska points to promising directions in feminist historiography; one of them consists in supplementing the seemingly universal — but in fact male-centered — history, the second one is herstory, and the last one is a gender studies path aiming at conceptualizing history anew.[15] These approaches could help retrieve the woman's position, previously omitted in the discussed period.

Although some of its concepts can be used to study Shoah-related issues, Ettinger's theory rarely refers to the Holocaust directly. That is to say, the matrixial paradigm helps rebuild the feminine perspective and experience, but the Shoah is present there mainly as a potential topic to be viewed through the affective prism or as an inherent — but veiled — inspiration for certain notions. However, Ettinger mentions art as the medium that carries the traces of the Holocaust trauma:

> We are carrying, at the beginning of the twenty-first century, enormous traumatic weight, and aesthetic wit(h)ness-ing in art brings it to culture's surface. […] The beautiful as accessed via artworks in our era — and I emphasize again in our era, since we are living through the massive effects of transitive trauma that different artworks capture and shed

---

14 "kobiety nie były postrzegane jako odrębna grupa ofiar, jako specyficzny podmiot historii." Aleksandra Ubertowska, "Niewidoczność, sprawczość, podmiot: Perspektywa feministyczna i genderowa w badaniach nad Holokaustem," in *Holokaust: Auto(tanato)grafie* (Instytut Badań Literackich PAN, 2014), 113. Translation mine.

15 Ibid., 116–22. See Joan Wallach Scott, *Gender and the Politics of History* (Columbia University Press, 1999), and Joan Wallach Scott, "Rewriting History," in *Behind the Lines: Gender and the Two World Wars*, ed. Margaret Randolph Higonnet et al. (Yale University Press, 1987), 19–30.

light upon — the beautiful carries new possibilities for affective apprehending and produces new artistic effects where aesthetics converges with ethics even beyond the artist's intentions or conscious control.[16]

As if a shelter, art is the space that stores fragments of the Holocaust trauma; these fragments can resurface and become accessible for the I provided that the I is able to become a wit(h)ness. As Ettinger argues, we are now all affected by the trauma of war, which makes it particularly important to become involved in the matrixial experience of art, which thus becomes a humanizing act. Indeed, while Ettinger does not overuse the Shoah as a point of reference in her psychoanalysis, in her artistic activity she deliberately chooses the Holocaust theme and reworks it countless times, creating images whose "enormous traumatic weight" is hard to be denied.

Burdened with traumatic content, the images hosting the Mizocz women can nevertheless be considered ethically dubious. First of all, the bodies of the women are decontextualized. Their surroundings are absent, but also — depending on the artwork — particular women are chosen to appear on the canvas while others are cut out; some of the women present in the historical photograph never reach the surface of the paintings. Furthermore, the appearances of the women are artistically manipulated with the usage of such techniques as cropping, applying layers of paint, or juxtaposing their bodies with other images. In some paintings, the women are altered to such an extent that they become as if ahistorical, extracted from their tragic moment of being on the verge of death. Also, if we return to the strategy of feminization of victims, the women from Mizocz can be considered easy to identify with, which leads us to the threat of appropriation. Empathic unsettlement is a notion introduced by Dominick LaCapra to characterize a reaction of secondary

---

16 Ettinger, "Wit(h)nessing Trauma," 147–48.

witnesses to trauma.[17] It is claimed to be valuable since empathy is a "virtual experience through which one puts oneself in the other's position while recognizing the difference of that position and hence not taking the other's place."[18] Simultaneously, LaCapra argues that if the clear-cut boundary between the actual witness touched by the trauma and the secondary witness is not maintained, the secondary witness may falsely identify with the victim, which can result in an appropriation of the pain of the Other.[19] For LaCapra, it is necessary to be empathetic and open in order to grasp the Other's trauma, but one has to both affirm the distance between oneself and the Other, and be careful not to appropriate the Other's position.[20] In this context, the situation of the Mizocz women in Ettinger's paintings becomes even more complex. The question that remains is: Are these women appropriated, or are they retrieved?

As I propose, although it is burdened with the perspective of the perpetrator, the original photograph may be viewed differently when being subject to Ettinger's artistic reworking. Hirsch postulates that the information about the author of the Holocaust photo is by no means irrelevant as it is made in particular circumstances and thus contributes to a specific viewing experience.[21] A kind of image Hirsch finds herself particularly interested in is one in which the victims and the perpetrators face each other, but also "in which the *photographer,* the *perpetrator,* and the *spectator* share the same space of looking

---

17 Dominick LaCapra, *Writing History, Writing Trauma* (Johns Hopkins University Press, 2001). The notion of emphatic unsettlement is used repeatedly in LaCapra's book, and mentioned for the first time on page xi.

18 Ibid., 78.

19 Ibid., 78–79.

20 LaCapra also argues that if one has not experienced the traumatic event directly, one cannot experience trauma, for it would be an abuse. Ibid., 102. I discuss the differences between LaCapra's approach and Ettinger's matrixial theory in more detail in my article: Anna Kisiel, "Uraz — bliskość — nie-pamięć: Psychoanalityczny dyskurs traumy od Freuda do Ettinger," *Narracje o Zagładzie* 2 (2016): 115–32.

21 Hirsch, "Nazi Photographs," 133.

at the victim,"[22] which would be the most accurate example of what she calls the Nazi gaze. This description is partly true if the image of the Mizocz women is considered. We cannot be certain where exactly the soldiers are (there are only two soldiers within the picture frame); most of the women standing in the row look ahead or at other women, and it is impossible to guess from the image alone whether the soldiers are in front of them or near the anonymous photographer. One of the women is looking in a different direction, and because of that she seems to respond to the Nazi gaze in the most striking manner. Still, as viewers we have to come to terms with the fact that most probably the photographer is also the perpetrator, and, consequently, we occupy the executioner's position. Having realized the place we are in, we are claimed to react as follows: "Too late to help, utterly impotent, we nevertheless search for ways to *take responsibility* for what we are seeing, to *experience,* from a remove, even as we try to redefine, if not repair, these ruptures."[23] Ettinger's artworks deal with the Nazi gaze, for she manipulates the image taken presumably by one of the perpetrators. Nevertheless, looking at her activity through the matrixial lens, we may assume that the gaze undergoes a change here. As I would like to argue, in the case of Ettinger's art, the gaze we can engage in is rather a com-passionate gaze: a gaze that can be portrayed as hospitable and respectful, responsible and engaging. Such a gaze involves wit(h)nessing and makes it impossible to objectify the intimate Other; finally, it entails suffering in the experience of trauma that the Other cannot work through. Ettinger's *Eurydices* open the space in which the viewer can gaze at the women's bodies in com-passion, acknowledging the perpetrator's position, but going beyond it in order to reach the women's fragility and shards of trauma.

Even if the gaze is com-passionate, it can still be considered "barbaric." Theodor W. Adorno famously proclaimed that

---

22 Ibid., 134. Emphasis mine.
23 Ibid., 138. Emphasis mine.

"[t]o write poetry after Auschwitz is barbaric"[24]; elsewhere, he explained that while it is not accurate to ask about the capacity to write poems after the Shoah, there is a more fundamental issue that can be tackled, namely, "whether after Auschwitz you can go on living."[25] As a daughter of the Holocaust survivors, Ettinger most probably has faced the latter dilemma. Still, when examining her art, we can — or even ought to — ask questions about its potential "barbaric" qualities.[26] Indeed, Ettinger has not experienced the Holocaust personally, being rather a secondary witness. Moreover, Ettinger's parents are the survivors, having been able to establish a family and to deal with the new reality; her position is, therefore, different from that of relatives of survivors who could not manage to "go on living." Moving on to the photo used in Ettinger's art, it may or may not present someone from her parents' family; we bear no actual knowledge of Ettinger's relation with the women. Last but not least, the author of this picture is probably a Nazi photographer, capturing the women's bodies without their consent, which Ettinger

---

24 Adorno, "Cultural Criticism and Society," 34.

25 Theodor W. Adorno, "Meditations on Metaphysics," in *Negative Dialectics*, trans. E.B. Ashton (Routledge, 2004), 363.

26 Pollock rejects the possibility of reading Ettinger's art through the prism of "barbarism," or potential ethical doubts. We read, "contemporary critics, who look too quickly and with prejudice, are liable to make mistaken judgments about the ethics of the *use* of historical photographs from the Holocaust or the family album, when the nature of this project involves no use at all. Bracha Lichtenberg Ettinger's work depends upon the potentiality of Painting — the category — and painting, the activity of a repeating bodily activity that encodes the duration of its making in the archaeology of its own surface and enshrines the time taken to create the space of 'almost missed encounter.'" Griselda Pollock, "Nichsapha: Yearning/Languishing. The Immaterial Tuché of Colour in Painting *after Painting after History*," in Bracha L. Ettinger, *Bracha Lichtenberg Ettinger: Artworking 1985–1999* (Ludion, 2000), 52. Emphasis in original. While, indeed, the question of the use of historical and personal photographs is rethought by Ettinger (in both theory and art), I believe one cannot close the discussion on possible "barbaric" qualities of Ettinger's art as such a discussion contributes to a broader set of reflections on the capacity to "go on living" in the post-Shoah reality. In this context, clear-cut judgements that do not take the arguments of the other side into consideration are reductive.

also cannot obtain in any way. Then, the question of consent applies to her as well. Keeping the above remarks in mind, can we think of an ethics of the *Eurydices*?

Facing the Bare Life

Agamben's reading of *homo sacer* casts light on the position of women photographed in Mizocz. As Agamben points out, in ancient Greece we can trace the dual understanding of "life." *Bios* stands for "political existence,"[27] wherein one exists through language and is included in society; yet, in order to be included, one needs to exclude one's *zoē*, understood as "bare life,"[28] or material existence prior to any norms. Agamben elucidates, "There is politics because man is the living being who, in language, separates and opposes himself to his own bare life and, at the same time, maintains himself in relation to that bare life in an inclusive exclusion."[29] This act of an inclusive exclusion is mirrored in the relation between the sovereign power and *homo sacer*. A figure that "may be killed and yet not sacrificed,"[30] *homo sacer* is excluded from the order of the secular and that of the divine.[31] It is the sovereign that performs such an exclusion by suspending the law, thus providing the space for an exception and reducing *homo sacer* to bare life. Beyond law, *homo sacer* nevertheless functions within the bounds of society, remaining a political entity. Finally, *homo sacer's* relation to death is defined as "an intimate symbiosis"[32]: they have not died yet, but they may be killed at any time and with no consequences for the perpetrator. The photograph of the women from Mizocz points to their status of *homines sacri*. Undressed, the women are humiliated and reduced to *zoē*. They are waiting for an execution which is

---

27 Giorgio Agamben, *Homo Sacer: Sovereign Power and Bare Life*, trans. Daniel Heller-Roazen (Stanford University Press, 1998), 8.
28 Ibid., 4.
29 Ibid., 8.
30 Ibid. Emphasis in original.
31 Ibid., 82.
32 Ibid., 100.

simultaneously beyond the law (being a mass killing that will not be penalized) and within the law (allowed by the sovereign as an exception). At the moment of taking the picture, the women are in "an intimate symbiosis" with their imminent death. The status of these women mirrors that of the Jewish nation during the war. As Agamben notes, the Jew is the twentieth century *homo sacer* figure, "exterminated not in a mad and giant holocaust but exactly as Hitler had announced, 'as lice,' which is to say, as bare life."[33] The women from Mizocz, and the Jewish people in general, are by no means sacrificed, as the etymology of "holocaust" would suggest.[34] Instead, being *homines sacri,* they are down-

---

33 Ibid., 114. LaCapra provides an interesting critique of Agamben's refusal to employ the notion of "Holocaust." He notes that, in Agamben, "The intolerability of the term 'Holocaust' derives from its ambiguity as a euphemism and an intimation that the events in question could possibly have sacred meaning," while, in fact, "no term is unproblematic for 'the events in question'"; in other words, there is no adequate name that can be ascribed to such incomprehensible, inhuman, and tragic circumstances. LaCapra proposes that one needs to, "recognize that there are no pure or innocent terms [...] and to avoid fixating on one term as innocent or as taboo." Therefore, LaCapra stands for using various names rather than focusing on one, and simultaneously for being aware of potential problematic implications of the chosen terms. Dominick LaCapra, "Approaching Limit Events: Siting Agamben," in *History in Transit: Experience, Identity, Critical Theory* (Cornell University Press, 2004), 169.

34 "Holocaust" is a translation of the Hebrew noun *'ōlā,* which means "that which goes up [in smoke]" and stands for a burnt offering: a sacrifice of an animal appearing in the bible. Baruch J. Schwartz, "Burnt Offering," in *The Oxford Dictionary of the Jewish Religion,* ed. Adele Berlin (Oxford University Press, 2011), 154. The English term originates in Greek *holokauston* and Late Latin *holocaustum,* meaning "a thing wholly burnt." *Online Etymology Dictionary,* s.v. "holocaust," https://www.etymonline.com/word/holocaust. After the Second World War, it begins to be associated with the Nazi genocide of European Jews. Bruno Bettelheim, for one, finds the word "holocaust" an improper name for the genocide of the majority of the nation, observing that, "this artificial and highly technical term" has not been chosen by the persecuted groups themselves but by "the Americans." Bruno Bettelheim, "The Holocaust — One Generation Later," in *Surviving, and Other Essays* (Alfred A. Knopf, 1979), 91. In his opinion, such an external decision is harmful from the religious point of view as it produces the otherwise inexistent linkages between the Nazi crimes and the Jewish faith and tradition. Bettelheim goes on to argue

graded and killed with the consent of the sovereign power. Still, assuming that these women are diminished to *zoē*, can we revive the ethical aspect of their bodies? What can Ettinger's art and theory "do" with this photograph to make it humanizing?

The bodies of women from Mizocz are incomprehensible, but, matrixially speaking, artistic practice is one of the means capable of producing the ethical relation with them. In the matrixial paradigm, there is no clear-cut opposition between the I and the non-I. Such a binary, however, is cherished in Nazi ideology, which places the Jewish nation in the position of the radical Other, depersonalized and reduced to bare — killable — life. Along with its atrocious historical context and the Nazi gaze indispensably attached to it, the Mizocz photograph cannot be accepted in its original form; yet, Ettinger works through this image in an attempt to alter the experience of the spectator. As Ettinger notes, "Aesthetic production already carries ethical aspects"[35]; an artist is, even unconsciously, capable of responding to the Other's call and establishing a canvas-space for an aesthetic encounter that can become ethical. Interestingly enough, what is encountered in this instance is, as I argue, *zoē*, provided that *zoē* is understood as material, non-linguistic existence, not governed by the phallic norms. To specify, an encounter with *zoē* can be ethical because, within the matrix, language is not a condition for ethics since meaning can be conveyed outside of it. While in the photograph these women's bodies may exist as *zoē*, matrixially — and aesth/ethically — speaking, they can turn into the carriers of sense and knowledge. Via art, they become the sites of painful shareable experience; having been reduced by Nazi perpetrators to bare lives, these women are affectively re-subjectified, but they are able to "speak" precisely — and

---

that, "Using a word with such strong unconscious religious connotations when speaking of the murder of millions of Jews robs the victims of this abominable mass murder of the only thing left to them: their uniqueness. Calling the most callous, most brutal, most horrid, most heinous mass murder a burnt offering is a sacrilege, a profanation of God and man." Bettelheim, "The Holocaust," 92.

35 Ettinger, "Wit(h)nessing Trauma," 151.

only — by means of their bodies, captured and transformed on the canvas by the artist. Interestingly enough, both the linguistic incomprehensibility of the message of the Mizocz women and their bareness build a bridge between Agamben's study of *homo sacer* to Levinas's ethics of the face.[36]

Levinas's category of the face of the Other is marked by nakedness and vulnerability. Nakedness of the face stands for "the absolute openness of the Transcendent."[37] The Other is open to the I, nevertheless remaining a radically separate entity; it is this openness that establishes an ethical relation. However, it also results in exposure, which makes the Other fragile. The face of the Other is, as we read, "exposed, menaced, as if inviting us to an act of violence."[38] Here, the correspondence between Agamben and Levinas becomes apparent as both philosophers render the Other vulnerable to dangers originating in the subject. In Ettinger's proposal of subjectivity-as-encounter, however, it is the subject that is unprotected. Fragile and open, the subject surrenders to the non-I, thus consenting to the potential pain and trauma to come. Of course, one cannot ignore the differences between the discussed types of threats; most of all, among the gravest possible consequences of an encounter that the Levinasian Other may face, there is death at the hands of the subject-perpetrator. Still, both positions — that of the Levinasian Other and that of the Ettingerian subject — are ethically meaningful and convergent, equally emphasizing the significance of openness to the point of defenseless vulnerability.

---

36 Similarly to Ettinger, Levinas rarely comments upon the Holocaust in his writings in a straightforward manner. Still, this tragedy has had a considerable impact on his life and work, which is why his reflections often prove useful in discussions concerning the Shoah. In his article, Jacob Meskin explores the main arguments for thinking Levinas and the Holocaust together. See Jacob Meskin, "The Jewish Transformation of Modern Thought: Lévinas and Philosophy after the Holocaust," *CrossCurrents* 47, no. 4 (Winter 1997–1998): 505–17.

37 Emmanuel Levinas, *Totality and Infinity: An Essay on Exteriority,* trans. Alphonso Lingis (Duquesne University Press, 1969), 199.

38 Emmanuel Levinas, *Ethics and Infinity: Conversations with Philippe Nemo,* trans. Richard A. Cohen (Duquesne University Press, 1995), 86.

Although the face eludes the field of vision, it is capable of communicating an ethical demand and anticipating a response. Regarding the appearance of the face, Levinas argues:

> I do not know if one can speak of a "phenomenology" of the face, since phenomenology describes what appears. So, [...] I wonder if one can speak of a look turned toward the face, for the look is knowledge, perception. I think rather that *access to the face is straightaway ethical.* You turn yourself toward the Other as toward an object when you see a nose, eyes, a forehead, a chin, and you can describe them. The best way of encountering the Other is not even to notice the color of his eyes! [...] The relation with the face can surely be dominated by perception, but what is specifically the face is what cannot be reduced to that.[39]

Once its appearance is described, the face is objectified, and the primary ethical relationship cannot be formed; then, it is not perception that should govern the encounter with the face but direct experience. Revealed affectively rather than phenomenologically, the face exists precisely "in its refusal to be contained,"[40] remaining incomprehensible for the subject. Still, it does utter an ethical demand. It is claimed to say "thou shalt not kill"[41] even if one is incapable of abiding by this commandment. Levinas admits that "the ethical exigency is not an ontological necessity."[42] As Adam Lipszyc notes, when facing the Other, "we always fail a little, we continually suffer a defeat, and we resort to violence."[43] Weak and vulnerable, the Other nevertheless demands not to be killed, which is described as "primor-

---

39 Ibid., 85–86. Emphasis mine.
40 Levinas, *Totality and Infinity,* 194.
41 Levinas, *Ethics and Infinity,* 87.
42 Ibid.
43 "zawsze trochę zawodzimy, nieustannie ponosimy klęskę i dopuszczamy się przemocy." Adam Lipszyc, *Ślad judaizmu w filozofii XX wieku* (Fundacja im. Prof. Mojżesza Schorra, 2009), 136. Translation mine.

dial *expression*" and "the first word"[44] — it becomes the primary ethical principle, because of which the encounter is subjectifying and humanizing by design. The act of speech the Other engages in marks also the entrance to discourse: "Face and discourse are tied. The face speaks. It speaks, it is in this that it renders possible and begins all discourse."[45] Through its speech, the face expects our reaction. Levinas observes that "the authentic relationship with the Other" is grounded upon "response or responsibility."[46] The act or responding to the non-I, therefore, equals responsibility, which turns out to initiate and shape the community. To be specific, one of the premises of humanizing responsibility is that one recognizes the absolute difference between oneself and the Other while not becoming unsympathetic or detached; this intimate relationship — "the *non-indifference* of responsibility,"[47] to use Levinas's words — is claimed to build the intersubjective community and solidarity.[48]

Unlike in the matrixial theory, in Levinasian ethics one ought not to associate responsibility with mutuality. The encounter with the face is not symmetrical; instead, the subject ought to assume the altruistic position regardless of the possibly non-reciprocal nature of the dialogic exchange.[49] Although responsible for the Other, the subject is not responsible for the Other's decision to engage further. Proposing the notion of response-ability, Ettinger diverges from Levinas and postulates

---

44 Levinas, *Totality and Infinity*, 199. Emphasis in original.

45 Levinas, *Ethics and Infinity*, 87.

46 Ibid., 88.

47 Emmanuel Levinas, *Humanism of the Other*, trans. Nidra Poller (University of Illinois Press, 2006), 6. Emphasis mine.

48 Emmanuel Levinas, "The Trace of the Other," in *Deconstruction in Context: Literature and Philosophy*, ed. Mark C. Taylor (University of Chicago Press, 1986), 353.

49 Levinas, *Ethics and Infinity*, 98–99. In his article, Ronald T. Michener comments upon this excerpt as follows: "Levinas calls for a *disinterested,* unconditional, asymmetrical relationship without mutuality or the expectation of equal exchange." Ronald T. Michener, "Face-to-Face with Levinas: (Ev)angelical Hospitality *and* (De)constructive Ethics?," *European Journal of Theology* 19, no. 2 (2010): 157. Emphasis in original.

the possibility of mutual—although not symmetrical—circulation of non-linguistic data.[50] Simultaneously, Ettinger by no means denies the primary significance of the act of caring for the Other in a compassionate and committed response. Ronald T. Michener delineates Levinas's ethics of the face as follows:

> An encounter with the other cannot be reduced to my own analysis, nor assimilated into my understanding or reasoning. The other with whom I am standing face to face beckons me to moral obligation. The call of the other precedes my own will and initiative. It ruptures my own ordered life of *being* (ontology) and morally obliges me to radical "corporeal" responsibility with sensitivity to embodied persons who become weary, experience pain and have physical and emotional needs.[51]

The face of the Other requires a caring response that precedes a conscious decision; this is why response-ability becomes embodied, just as the Other is "embodied" per se. Responsibility, however, becomes even more urgent when one faces the Other in agony.

A response is expected as a primary reaction to the horror of the Shoah. As Levinas observes, the twentieth century is marked by unimaginable and pointless pain, and because of that "the suffering for the useless suffering of the other person, the just suffering in me for the unjustifiable suffering of the Other, opens upon suffering the ethical perspective of the inter-human."[52] Suffering makes sense in so far as one suffers for the Other who experiences pain; only then can it become a humanizing process since it offers an interpersonal relation within which one attends to the Other. Such careful attentiveness also applies to the gen-

---

50 See Bracha L. Ettinger, "Weaving a Woman Artist with-in the Matrixial Encounter-Event," in Ettinger, *The Matrixial Borderspace*, 190.
51 Michener, "Face-to-Face with Levinas," 156. Emphasis in original.
52 Emmanuel Levinas, "Useless Suffering," trans. Richard Cohen, in *The Provocation of Levinas: Rethinking the Other*, ed. Robert Bernasconi and David Wood (Routledge, 1988), 159.

erations that follow — ones who have not experienced the incomprehensible tragedy personally. Georges Didi-Huberman argues for the necessity of trying to conceive of the unconceivable. In the context of photographs taken in Auschwitz, we read:

> In order to know, we must *imagine* for ourselves. We must attempt to imagine the hell that Auschwitz was [...]. Let us not invoke the unimaginable. Let us not shelter ourselves by saying that we cannot, that we could not by any means, imagine it to the very end. We *are obliged* to that oppressive imaginable. It is a response that we must offer, as a debt to the words and images that certain prisoners snatched, for us, from the harrowing Real of their experience.[53]

The next generations are required to respond compassionately, and such responses should incorporate an attempt to see through the eyes of the Other, in order not to usurp the pain, but to grasp at least the fragment of it. When facing the suffering Other, one ought not to protect oneself because such an attitude is not open to the ethical encounter; one is in a sense indebted to the Other, and the only way to repay is to answer the call.

The necessity of facing the Holocaust victims corresponds to Derrida's hauntology. One of the characteristics of Derridean specter is its constantly displaced position on the verge or at the intersection of different temporalities: "Before knowing whether one can differentiate between the specter of the past and the specter of the future, of the past present and the future present, one must perhaps ask oneself whether the *spectrality effect* does not consist in undoing this opposition, or even this dialectic, between actual, effective presence and its other."[54] As Ubertowska notes, the specter is also prone to such mechanisms

---

53 Georges Didi-Huberman, *Images in Spite of All: Four Photographs from Auschwitz*, trans. Shane B. Lillis (University of Chicago Press, 2008), 3. Emphasis in original.

54 Jacques Derrida, *Specters of Marx: The State of Debt, the Work of Mourning and the New International*, trans. Peggy Kamuf (Routledge, 2006), 48. Emphasis in original.

as repetition, duplication, manipulation, and translation. A twofold relation of the specter to language thus emerges; on the one hand, the two bear a striking resemblance to each other, for they are liable to the above types of transformations, and, on the other, language becomes the space in which the specter may be conjured up.[55] This duality, I believe, is not reducible to the field of language as it can be also transferred to the field of art, which — especially if we consider Ettinger's "Eurydicial" art — is governed by a corresponding set of rules. When encountering the spirits, one is claimed to be given a unique chance of "learning to live"[56] from these evanescent figures suspended between life and death. Counterintuitively, the dialogue is supposed to take place despite their doubtful presence; after all, "this, the spectral, is *not*," or it "is *never present as such*."[57] Gaining knowledge about life embraces the movement towards positive change and justice. For this reason, "*talk[ing] with or about some ghost*"[58] becomes an essential activity of a human being even if the faced ghost is not comprehensible. Unintelligibility is, in fact, an inescapable trait of an apparition. The spirit cannot be seen in its entirety, thus resisting identification, and yet it sees the subject. The subject, then, is left with nothing but trust. Nevertheless, the subject is demanded to obey, that is, to respond to the encountered spirit by taking an oath.[59] In the context of the Shoah, the basic elements of the pledge given to the spectral victims are compassion, responsibility, memory, attentiveness, and radical, fragilizing openness despite potential suffering.

Responding to the Mizocz Women

The specter corresponds to the Mizocz women in Ettinger's art. Historically speaking, the women belong to the bygone past, but

---

55 Aleksandra Ubertowska, "Rysa, dukt, odcisk (nie)obecności: O spektrologiach Zagłady," *Teksty Drugie*, no. 2 (2016): 107–8.

56 Derrida, *Specters of Marx*, xvii.

57 Ibid. Emphasis in original.

58 Ibid. Emphasis in original.

59 See Ibid., 6–7 and 34.

in Ettinger's aesthetic work they become Eurydices: figures of varying temporalities who resist being confined to one of the times. Trapped between presence and absence on the one hand, and between the past, present, and future on the other, the Eurydices from Mizocz are ghostly entities haunting the canvas. Their confinement — along with the possibility of grasping them — is directly connected to artistic techniques employed by Ettinger. The *Eurydice* series incorporates a multiplicity of canvases, repetitiveness of themes, and manipulation of the background photograph(s); the very series, therefore, becomes not only a haunted borderspace, but also a haunting one, a spectral, serial, ceaselessly becoming oeuvre. The women from Mizocz seem to follow Derridean logic of conjuration. The French term carries several meanings. One of them is conspiracy, associated with an act of vowing, undertaken possibly under a veil of secrecy.[60] Another understanding embraces "the magical incantation destined to *evoke,* to bring forth with the voice, to convoke a charm or a spirit."[61] Finally, conjuration signifies the opposite of the second meaning; "conjurement" stands for an exorcism that aims at expelling the ghost once and for all.[62] Similarly to that with the specter, the relationship with the Mizocz women made possible via Ettinger's art is, indeed, an ambiguous alliance. By means of various artistic techniques, these women are convoked and cast out at the same time; when appearing in art, they call the viewer to conspire with them, that is, to enter a more intimate relation than merely an aesthetic one. Occupying Ettinger's works, the Mizocz women are specters haunting both the viewer and — arguably — the artist herself.

The spectral pres-absence of the women from the Mizocz ghetto poses an ethical demand, whose aspects can be portrayed by means of two major tendencies in the *Eurydice* series and other images employing the analyzed theme. We cannot draw a line between the two tendencies as they constantly overlap in

---

60 Ibid., 49–50.
61 Ibid., 50. Emphasis in original.
62 Ibid., 58.

this nonlinear and mostly unchronological oeuvre. Still, we can make a tentative distinction into the early and the late *Eurydice* series in order to examine varying artistic interventions and their effects on viewers. The first aspect of the demand is that of being attentive towards the Other, portrayed in particular in Ettinger's early paintings and sketches. Artworks such as *No Title — Sketch* (1985) (fig. 10) — not belonging to the series but united with it by means of the background image — are ethical in Levinas's understanding of the word; the canvases host the women along with their almost uncovered bodies, and thus the spectator is expected to gaze in a non-voyeuristic and non-aggressive way, and to respond to the women's painful position. The other aspect of the demand is that of trust. Interacting with the late *Eurydice* series is based entirely on the viewer's trust. One is required to surrender to the image and follow it beyond its quality of representation — towards disruptive un-intelligibility. If one is unable to do so, that is, if one cannot trust that which cannot be fully comprehended, the women's desire to be acknowledged cannot be fulfilled and the ethical demand remains unanswered. Trust and attentiveness are thus two inextricably linked — yet distinct — qualities that the potential viewer needs to possess to respond to the Other.

What makes the viewer respond to Ettinger's *Eurydices*? One of the key themes connected to the Mizocz women is the recurring face of one of them in semi-profile, looking away; what seems to captivate us is her ambiguous gaze, which cannot be reduced to one interpretation because of Ettinger's various artistic reworkings. In her psychoanalysis, Ettinger also takes up the notion of the gaze. The Lacanian gaze is a split- and loss-based type of *objet petit a*, the unsatisfiable object of one's desire; Lacan writes, "In our relation to things, in so far as this relation is constituted by the way of vision, and ordered in the figures of representation, something slips, passes, is transmitted, from stage to stage, and is always to some degree eluded in it."[63] The gaze is

---

63 Jacques Lacan, "Of the Gaze as Objet Petit a," in *The Seminar of Jacques Lacan, Book XI: The Four Fundamental Concepts of Psychoanalysis*, ed.

precisely this "something" which, when encountered, is doomed to be missed. Nevertheless, the fragments of it remain in the visual field, so to a degree the gaze can be accessed.[64] Putting the aesthetic experience at the center of her reflections, Ettinger provides us with a non-phallic, supplementary rereading of the gaze. The relation between the viewer, the gaze, and the work of art is explicated as follows:

> The visual artwork attracts, shifts, or originates a desire for a subjective-object that is mysteriously embodied in the artwork as a gaze. The gaze calls to the viewer to follow it into a space beyond, yet inside the visible, to abandon defenses and become fragmented and fragile, to become open to sharing and absorbing and a further redistributing of fragments of trauma — all this on the condition of weaving into the artwork one's own matrixial threads and letting the artwork penetrate one's own psychic sphere of severality.[65]

The matrixial gaze is grounded not upon separation or loss but upon fragilization, transformation, and sharing. "Touched" by the gaze, one is claimed to give in to its power in order to reach partial traces of the Other's trauma; however, what takes place is not only a change, but also an exchange — the gaze itself within the work of art is also transformed in the process. When the impact of the gaze on the viewer is considered, Ettinger elucidates that "[t]he matrixial gaze thrills us while fragmenting, scattering, and joining grains together, turning us into participatory witnesses; it enchants and horrifies us, attenuating us into connected particles that participate in a drama wider than that of our individual selves."[66] Within the matrixial realm, the gaze is marked by vulnerability, involvement, and openness to

---

Jacques-Alain Miller, trans. Alan Sheridan (W.W. Norton & Company, 1981), 73.

64 Ibid., 101.

65 Bracha L. Ettinger, "Wit(h)nessing Trauma," 152.

66 Bracha L. Ettinger, "The With-In-Visible Screen," in Ettinger, *The Matrixial Borderspace*, 117–18.

Fig. 29. Bracha L. Ettinger, *Eurydice,* No. 35, 1994–2001, oil, xerography, photocopic pigment, and ashes on paper mounted on canvas, 40 × 27 cm. Collection: Marguerite Steed Hoffman, Dallas, featured at the exhibition *Bracha Lichtenberg Ettinger: Eurydice — Pieta* in Muzeum Śląskie (Silesian Museum), Katowice, July 7–September 2, 2017. © Courtesy of the artist.

the traumatic information originating in the Other. Emphatically, the gaze as a psychoanalytic notion and the gaze as a potentially com-passionate mode of spectatorship share such qualities as participation and response-ability without objectification, and also the experience of the Other's trauma without appropriation.

When found, the woman from Mizocz returns the viewer's gaze. In *Eurydice,* No. 35 (1994–2001), the central part of the image seems to have disappeared to a great extent; the sand-like beige occupies the middle of the canvas, but it is by no means only a color, pattern, or texture with no other data covered (fig. 29). Almost invisible and yet present, the phrases recurring in Ettinger's art resurface in the upper part of this area: *maternelle* and, slightly below, *vivante/morte*.[67] This time, *langage* (language) is absent, or perhaps simply irrelevant; it is the maternal connotation of the state between life and death that plays a major role in the artwork. Above the desert of grainy colors and letters, a face of the woman is placed. While in the original photograph she is looking towards the perpetrator — and thus viewer — but does not meet the camera's eye, here it remains uncertain whether the woman looks away or exactly at the potential spectator. Moreover, if we assume that she does look at the viewer, we may go on to claim that her gaze invites one "into a space beyond, yet inside the visible": the space within which her tragic fate is reworked and the traces of the Holocaust trauma are carried on. The matrixial gaze, in this context, is undeniably feminine and humanizing, and these two qualities are inextricably linked. It is feminine, for it belongs to the anonymous woman and its *maternelle* nature is hinted at on the canvas. It becomes ethical since it guides one to the motherly-matrixial sphere, makes one vulnerable, and does not allow one to forget the past and move on; instead, it poses a demand of passing the history on to others and of being transformed by the newly acquired non-linguistic knowledge.

Attentiveness, trust, the capacity to be influenced by the Other's painful history and to share it — these qualities boil down to Levinas's ethical message: *respond without killing*. The historically hopeless request — considering the woman's fate — becomes a potentially humanizing one in artistic practice since the spectator, unlike the perpetrator, may "glean something of the hidden gaze if s/he refrains from any conscious attempt to capture it, if — to use Lacan's expression — *s/he lays down her/his weapons at the painting's threshold and gives in*."[68] Should one surrender to the gaze and renounce violence or appropriation,

---

67 In fact, the majority of the canvas is covered with words and phrases from a French–Hebrew dictionary, but it is these two entries that are most easily decipherable. Also, the lower part of the artwork seems to carry a sketch-like image, but I am unable to identify it.

68 Ibid., 100. Emphasis mine.

one may grasp the partial imprints of trauma encrypted within the space of the artwork, but beyond its representational aspect. At this point of an encounter, it is necessary to remain non-aggressive: to refrain from turning one's back at this knowledge and from objectifying or abjectifying the Other. Rather, one is asked to process the information, to respond to it with compassion, and to remember it for and instead of the non-I. The Mizocz Eurydices — and among them the woman from *Eurydice,* No. 35 — beseech us to look back but without killing them again; already dead and yet relentlessly present in Ettinger's artworks, they seem to hope that fragments of their trauma will be embraced, worked through, and imparted further.

Living After Auschwitz

The question that still has been left unanswered is whether Ettinger's art is "barbaric" or not. One cannot deny the inherent danger of including Holocaust-related themes and documents in art; similarly, there are qualities of Ettinger's art that may seem to render it close to barbarism, that is, the artist's position of a secondary witness to the experiences of her parents-survivors, the dubious nature of her connection with the photo from Mizocz, and the issue of (missing) consent. These properties may be used as arguments portraying Ettinger's artistic activity as ethically questionable, and it would be ignorant to reject them straightaway; quite the contrary, numerous subtleties and threads in Ettinger's art make an unequivocal judgement for any side impossible. Nevertheless, if this art is read through the prism of the matrixial theory alongside Levinas, Agamben, and Derrida, its proto-ethical potential is uncovered.

If one puts aside the issues of appropriateness and appropriation in Ettinger's artistic and theoretical oeuvre while still keeping in mind their inevitability and validity, one can discover numerous emerging ethics-related tropes. When the question of femininity and the Holocaust is concerned, Ettinger de-objectifies the Mizocz women and protects them from the Nazi gaze inherent in the original photograph; by that, she opens the potential path towards a more com-passionate encounter with them. Although the women from Mizocz may be identified as Agamben's *homines sacri,* art in its matrixial understanding makes it possible to communicate with them despite their burden of being *zoē.* Nevertheless, when we employ Levinas's categories of the face and responsibility, we learn that these women do utter a call: "thou shalt not kill." Defenseless and naked, these spectral figures wish the reader to respond compassionately and openly to their painful position. This demand includes not only attentiveness and trust, but also a different — matrixial and *maternelle* — gaze. In the world that has witnessed, participated in, and survived the failure of humanity, one's hope can be found — perhaps only — in a devoted humane response.

Conclusion

The underlying assumption of the proposed project of the matrixial corporeal aesth/ethics is that corporeality, inherent in Ettinger's oeuvre, and humanism are inextricably conjoined since the (female) body is the primary space and source of a proto-ethical encounter. Rooted in the intrauterine/pregnancy phase, such an encounter becomes the elementary mode of subjectivity, and thus it redefines the position of the subject in the world. This shift of emphasis from radical separation to coexistence and mutual transformation leads to further ethical implications. Namely, when the maternal body becomes a psychoanalytical model of relationships, the hospitable acts of caring for and carrying the Other testify to the foundational bond that challenges the stability of borders between subjects and their seeming individuality.

As has been shown, Ettinger's theoretical propositions are indebted to and immersed in the body. The matrix is inspired by the qualities of the womb and pregnancy. The matrixial womb-like sphere is a non-passive realm governed by severality, and it initiates an Other subjectivizing process, subjectivity-as-encounter, characterized by the act of becoming-together. It is exactly the capacity to produce and partake in connections that constitutes the basic ethical promise of the motherly-feminine body, but this does not mean that such a capacity belongs to women only. Grounded upon the relation between the becoming-mother and the becoming-infant, an embodied encounter is marked by hospitality. In this covenant, the two subjects not only meet, but also share traces of information — they communicare. Importantly, the very fact that this model is based on the female body does not reduce its scope: The matrix is a universal human(e) potentiality as every person has already experienced being with and in the maternal body in the prenatal period. Moreover, the possibility to transmit and share information gains particular significance when Holocaust issues are considered; in this context, the transmissibility of knowledge becomes a chance to preserve the partial memory of a traumatic event and work through it when those who were directly affected are not able to do so anymore. This is where Ettinger's art comes in; her "Eurydicial" artworks can be argued to carry an affective load that consists of traces of disruptive data originating in the women from Mizocz, Ettinger's parents, and the artist herself. While the female body is an archaic prenatal experience, art becomes one of postnatally accessible spaces of humanizing proximity to the Other.

Inspired by the events within the female body, the category of an encounter reveals its humanizing potential not only in matrixial psychoanalysis and Ettinger's art, but also in dialogues with Judeo-Christian theology and Holocaust studies. The covenant's bodily nature and meetings *with* the actual bodies point to entanglement of the body and encounter. Interestingly, an encounter remains asymmetrical and poses requirements such as commitment, attentiveness, decision, and trust; also, there are two prevailing needs of the matrixial covenant, compassion and a response to a call. Such an encounter cannot take place if the Other is recognized as an object, so de-objectification of the Other gains the status of a humanizing strategy. Sacrifice is a category directly linked to a compassionate encounter. An Ettingerian, *mère*-verse sacrifice is a partial offering of oneself for the sake of the Other, inspired by the prenatal/pregnancy encounter: One chooses to abandon one's security and borders and expose oneself to suffering, motivated by the prospect of a humane reciprocal relation.

Even though the potential of theorizing the proto-ethical dimension of the body is considerable, the matrixial theory and Ettinger's art raise problematic questions that cannot be left unnoticed. Starting with gender-related issues, while the matrixial realm refers to a universal experience (that of having encountered the maternal body), the matrixial feminine difference is undeniably gendered, and women have a privileged access to it. Next, despite the fact that her theory draws inspiration from such encounter-events as prenatality, pregnancy, and maternity, Ettinger disagrees with the possibility of essentialist and biologically determined readings, or interpretations that undermine women's rights; we cannot, however, reject the rhetorical appeal of certain matrixial notions. When we turn to Ettinger's use of male and female figures in her works, other curious implications resurface. In matrixial psychoanalysis, mainly biblical and mythical women contribute to the structure of the matrixial domain, but there are notable exceptions — such as Isaac and Moses — who prove that the matrixial bodily connection transcends gender divisions. In Ettinger's art, it is female family members who prevail (especially Bluma Lichtenberg); yet, as I suggest, it is rather the question of a mother–daughter relation than that of a gender bias. Gender issues are not the only potentially problematic aspect of Ettinger's oeuvre. When her artistic activity is scrutinized, it is difficult not to address the doubts raised by the use of the Holocaust. One cannot ignore the threat of appropriation, Ettinger's status of a secondary witness, her unknown relation to the Mizocz women, and the inevitable lack of consent of the photographed people. Still, I do believe that the matrixial theory and Ettinger's art, when combined, can contribute to a trans-formation of ethics through, with, and in corporeality.

The body is a dynamic force. The body not only is, or is had; it also does, or even makes. The body is a feel-know-seeing entity — it is affected by an encounter or an event, it remembers, and thus it becomes a bearer of knowledge. Bearing, however, is not sufficient; the body needs to pass the knowledge on, even if the transfer is painful, and even if the transmitted information is not entirely comprehensible. This transfer is communication of sorts, but the language of such communication is corporeal, that is, governed by the body's capacities and flows. The body is lively; among its movements, we can distinguish an embrace — a hospitable gesture of caring for or taking care of another body. When it embraces, the body can venture to carry another body, but this activity transcends and precedes conscious decision as it is inscribed within the body's archaic potential. To specify, the body is capable of carrying because it remembers being carried; the first encounter — that with the female-motherly body — is originarily inscribed within it. Interestingly, what the maternal body encounters already becomes part of it — an influential, becoming, intimate border-Other. The becoming-bodily-entity and the maternal-female body: The two cherish their linkages and mutual transformations despite still being anonymous to each other. A site of a tender covenant and its source, the (female) body is more than dynamic; rather, it becomes the core of human(e)ness. The matrixial body allows us to adopt vulnerability as an ethical statement responding to times afflicted by trauma and unrest.

Bibliography

Adorno, Theodor W. "Cultural Criticism and Society." In *Prisms,* translated by Samuel Weber and Shierry Weber. MIT Press, 1983.

———. "Meditations on Metaphysics." In *Negative Dialectics,* translated by E.B. Ashton. Routledge, 2004.

Agamben, Giorgio. *Homo Sacer: Sovereign Power and Bare Life.* Translated by Daniel Heller-Roazen. Stanford University Press, 1998.

———. *The Time That Remains: A Commentary on the Letter to the Romans.* Translated by Patricia Dailey. Stanford University Press, 2005.

Barthes, Roland. *Camera Lucida: Reflections on Photography.* Translated by Richard Howard. Hill and Wang, 2010.

Bettelheim, Bruno. "The Holocaust — One Generation Later." In *Surviving, and Other Essays.* Alfred A. Knopf, 1979.

Bevis, Kathryn. "'Better Than Metaphors'? Dwelling and the Maternal Body in Emmanuel Levinas." *Literature and Theology* 21, no. 3 (2007): 317–29. DOI: 10.1093/litthe/frm028.

Burke, Nancy, ed. *Gender & Envy.* Routledge, 1998.

Butler, Judith. "Foreword: Bracha's Eurydice." In Bracha L. Ettinger, *The Matrixial Borderspace,* edited by Brian Massumi. University of Minnesota Press, 2006.

————. *Gender Trouble: Feminism and the Subversion of Identity*. Routledge, 2007.

Caputo, John D. *The Prayers and Tears of Jacques Derrida: Religion without Religion*. Indiana University Press, 1997.

Cavanagh, Sheila L. "Tiresias: Bracha L. Ettinger and the Transgression With-In-To the Feminine." In *Femininity and Psychoanalysis: Cinema, Culture, Theory*, edited by Agnieszka Piotrowska and Ben Tyrer. Routledge, 2019.

————. "Transgender, Hysteria, and the Other Sexual Difference: An Ettingerian Approach." *Studies in Gender and Sexuality* 20, no. 1 (2019): 36–50. DOI: 10.1080/15240657.2019.1559517.

————. "Transsexuality as Sinthome: Bracha L. Ettinger and the Other (Feminine) Sexual Difference." *Studies in Gender and Sexuality* 17, no. 1 (2016): 27–44. DOI: 10.1080/15240657.2016.1135681.

Celan, Paul. *Breathturn*. Translated by Pierre Joris. Sun & Moon Press, 1995.

Chromik, Anna. "Eurydice and Pieta, Fire and Water, Rescue and Evacuation: Traces of Trauma in Bracha Lichtenberg Ettinger's Art." In *Bracha L. Ettinger: Eurydyka — Pieta / Eurydice — Pieta*, edited by Anna Chromik. Muzeum Śląskie, 2018.

Cixous, Hélène. "The Laugh of the Medusa." Translated by Keith Cohen and Paula Cohen. *Signs: Journal of Women in Culture and Society* 1, no. 4 (1976): 875–93. https://www.jstor.org/stable/3173239.

Condren, Mary. "Relational Theology in the Work of the Artist, Psychoanalyst and Theorist Bracha Lichtenberg Ettinger." In *Through Us, with Us, in Us: Relational Theologies in the Twenty-First Century*, edited by Lisa Isherwood and Elaine Bellchambers. SCM Press, 2010.

Deleuze, Gilles, and Félix Guattari. *A Thousand Plateaus: Capitalism and Schizophrenia*. Translated by Brian Massumi. University of Minnesota Press, 1987.

Derrida, Jacques. "Faith and Knowledge: The Two Sources of 'Religion' at the Limits of Reason Alone." Translated by

Samuel Weber. In *Religion,* edited by Jacques Derrida and Gianni Vattimo. Polity Press, 1998.

———. *Specters of Marx: The State of the Debt, the Work of Mourning and the New International.* Translated by Peggy Kamuf. Routledge, 2006.

———. *The Gift of Death.* Translated by David Wills. University of Chicago Press, 1995.

Didi-Huberman, Georges. *Images in Spite of All: Four Photographs from Auschwitz.* Translated by Shane B. Lillis. University of Chicago Press, 2008.

Ettinger, Bracha L. *And My Heart Wound-Space.* Wild Pansy Press, 2015.

———. "Antigone with(out) Jocaste." In *Interrogating Antigone in Postmodern Philosophy and Criticism,* edited by S.E. Wilmer and Audronė Žukauskaitė. Oxford University Press, 2010.

———. *Bracha Lichtenberg Ettinger: Artworking 1985–1999.* Ludion, 2000.

———. "Copoiesis." *Ephemera: Theory and Politics in Organization* 5, no. X (2005): 703–13. https://www. ephemerajournal.org/sites/default/files/2022-01/5-Xettinger. pdf.

———. "Demeter–Persephone Complex, Entangled Aerials of the Psyche, and Sylvia Plath." *ESC: English Studies in Canada* 40, no. 1 (2014): 123–54. DOI: 10.1353/esc.2014.0010.

———. "Diotima and the Matrixial Transference: Psychoanalytical Encounter-Event as Pregnancy in Beauty." In *Beyond the Threshold: Explorations of Liminality in Literature,* edited by Hein Viljoen and Chris N. Van der Merwe. Peter Lang, 2007.

———. "*Fascinance* and the Girl-to-m/Other Matrixial Feminine Difference." In *Psychoanalysis and the Image: Transdisciplinary Perspectives,* edited by Griselda Pollock. Blackwell Publishing, 2006.

———. "Fragilization and Resistance." *Studies in the Maternal* 1, no. 2 (2009): 1–31. DOI: 10.16995/sim.141.

———. "From Proto-Ethical Compassion to Responsibility: Besideness and the Three *Primal* Mother-Phantasies of Not-Enoughness, Devouring and Abandonment." *Athena* 2 (2006): 100–135. https://athena.lt/files/pdf/2/II-1.pdf.

———. "Laius Complex and Shocks of Maternality: With Franz Kafka and Sylvia Plath." In *Interdisciplinary Handbook of Trauma and Culture,* edited by Yochai Ataria, David Gurevitz, Haviva Pedaya, and Yuval Neria. Springer, 2016.

———. "Matrix and Metramorphosis." *differences* 4, no. 3 (1992): 176–208. DOI: 10.1215/10407391-4-3-176.

———. *Matrix Halal(a): Lapsus: Notes on Painting.* Translated by Joseph Sims. Museum of Modern Art, 1993.

———. *The Matrixial Borderspace.* Edited by Brian Massumi. University of Minnesota Press, 2006.

———. "Transgressing With-In-To the Feminine." In *Differential Aesthetics: Art Practices, Philosophy and Feminist Understandings,* edited by Penny Florence and Nicola Foster. Routledge, 2018.

———. "Trans-Subjective Transferential Borderspace." In *A Shock to Thought: Expression after Deleuze and Guattari,* edited by Brian Massumi. Routledge, 2002.

———. "Uncanny Awe, Uncanny Compassion and Matrixial Transjectivity Beyond Uncanny Anxiety." In *Psychoanalysis in French and Francophone Literature and Film,* edited by James Day. Brill, 2011. DOI: 10.1163/9789401207591_002.

———. "Woman-Other-Thing: A Matrixial Touch." In *Matrix–Borderlines.* Museum of Modern Art, 1993.

Ettinger, Bracha L., and Kyoko Gardiner. "Affectuous Encounters: Feminine-Matrixial Encounters in Duras/Resnais' *Hiroshima Mon Amour.*" In *PostGender: Gender, Sexuality and Performativity in Japanese Culture,* edited by Ayelet Zohar. Cambridge Scholars, 2009.

Fink, Bruce. *A Clinical Introduction to Lacanian Psychoanalysis: Theory and Technique.* Harvard University Press, 1997.

———. *Lacan to the Letter: Reading* Écrits *Closely.* University of Minnesota Press, 2004.

Freud, Sigmund. "On the Sexual Theories of Children." In *The Standard Edition of the Complete Psychological Works of Sigmund Freud*, Vol. 9: *Jensen's "Gradiva" and Other Works (1906–1908)*, edited and translated by James Strachey with Anna Freud. Hogarth Press, 2001.

———. "Some Psychical Consequences of the Anatomical Distinction between the Sexes." In *The Standard Edition of the Complete Psychological Works of Sigmund Freud*, Vol. 19: *The Ego and the Id and Other Works (1923–1925)*, edited and translated by James Strachey with Anna Freud. Hogarth Press, 2001.

———. "The Infantile Genital Organization (An Interpolation into the Theory of Sexuality)." In *The Standard Edition of the Complete Psychological Works of Sigmund Freud*, Vol. 19: *The Ego and the Id and Other Works (1923–1925)*, edited and translated by James Strachey with Anna Freud. Hogarth Press, 2001.

———. "The Question of Lay Analysis: Conversations with an Impartial Person." In *The Standard Edition of the Complete Psychological Works of Sigmund Freud*, Vol. 20: *An Autobiographical Study, Inhibitions, Symptoms and Anxiety, Lay Analysis and Other Works (1925–1926)*, edited and translated by James Strachey with Anna Freud. Hogarth Press, 2001.

———. "The 'Uncanny.'" In *The Standard Edition of the Complete Psychological Works of Sigmund Freud*, Vol. 17: *An Infantile Neurosis and Other Works (1917–1919)*, edited and translated by James Strachey with Anna Freud. Hogarth Press, 2001.

Goldenberg, Myrna, and Amy H. Shapiro, eds. *Different Horrors, Same Hell: Gender and the Holocaust*. University of Washington Press, 2013.

Grosz, Elizabeth. *Sexual Subversions: Three French Feminists*. Allen & Unwin, 1989.

———. *Volatile Bodies: Toward a Corporeal Feminism*. Indiana University Press, 1994.

Guenther, Lisa. "'Like a Maternal Body': Emmanuel Levinas and the Motherhood of Moses." *Hypatia* 21, no. 1 (2006): 119–36. DOI: 10.1111/j.1527-2001.2006.tb00968.x.

Haraway, Donna. "A Cyborg Manifesto: Science, Technology, and Socialist-Feminism in the Late 20th Century." In *International Handbook of Virtual Learning Environments*, edited by Joel Weiss, Jason Nolan, Jeremy Hunsinger, and Peter Trifonas. Springer, 2006.

Hirsch, Marianne. "Nazi Photographs in Post-Holocaust Art." In *The Generation of Postmemory: Writing and Visual Culture after the Holocaust.* Columbia University Press, 2012.

Homer, Sean. *Jacques Lacan.* London: Routledge, 2005.

Horney, Karen. "The Dread of Woman: Observations on a Specific Difference in the Dread Felt by Men and by Women Respectively for the Opposite Sex." In *Feminine Psychology.* W.W. Norton & Company, 1973.

Huhn, Rosi. "The Folly of Reason." In *Art as Compassion: Bracha L. Ettinger,* edited by Catherine de Zegher and Griselda Pollock. ASA Publishers, 2012.

Irigaray, Luce. *This Sex Which Is Not One.* Translated by Catherine Porter and Carolyn Burke. Cornell University Press, 1985.

Kaiser, Brigit M., and Kathrin Thiele. "If You Do Well, Carry! The Difference of the Humane: An Interview with Bracha L. Ettinger." *philoSOPHIA: A Journal of Continental Feminism* 8, no. 1 (2018): 101–25. DOI: 10.1353/phi.2018.0005.

Kisiel, Anna. "Aesth/Ethical Bodies: Bracha Ettinger's Eurydices and the Encounter with the Other's History." In *The Body in History, Culture, and the Arts,* edited by Justyna Jajszczok and Aleksandra Musiał. Routledge, 2019.

———. "Dis-Obedience to the Father: Bracha L. Ettinger's Theory and Installation Confronted with Freud and Lacan." *Romanica Silesiana* 12 (2017): 53–63. https://journals.us.edu.pl/index.php/RS/article/view/7154.

———. "Gazing at Eurydice: Authorship and Otherness in Bracha L. Ettinger." *Analyses/Rereadings/Theories: A Journal*

Devoted to Literature, Film and Theatre 6, no. 1 (2020): 7–17. DOI: 10.18778/2353-6098.6.02.

———. "Uraz — bliskość — nie-pamięć: Psychoanalityczny dyskurs traumy od Freuda do Ettinger." *Narracje o Zagładzie* 2 (2016): 115–32. https://journals.us.edu.pl/index.php/NoZ/article/view/6773.

Klein, Melanie. "Envy and Gratitude." In *The Writings of Melanie Klein,* Vol. 3: *Envy and Gratitude and Other Works, 1946–1963.* The Free Press, 1975.

———. "Love, Guilt and Reparation." In *The Writings of Melanie Klein,* Vol. 1: *Love, Guilt and Reparation and Other Works, 1921–1945.* The Free Press, 1975.

———. *The Psychoanalysis of Children.* Translated by Alix Strachey. Grove Press, 1960.

Kristeva, Julia. "Motherhood According to Giovanni Bellini." In *Desire in Language: A Semiotic Approach to Literature and Art,* edited by Léon S. Roudiez, translated by Thomas Gora, Alice A. Jardine, and Léon S. Roudiez. Columbia University Press, 1980.

———. *Powers of Horror: An Essay on Abjection.* Translated by Léon S. Roudiez. Columbia University Press, 1982.

———. *Revolution in Poetic Language.* Translated by Margaret Waller. Columbia University Press, 1984.

———. "Women's Time." Translated by Alice Jardine and Harry Blake. *Signs: Journal of Women in Culture and Society* 7, no. 1 (1981): 13–35. https://www.jstor.org/stable/3173503.

Lacan, Jacques. "Of the Gaze as Objet Petit a." In *The Seminar of Jacques Lacan,* Book XI: *The Four Fundamental Concepts of Psychoanalysis,* edited by Jacques-Alain Miller, translated by Alan Sheridan. W.W. Norton & Company, 1981.

———. "Seminar on 'The Purloined Letter.'" In *Écrits: The First Complete Edition in English,* translated by Bruce Fink, Héloïse Fink, and Russel Grigg. W.W. Norton & Company, 2006.

———. "The Freudian Unconscious and Ours." In *The Seminar of Jacques Lacan,* Book XI: *The Four Fundamental Concepts of Psychoanalysis,* edited by Jacques-Alain Miller, translated by Alan Sheridan. W.W. Norton & Company, 1981.

———. "The Instance of the Letter in the Unconscious, or Reason Since Freud." In *Écrits: The First Complete Edition in English,* translated by Bruce Fink, Héloïse Fink, and Russel Grigg. W.W. Norton & Company, 2006.

———. *The Seminar of Jacques Lacan,* Book III: *The Psychoses, 1955–1956.* Edited by Jacques-Alain Miller. Translated by Russell Grigg. Routledge, 1993.

———. *The Seminar of Jacques Lacan,* Book XX: *On Feminine Sexuality, the Limits of Love and Knowledge, Encore 1972–1973.* Edited by Jacques-Alain Miller. Translated by Bruce Fink. W.W. Norton & Company, 1999.

———. "The Signification of the Phallus." In *Écrits: The First Complete Edition in English,* translated by Bruce Fink, Héloïse Fink, and Russel Grigg. W.W. Norton & Company, 2006.

LaCapra, Dominick. "Approaching Limit Events: Siting Agamben." In *History in Transit: Experience, Identity, Critical Theory.* Cornell University Press, 2004.

———. *Writing History, Writing Trauma.* Johns Hopkins University Press, 2001.

Laub, Dori. "An Event without a Witness: Truth, Testimony and Survival." In Shoshana Felman and Dori Laub, *Testimony: Crises of Witnessing in Literature, Psychoanalysis, and History.* Routledge, 1992.

Levinas, Emmanuel. *Ethics and Infinity: Conversations with Philippe Nemo.* Translated by Richard A. Cohen. Duquesne University Press, 1995.

———. *Existence and Existents.* Translated by Alphonso Lingis. Nijhoff, 1978.

———. *Humanism of the Other.* Translated by Nidra Poller. University of Illinois Press, 2006.

———. *Otherwise Than Being, or Beyond Essence.* Translated by Alphonso Lingis. Kluwer Academic Publishers, 1991.

———. "The Trace of the Other." In *Deconstruction in Context: Literature and Philosophy,* edited by Mark C. Taylor. University of Chicago Press, 1986.

———. *Time and the Other [and Additional Essays].* Translated by Richard A. Cohen. Duquesne University Press, 1987.

———. *Totality and Infinity: An Essay on Exteriority.* Translated by Alphonso Lingis. Duquesne University Press, 1969.

———. "Useless Suffering." Translated by Richard Cohen. In *The Provocation of Levinas: Rethinking the Other,* edited by Robert Bernasconi and David Wood. Routledge, 1988.

Levinas, Emmanuel, and Bracha L. Ettinger. "What Would Eurydice Say?" Translated by Joseph Simas and Carolyne Ducker. *Athena: Philosophical Studies* 2 (2006): 137–45. https://athena.lt/files/pdf/2/II-1.pdf.

Lipszyc, Adam. *Ślad judaizmu w filozofii XX wieku.* Fundacja im. Prof. Mojżesza Schorra, 2009.

Manning, Erin. "Vertiginous before the Light: The Form of Force." In *Art as Compassion: Bracha L. Ettinger,* edited by Catherine de Zegher and Griselda Pollock. ASA Publishers, 2012.

Massumi, Brian. "Afterword. Painting: The Voice of the Grain." In Bracha L. Ettinger, *The Matrixial Borderspace,* edited by Brian Massumi. University of Minnesota Press, 2006.

Meskin, Jacob. "The Jewish Transformation of Modern Thought: Lévinas and Philosophy after the Holocaust." *CrossCurrents* 47, no. 4 (Winter 1997–1998): 505–17. https://www.jstor.org/stable/24460603.

Michener, Ronald T. "Face-to-Face with Levinas: (Ev)angelical Hospitality and (De)constructive Ethics?" *European Journal of Theology* 19, no. 2 (2010): 153–62.

Mitchell, Juliet. *Fratriarchy: The Sibling Trauma and the Law of the Mother.* Routledge, 2023.

Nancy, Jean-Luc. "In the Midst of the World." In *Adoration: The Deconstruction of Christianity II,* translated by John McKeane. Fordham University Press, 2013.

Pine, Lisa. "Gender and Holocaust Victims: A Reappraisal."
Journal of Jewish Identities 1, no. 2 (2008): 121–41. DOI:
10.1353/jji.0.0022.

Pollock, Griselda. "Aesthetic Wit(h)nessing in the Era of
Trauma." *EurAmerica* 40, no. 4 (2010): 829–86. https://www.
ea.sinica.edu.tw/allQuarterly_main.aspx?QSID=334.

———. *After-Affects/After-Images: Trauma and Aesthetic
Transformation in the Virtual Feminist Museum.* Manchester
University Press, 2013.

———. "A Matrixial Installation: Artworking in the Freudian
Space of Memory and Migration." In *Art as Compassion:
Bracha L. Ettinger,* edited by Catherine de Zegher and
Griselda Pollock. ASA Publishers, 2012.

———. *Art in the Time-Space of Memory and Migration:
Sigmund Freud, Anna Freud, and Bracha L. Ettinger in the
Freud Museum, Artwriting after the Event.* Wild Pansy Press,
2015.

———. "Between Painting and the Digital: Matrixial
Aesthetics Creates Matrixial Thought-Forms." In Bracha L.
Ettinger, *And My Heart Wound-Space.* Wild Pansy Press,
2015.

———. "Beyond Oedipus: Feminist Thought, Psychoanalysis,
and Mythical Figurations of the Feminine." In *Laughing
with Medusa: Classical Myth and Feminist Thought,* edited
by Vanda Zajko and Miriam Leonard. Oxford University
Press, 2006.

———. "From Horrorism to Compassion: Re-Facing Medusan
Otherness in Dialogue with Adriana Caverero and Bracha
Ettinger." In *Visual Politics of Psychoanalysis: Art and
the Image in Post-Traumatic Cultures,* edited by Griselda
Pollock. I.B. Tauris, 2013.

———. "Introduction. Femininity: Aporia or Sexual
Difference?" In Bracha L. Ettinger, *The Matrixial
Borderspace,* edited by Brian Massumi. University of
Minnesota Press, 2006.

———. "Mother Trouble: The Maternal-Feminine in Phallic
and Feminist Theory in Relation to Bracha Ettinger's

Elaboration of Matrixial Ethics/Aesthetics." *Studies in the Maternal* 1, no. 1 (2009): 1–31. DOI: 10.16995/sim.114.

———. "Nichsapha: Yearning/Languishing. The Immaterial Tuché of Colour in Painting *after Painting after History*." In Bracha L. Ettinger, *Bracha Lichtenberg Ettinger: Artworking 1985–1999*. Ludion, 2000.

———. "Thinking the Feminine: Aesthetic Practice as Introduction to Bracha Ettinger and the Concepts of Matrix and Metramorphosis." *Theory, Culture & Society* 21, no. 1 (2004): 5–65. DOI: 10.1177/0263276404040479.

———. "Trauma, Time and Painting: Bracha Ettinger and the Matrixial Aesthetic." In *Carnal Aesthetics: Transgressive Imagery and Feminist Politics*, edited by Bettina Papenburg and Marta Zarzycka. I.B. Tauris, 2013.

Potkański, Jan. "Przeciw lacanowskiej prawicy." *Śląskie Studia Polonistyczne*, no. 1 (2013): 53–72. https://journals.us.edu.pl/index.php/SSP/article/view/3279.

Ragland-Sullivan, Ellie. *Jacques Lacan and the Philosophy of Psychoanalysis*. University of Illinois Press, 1987.

Riviere, Joan. "Public Lectures: Hate, Greed and Aggression." In *The Inner World and Joan Riviere: Collected Papers, 1920–1958*, edited by Athol Hughes. Karnac Books, 1991.

Rose, Jacqueline. "Feminine Sexuality: Jacques Lacan and the école freudienne." In *Sexuality in the Field of Vision*. Verso, 2020.

———. *Mothers: An Essay on Love and Cruelty*. Faber & Faber, 2019.

Rupp, Leila J. "Mother of the *Volk*: The Image of Women in Nazi Ideology." *Signs: Journal of Women in Culture and Society* 3, no. 2 (1977): 362–79. DOI: 10.1086/493470.

Schwartz, Baruch J. "Burnt Offering." In *The Oxford Dictionary of the Jewish Religion*, edited by Adele Berlin. Oxford University Press, 2011.

Scott, Joan Wallach. *Gender and the Politics of History*. Columbia University Press, 1999.

———. "Rewriting History." In *Behind the Lines: Gender and the Two World Wars*, edited by Margaret Randolph

Higonnet, Jane Jenson, Sonya Michel, and Margaret Collins Weitz. Yale University Press, 1987.

Sontag, Susan. *On Photography.* Penguin, 1979.

Stephenson, Jill. *Women in Nazi Germany.* Pearson Education, 2001.

Tec, Nechama. *Resilience and Courage: Women, Men, and the Holocaust.* Yale University Press, 2003.

Ubertowska, Aleksandra. "Niewidoczność, sprawczość, podmiot: Perspektywa feministyczna i genderowa w badaniach nad Holokaustem." In *Holokaust: Auto(tanato) grafie.* Instytut Badań Literackich PAN, 2014.

———. "Rysa, dukt, odcisk (nie)obecności: O spektrologiach Zagłady." *Teksty Drugie,* no. 2 (2016): 102–21. DOI: 10.18318/td.2016.2.7.

Wild, John. "Introduction." In Emmanuel Levinas, *Totality and Infinity: An Essay on Exteriority,* translated by Alphonso Lingis. Duquesne University Press, 1969.

Winnicott, D.W. *Therapeutic Consultations in Child Psychiatry.* Routledge, 2018.

Zegher, Catherine de. "Drawing Out Voice and Webwork." In *Art as Compassion: Bracha L. Ettinger,* edited by Catherine de Zegher and Griselda Pollock. ASA Publishers, 2012.

Zegher, Catherine de, and Griselda Pollock, eds. *Art as Compassion: Bracha L. Ettinger.* ASA Publishers, 2012.

www.ingramcontent.com/pod-product-compliance
Lightning Source LLC
Chambersburg PA
CBHW070825250726
48662CB00003B/1092